CREATIVITY & MADNESS

PSYCHOLOGICAL STUDIES OF ART AND ARTISTS

CREATIVITY
&MADNESS

PSYCHOLOGICAL STUDIES OF
ART AND ARTISTS

Edited by
Barry Panter, M.D., Ph.D.,
Mary Lou Panter, R.N.,
Evelyn Virshup, Ph.D., A.T.R.,
and Bernard Virshup, M.D.

AIMED PRESS

Second printing July 1996

Published by AIMED PRESS
AMERICAN INSTITUTE OF MEDICAL EDUCATION
2625 West Alameda Avenue, Burbank, CA 91505
800/348-8441 FAX 818/789-9857

Cover art by Mary Lou Panter

Creativity and madness : psychological studies of art and artists/
  edited by Barry Panter, May Lou Panter, Evelyn Virshup & Bernard Virshup.
    p. cm.
    Includes bibliographical references and index.
    ISBN 0-9641185-1-3

    1. Artists—Biography. 2. Artists—Psychology. 3. Creative
ability. 4. Psychology—Biographical methods. I. Panter, Barry.
II. Panter, Mary Lou. III. Virshup, Evelyn. IV. Virshup, Bernard.

N40.C743 1994   709.22
                                 QB194-1319

Library of Congress Catalog No. 94-94521

Acknowledgments

We would like to thank the authors who made contributions to this book: Susan Backes, M.D., Lee Berman, M.D., Alma Bond, Ph.D., Scott Carder, M.D., Ph.D., Linda Carder, M.A, Joan DiGiovanni, Ph.D., Sara Epstein, M.D., Benjamin Garber, M.D., Kay Goebel, Ph.D., Warren Jones, M.D., Ph.D., Kate Kavanagh, R.N., Ph.D., Ron Lee, Ph.D., Dea Mallin, M.A., Mary Lou Panter, R.N., Melissa Robertson, Ph.D., Vivian Rogers, Ph.D., Elaine Warick, B.A., and Larry Warick, M.D., Ph.D. Many of their works were given originally as presentations at the conferences of the same name, CREATIVITY & MADNESS—*Psychological Studies of Art and Artists,* sponsored by the *American Institute of Medical Education.* It was in the fine work that the authors did as presenters, and the warm reception their work received, that this volume was conceived.

We would like to thank Joseph Simon of Pangloss Press, Malibu, California for his help with designing the book, and Annette Alexander, our Executive Secretary, for her invaluable help and support throughout this project.

Many people read the manuscript and made valuable comments. Among them are Sheldon Coburn, M.D., Jose Luis de la Rosa, M.D., Elvie de la Rosa, B.S., Heidi Haden, M.A., Lauren Kaplan, Ph.D., J. Dan Kubelka and Marilou Kubelka, educators, Joyce Rumack, artist and CSUN docent, and Allan Rumack, M.D.

We would also like to thank all the presenters and attendees at our conferences over the past 12 years. They greatly enriched and broadened our lives, and it was their support and interest that encouraged us to bring this work to fruition.

Finally, we would like to dedicate this book to our creative children: Amy, Adrienne, and David; and David, Gary, and Steven.

The editors

We are gratified that our book has been so well received.
This is our third printing.
It was first published in 1995, reprinted in 1999.

Look for Volume Two—coming soon!

Please feel free to contact us at our new location

Aimed Press
A Division of
The American Institute of Medical Education
and
The Creativity & Madness Conferences
3837 Winford Drive
Tarzana, CA 91356

800 348 8881   818 776 0344
Fax 818 776 0269
www.aimed.com
Email   BarryP15@aol.com

January 2006

Contents

Preface

The material artists use for their art comes from the primitive levels of their inner lives. As we mature and are "civilized" we suppress these forces. But the artist stays in touch with, and struggles to understand, them. And to remain so in touch with that primitive self is to be on the fine line between sanity and madness.

The passions and inner conflicts of the creative artist are often revealed in studies of the artists' lives and works. They are the passions and conflicts with which we all struggle. Our studies illustrate what we all know to be true—pain and turmoil do not always result in disability and disease, but can lead to that triumph of the human spirit we call creativity.

Creativity, uniquely human, has allowed mankind to reach its highest levels of achievement. We can approach the understanding of creativity in many ways—psychological, neurological, sociological, biochemical, genetic, environmental, political. This book emphasizes the psychological aspect, and gains understanding of the artist's personality. What forces—parental, societal, internal—mold an individual's psyche to allow use of creativity as a reaction to the world?

A major thread throughout this book is that creativity, a factor in the lives of many artists, is the highest level of reaction to injury. The artist is wrestling with inner demons that torment many of us—depression, as in Elizabeth Layton; lack of self-cohesion and aggression as in Jackson Pollock; feelings of unworthiness and the inability to tolerate success as in Vincent van Gogh; fear of success as in Sylvia Plath. Instead of being paralyzed or beaten by their psychological problems, artists wrestle with the problems and use the conflicts and torments as elements of the creative process. In this way, the artist discovers a transcendent path through the great universal emotional issues that confront all of us.

Dr. Goebel's article on Michelangelo emphasizes this. She states that Michelangelo's creativity was his attempt to externalize in his sculptures his conflicts with and yearnings for male figures of authority, as well as his longing to be re-united with the gratifying mother of his infancy. His ability to wrestle with his inner conflicts in this visual manner made him a resilient survivor of psychological trauma, helping him to live a long and productive life. Others were not so fortunate. We can see in the tragedies and suicides of van Gogh, Plath, Woolf, Pollock, and others, the failed attempts to resolve the emotional wounds of early life.

Artists are driven to create by their psychological issues. Yet paradoxically, the artist does not need to be consciously aware of these issues or conflicts. Indeed, many artists shun anything, and especially psychotherapy or psychoanalysis, that would bring these issues into awareness, fearing that such knowledge would cause their creativity to dry up. They may be right. As Dr. and Mrs. Warick describe in their article on Munch, his somewhat successful psychiatric treatment led to a change in the nature of his paintings. Many art critics think his later works are not as powerful as the early ones. Dr. Jones, in his article on Leonardo and Magritte, states the opposite—that neurosis or psychological conflicts are obstacles to creativity rather than the fuel for the artist.

The psychological approach to creativity is only one of many approaches to understanding art and artists. For us, it is the most interesting way of studying our greatest abilities. However, we realize that no matter how comprehensive our psychological studies are, they constitute only one of many avenues into the secrets of creativity. Even if all the known avenues were traveled, the innermost secrets would still remain. We can know parts of the truth about creativity; we are unlikely to know all of it.

The book is intended for both the lay person interested in psychology, art and the creative process, as well as the mental health professional. We appreciate that, although many of the chapters deal with sophisticated psychological theories, the authors have followed our request to make the concepts easily understood.

Barry M. Panter
Sherman Oaks, California

Introduction

What is creativity?

Creativity is the ability to bring something new into existence, by seeing things in a new way. Those who have this in the greatest degree are considered geniuses, and greatly honored and rewarded, but frequently considered strange, disturbing, and even mad. Picasso liked to live in a house of chaos—paintings, object, clothes strewn in disarray—in which his eye would behold unusual combinations. One of his most famous works is the handlebar of a bicycle above the metal seat of the bicycle making the form of a bull's head. He saw it that way in his house. Einstein was riding the trolley to work one day when, his attention caught by a clock tower he passed every day, he wondered what would happen to his perception and understanding of time if he were traveling at the speed of light. His musings turned into the theory of relativity, and changed the world we live in. Freud wondered about the bizarre behavior of patients few other physicians wanted to treat. His early musings led to the opening of the unconscious—and he too changed the world we live in.

From where does creativity come?

Perhaps Plato knew as much as anyone can know, when he wrote that creativity is a *"divine madness...a gift from the gods."* There are many examples of inspirations that seem to come from the gods. The chemist Kekule was trying to discover the chemical structure of the benzene ring. One night during his sleep he dreamed of snakes chasing their own tails—and when he awoke, he realized he had discovered in his dream exactly what he had been looking for. George Handel was asked how he composed the magnificent *Hallelujah Chorus.* He replied he really hadn't composed it—he heard it. Sleeping, he dreamed of huge doors opening. As they opened he heard music. The wider they opened, the louder the music became. When he awoke, he wrote down the music he had heard.

So creativity is not limited to conscious effort. Freud would say that creativity takes place in the unconscious.

Who is creative?

On the one hand there are those precious few—Mozart, Michelangelo, da Vinci, Shakespeare, Einstein—whose creativity is so great that the gifts they give the world are unfathomable, except as gifts of the gods. But there is also the creativity of everyday life. The simple task of making a meal is an act of creativity. No two people do it the same way. It combines elements into something new. It brings pleasure. The same can be said for giving a party or writing a letter. In this sense we all are creative.

What fosters creativity?

Pasteur wrote, "Chance favors the prepared mind." Artists must learn their craft. Usually early in life the artist learns the technique necessary for his or her medium. Michelangelo grew up among the stone cutters of Carrera from whom he learned how to carve marble. Being exposed to the techniques of art was once considered a necessary part of an education. Children were expected to learn a musical instrument or to paint or to mold clay. Unfortunately, these skills increasingly are seen as not useful for making a living, and they are being dropped from curricula. Elizabeth Layton shows that the craft may be learned at any age.

But craft is not enough. The prepared mind includes a willingness to experience and express without inhibition. The favorable soil frequently is the accepting, approving, non-critical atmosphere created by a parent or benefactor. In the early stages of creation there should be no editing. Unusual questions should be encouraged; unusual responses should be admired. Everything should be allowed to flow—to find its expression on paper, or canvas, or stone. Editing comes later. To edit early, to feel disapproval or criticism too early, stifles the creative process. Parents can provide the encouraging, approving, educating environment for their children that fosters the joy of creativity, as well as helping them learn healthy techniques for coping with life's adversities.

> I am convinced that genius is a "gift of the Gods," and is already laid down at birth, probably as a sport development which finds specially favorable soil for its evolution in families where there is also a good inheritance of intellect, and a favorable background for identification.
>
> Phyllis Greenacre

Families of creative people are often open to creative expression, are often creative themselves. Virginia Woolf came from a long line of writers. She observed her father and her mother in the act of writing and discussing the process. Rossini's parents were musicians. The child's natural idealization of the parent turns into the wish to be like the parent, to learn what the parent knows, and to become the artist the parent was perceived to be. Mozart's father was a skilled and accomplished musician and composer. Van Gogh's mother was only marginally talented—but in her son's eyes she was an artist, and that was enough for him to idealize the act of painting, and one of the factors that led to his drive to be a painter himself. It is no accident that families of musicians produce musicians. Parents are models for idealization and emulation.

The fostering, encouraging person need not be a parent. Michelangelo's parent punished him for wanting to be an artist, but he found another fostering benefactor, Lorenzo de Medici of Florence. There are certain people and times in history who have provided the fertile soil for creativity. Among these was Lorenzo, in the second half of the 15th century. He loved the arts and wanted Florence to be a world leader. He supported and encouraged artists, and among his rewards, and the world's rewards, are Botticelli, Michelangelo, Fra Angelico, and Leonardo da Vinci. Other enlightened governments include Paris in the late 1800's and Vienna at the turn of the century. Their leaders encouraged the arts—and their cities and the arts flowered.

The artist must tolerate and enjoy being alone. He or she needs the time to allow thoughts and feelings to roll around in the head, to ruminate, to come together in new combinations. Einstein said he got his best ideas while shaving. Beethoven, Brahms and Strauss loved to walk in the Vienna woods. How many of us have had wonderful, creative ideas while on vacation, when our minds are not occupied with the usual tasks and routine of life?

> Certain springs are tapped only when we are alone.
> Anne Morrow Lindbergh

> Genius, whether locked up in a cell or roaming at large, is always solitary.
> George Sand

The artist must be courageous, with the strength and boldness to stand behind the new ideas, new combinations, new techniques that emerge. Many new ideas are greeted at first with scorn or ridicule. Sometimes the worth of a creation is appreciated at first only by the artist—sometimes until long after the artist's death.

> Greatness breaks laws.
> Louise Nevelson

> Every work of art is an act of faith, or we wouldn't bother to do it. It is a message in a bottle, a shout in the dark. It's saying, "I'm here, and I believe you are somewhere, and that you will answer, if necessary, across time."
> Jeanette Winterson

Are creative artists "mad"?

Artists see the world differently, and for this they pay a price. Dr. Kay Jamison and Dr. Nancy Andreason have found in recent studies that a high percentage of artists have manic-depressive and depressive disorders. Many artists have disturbances in the regulation of their moods, with a higher than normal degree of alcoholism, drug addiction, depression, and mood swings than is found in the general population. Is this a natural association with creativity? Is it caused by the way they perceive the world, or the way the world receives them? Or is creativity a response to trauma? Artists may have a greater sensitivity to emotional trauma than others. They must be able to experience and endure their primitive emotional storms, with the capacity and technical ability to express their torment in their art form. Artists, like Orpheus, must descend into their particular Hades, and return to tell about it. If they turn back to look at Eurydice, she will be lost. Only by turning toward life can artists emerge with their treasure. For many artists, art is their salvation.

Must the artist suffer?

Not all artists suffer. Marc Chagall and Felix Mendelsohn are among many artists who seemingly did not suffer from neurotic problems and who did not live lives of misery; but many artists attribute their works to their misfortunes, which they see as the fuel for their creativity. We think that emotional suffering, and the struggle against it, is found in most great artists. Creativity is humanity's most heroic struggle against adversity. The artists studied in this book are examples of this.

Why do we enjoy art?

The works of great artists put us in touch, often on a subliminal level, with unconscious parts of ourselves. Great works of art are great because the artists have put into their work something that is universal, that touches each of us. The *Scream* by Munch is a good example of something that expresses what each of us, on some level, has felt. Looking at great art acts as a catharsis, helping us relieve the tension of some of our own repressed elements. This may explain why two hours in a great museum, or an evening at a concert or play, is followed by a sense of comforting, of gladdening, of feeling uplifted, of euphoria.

> Even in the most sophisticated person, it is the primitive eye that watches the film.   Jack Nicholson

What can we learn from these creative artists?

Creativity is a constructive outlet for painful feelings and confused states of being. Creativity is a healing force in an individual, and in a society in turmoil. Teaching our children, and learning ourselves, how to paint or play an instrument or sculpt is not just idle use of time. It is an important, even a necessary element if we are to deal with the inevitable problems in our lives, if we are to be a civilized society, and, possibly, if we are to survive as a society.

Barry M. Panter
Evelyn Virshup

Barry M. Panter is the co-founder and co-director of the American Institute of Medical Education, a non-profit educational organization that conducts conferences on Creativity and Madness, Emotional Growth and Creativity in Adult Life, Self Psychology, and Psychodynamic Psychotherapy. He is a training and supervising analyst at the Southern California Psychoanalytic Institute and the Institute for Contemporary Psychoanalysis, Los Angeles, and a Clinical Professor of Psychiatry at the University of Southern California School of Medicine. He served for a year aboard the hospital ship SS Hope in Sri Lanka as director of the pediatric program.

Art is a protest against death.   *—Audrey Flack*

Vincent van Gogh
Creativity and Madness
by Barry Panter, M.D., Ph.D.

The sunflower was one of Vincent van Gogh's favorite subjects. He painted it a dozen or more times. It is also one of nature's most brilliant creations. It lies dormant for a long time, then suddenly pushes through the crust of the earth and, in a dazzling burst of energy, reaches toward the sun. Its productivity, its seeds, are in the head of the flower at the end of a slender stalk. If the productivity is excessive the head is too heavy to be supported by the stalk, and the flower, after rising to a great height, falls back rapidly toward the earth.

Van Gogh's life parallels that of his beloved sunflower. He, too, was so brilliantly creative and productive near the end—sending forth sometimes two or three paintings a day—that he could not survive at that height. He, too, fell to earth suddenly, struck down by his own hand. But his brilliance remains. I hope to share in this chapter some thoughts and feelings of appreciation and enjoyment of his brilliance, his tragedy and the glory of his work.

Vincent's childhood and young adulthood

Vincent was born March 30, 1853, in Zundert, Holland, near the Belgian border. Exactly one year prior to the day of his birth, his mother had given birth to a stillborn child who was named Vincent

1

Wilhelm van Gogh. The stillborn child was buried in the graveyard behind the church where Vincent's father was minister. For the first 12 years of his life he walked past a grave with his name on it.

His mother was thirty years old when she married, and thirty three when Vincent was born. Probably as a result of the stillbirth of her first-born occurring late in her life, she was depressed during her pregnancy with Vincent, and the years of his infancy and early childhood. In his letters to his brother Theo, Vincent referred to their mother as "Mater Dolorosa" (Mother of Sorrow). Because of her depression, she was probably withdrawn and emotionally unavailable to the young Vincent for much of the time. From this ongoing experience with her, during these formative years of his life, Vincent may have developed the ideas and feelings of unworthiness and isolation that plagued him constantly. His painting of an infant being held at the end of outstretched arms shows the distance and isolation that he probably felt most of his life. Compare this to the Madonnas and Child that are so frequent in the art world, in which there is an enfolding, a caressing, and obvious love and entwining of mother and child.

Augustine Roulin with baby

Vincent's mother was known to sketch drawings of flowers and portraits. Vincent probably observed her doing this during his childhood. Thus, in his child's eye, his mother was "an artist." Five more children were born after Vincent. The family history of mental illness is seen in them. Vincent experienced hallucinations and probably delusions, his brother, Theo, with whom he was so close, had a psychotic episode within several months of Vincent's death, and their sister, Wilhelmiena, spent 50 years of her life in an asylum, dying at the age of 79.

Vincent's father was a Protestant minister in the predominantly Catholic town. This may have led to another form of isolation for Vincent—from children his own age who perhaps were more likely to play with other Catholic children than with the Protestant Vincent. The teachings of his Church at the time included that it was sinful for a father to take pride in his son, that the seeking of recognition was vanity, and that humility, modesty, and sacrifice were the paths to salvation. From this, Vincent probably internalized his feelings of being a sinner, deserving of punishment, and undeserving of praise or recognition. These ideas and feelings were in conflict with his career as a artist, which would ordinarily require recognition and praise in order to make a living, which Vincent never did. After he started paintint, he was supported by his parents, and then by his brother, Theo, for the rest of his brief life.

Vincent and his father had a tumultuous relationship, with many arguments. When Vincent was twelve, the family sent him to a private boarding school. This may have been because he didn't get along with his father, or because they recognized special ability, talent or intelligence in their son. A loner, he had difficulty getting along with other children.

At sixteen, he left school to work in The Hague at the art dealers, Goupil and Son, who were extended members of his mother's family. He did well and was sent at the age of twenty for more experience to a branch of the business in London. In London, he developed an infatuation with Ursula, his landlady's daughter. For months he fantasized about her, but never indicated his feelings for her, until one day he suddenly declared his love. Taken by surprise, she said that she definitely was not interested in him. Vincent was deeply hurt. This is an early example of his lack of social awareness and awkwardness. After this, he began to isolate himself, became very religious, and began to be rude to the art dealers' customers and co-workers. Previously well-dressed, he became slovenly in his habits. He was described at this early age as being peculiar and strange.

He was transferred to a branch in Paris, probably because the family wanted to keep a closer eye on him. His rudeness and other inappropriate behavior continued. He was known to tell customers, "Don't buy this painting. Art dealers are thieves. They steal from the artists and they steal from the customers." He was fired from his job, and returned to his parents' home in Holland, where he stayed until he found a job in a boys' school at Ramsgate, England.

Vincent becomes a minister

One of the reasons he took the job was that he was permitted to give a sermon to the boys, once a month. In this, he was identifying with his father, and following in his footsteps. However, he argued with the headmaster, who wanted Vincent to assist him in collecting fees for the school, a repetition of his conflicts with his father. He was let go from this position, too. He then decided that he would become a minister like his father. He studied in preparation for exams to gain entrance to the seminary. His harsh conscience and need to punish himself can be heard in the words of his tutor, Mendes DeCosta, who wrote, "Whenever Vincent felt that he hadn't been diligent enough, he would belabor his back with a cudgel, and sleep outdoors on the ground. He preferred to do this in the winter."

Vincent failed to gain entrance to the seminary, but did attend a school for lay ministers. Although he was extremely intelligent, a voracious reader, and fluent in several languages, he failed to graduate; however, he found a position for himself, without the school's permission, among the poor miners in the Borinage, an area in Belgium. While there, he became even more strange, and was noted for giving away much of his clothing and food to the miners and their families. Because of his inappropriate behavior, the school asked him to desist from his activities there, and wrote his father asking him to remove Vincent. He wrote to Theo that he felt broken and forlorn. He again isolated himself. He told Theo that this was "his molting time."

Vincent becomes an artist

The skin that he threw off was that of religion and his identification with his minister father. The new skin that emerged was that of being an artist—identification with his mother. This was a regression from following in his father's footsteps, or competing with his

4

father, to trying to find solace and comfort in his merging with his mother through drawing and painting, which he had seen her do as a child. He wrote to Theo that he would devote his life "to Art, only Art," which he did. In the remaining eight years of his short career, he created over 800 works, 400 of them in the last year of his life.

He moved to Antwerp and enrolled in an art school, where he remained for a brief stay. During this time, he met and fell in love with his cousin Kee Vos, a widow with a small child. Once again he abruptly declared his love. She replied to his declaration, "No—never, never." He followed her to her parents' home in Brussels. When he asked to see her, they refused him. While he pleaded with them, he held his hand in the flame of a candle, and said, "Let me see her for as long as I can hold my hand in the flame." He passed out and was taken to a nearby hotel, without seeing Kee again. This was not just a neurotic act, the simple Freudian slip that all of us commit from time to time. This is an example of a psychotic act, by a desperate and self-destructive man. Certainly one of the worst things an artist could do to himself would be to destroy his hand.

Sien

His despondency continued. He began to live with a woman named Christine, known as "Sien," who was probably a prostitute. She, too, had a young child. His parents were very distressed about this relationship. He wrote to Theo, "She is a whore, pock marked and coarse. Life has been rough on her. She is ill-mannered and has a bad temper. I see in her exactly what I need—to me, she is beautiful." He wrote, "I cannot, I will not live without love. I want to touch people. I want them to know what is in the soul of this man, so rejected and unwanted by everyone. The clergymen call us sinners, conceived and born in sin. Bah, what dreadful nonsense that is! Is it a sin to love, to need love, not to be able to live without love? I think a life without love a sinful condition and an immoral condition... When you wake up in the morning and find yourself not alone, but see there in the morning light a fellow creature beside you, it makes the world look so much more friendly." But this relationship didn't last either. After several months Vincent and Sien separated.

During these years he was being supported by Theo, and was devoting himself to studying art. He sketched in pen and ink, and charcoals. After his separation from Sien, he returned to live with his parents. At the age of thirty, he began to use oils for the first time. His early works are very dark in color and dreary in mood—probably expressing his sadness and pessimism.

The Potato Eaters

In 1885, when Vincent was thirty two years old, his father died. Perhaps this released Vincent from the hold of some unconscious beliefs about himself—that he was a sinner, undeserving, and should not attempt anything for recognition or praise. Within 6 months of his father's death, Vincent painted his first masterpiece, *The Potato Eaters*, which depicts a poor, sad-appearing, hopeless family.

In Paris, he meets the impressionists

He then moved to Paris and lived with Theo, who was working at Goupil and Sons. While there, he met and saw the works of the Impressionists, members of the new movement in art. Through his brother's contacts with artists, he met Gauguin, Toulouse-Lautrec, Degas, and others. With this new influence in his life, his works began to change. He began to use brighter colors, and the works became more exciting. However, he was not able to change his difficulties in getting along with people. He argued with his fellow painters and even with Theo.

Probably as an attempt to control the anger that welled up in him with closer contact with people, he began drinking heavily. He drank absinthe—a drink that has since been banned in most countries because it is known to cause permanent brain damage. He was aware that he was deteriorating psychologically, and in an effort to find a less stressful environment, he decided to move to the south of

La Berceurse

France. This may have been due to the influence of Henri Toulouse-Lautrec who was from Albi in the south, and had told Vincent about the beauty and light of the area.

The Yellow House in Arles

He took a train to Arles in February of 1888. Within several months he was living in "The Yellow House," which he apparently selected as his home because of its color—yellow was his favorite. At a later time, he wrote to Theo when he was painting feverishly, that he was in the high yellow. "I'm very excited. The work goes very well."

He made friends with the postman, Roulin, and his family. Some of his most beautiful paintings of this period are of the Roulins. His *Berceuse* or *Lullaby* is a portrait of Mme. Roulin in which he expressed his loneliness and longing to be with people. He wrote of the painting, "I hope some day, it will be on a ship at sea, with men far from their homes and mothers, and that it will comfort them, as a mother comforts her children."

He wrote of his paintings, "I want to do works that will touch people. So that they will see that inside this wretch of a man, cast out by everyone, there is a soul that is beautiful, that despite all, is motivated more by love than by anything else." He had withdrawn from the world of people, and was living and trying to relate to people through his paintings.

He wrote to Theo of his dream of founding a school of artists in Arles, which was to have been called *The Colorists*. He hoped that other artists would join him in Arles. Theo was supportive of the idea, and wrote to a number of artists about it. Gauguin was the only one interested enough to actually move there—a move probably motivated by Gauguin's impoverished state, his distaste for the cold of winter in Pont Aven, Brittany, where he was living, and Theo's willingness to underwrite his move and living with Vincent in Arles.

Gauguin joins him in Arles

Prior to Gauguin's arrival in October of 1888, Vincent excitedly prepared for his companion by painting several pictures—the *Poet's Garden*, which expressed the fantasy and wish of the two painters strolling together discussing art, *Sunflowers*, which was to be on the wall of Gauguin's room, and several other works. The two artists lived together in "The Yellow House," painted views of the countryside with their easels side by side, ate together, and discussed art.

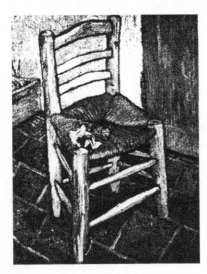

Vincent's Chair

Gauguin's Chair

There is a suggestion of latent homosexuality in Vincent's behavior toward Gauguin. He prepared for his arrival as one would for the arrival of a lover. "The room Gauguin will have—if he comes—will be the prettier room upstairs, which I shall try to make as much as possible like the boudoir of an artistic woman." He dreamt of their closeness—of walking, discussing, enjoying each other. Two of his paintings done at this time give further support to this. In *Vincent's Chair*, we see a strong, masculine chair, with a pipe and tobacco—accouterments of masculinity. In *Gauguin's Chair*, we see a chair with curved arms and back, with a soft tufted seat and a flaming candle arising from the seat—signs of femininity.

Not surprisingly, they soon began to quarrel. The disagreements of these two emotionally volatile men reached an apex on the evening of December 23rd, 1888. Gauguin stormed out of the house in which they were having dinner and discussing art, into the snow outside. Vincent followed with a knife in his hand. Gauguin heard the footsteps behind him, turned, and stared at the enraged Van Gogh. Their eyes locked for a moment, Vincent turned back, went upstairs to his room, and cut off a portion of his left ear. This was a displacement of his anger toward Gauguin to himself, and another self-mutilation or displaced castration of himself. He put the portion of his ear into a box, took it to Rachel, a prostitute he knew in Arles, and then passed out. Taking the ear to Rachel probably expressed his wish to escape from the unbeatable father, represented by Gauguin, and to be comforted by the mother.

Vincent's misfortune with Gauguin is an expression of his difficulties with many people throughout his life. He desperately wanted a close intimate relationship. But his feelings of unworthiness and unacceptability made him extremely vulnerable to narcissistic injuries. When these occurred, as they inevitably will, Vincent reacted with anger and sometimes rage, which eventually led to failure of every one of his relationships, even with his saint-like brother, Theo.

Vincent is hospitalized

Vincent was hospitalized at the hospital in Arles, and then in the asylum at St. Remy, where he stayed for approximately a year.

Eighty of the townspeople of Arles signed a petition given to the mayor, asking that Vincent not be allowed to live in the village—another injury to the heart of a man who yearned to live with and touch his fellow men. In Vincent's words, "A number of people here addressed to the mayor a petition describing me as a man not fit to be at liberty. The inspector of police then gave the order to shut me up again. So here I am shut up the livelong day under lock and key and with keepers in a cell... Needless to say in the secret tribunal of my soul, I have much to say."

During this time he tried unsuccessfully to sell his paintings for five francs (several US dollars). He made several suicide attempts by swallowing paints and turpentine. He continued to paint, sometimes in a frenzied manner and wrote to Theo that he was "a painting engine, turning out two, sometimes three paintings a day."

I have two speculations about the drivenness of his painting at this time. One of Vincent's life-long unfulfilled goals was to connect with others. The act of painting was a way to merge with his mother—the painter he had observed during his childhood. In addition, he hoped that others, viewing his paintings, would understand him, would relate to him, would bond with him. His work was his last desperate attempt to reach this goal.

Other inner conflicts and wishes were being expressed in his pictures. The clutching branches of the olive trees appear ominous and threatening—perhaps expressing his fear of and longing for death. The cypress trees are a symbol of death which was frequently on his mind. *Starry Night*, painted during this time, expressed his turmoil and frenzy as he tried to maintain his sanity which he knew was impaired.

More than 150 different diagnoses have been given to Vincent—both organic and psychological, including manic-depressive psychosis, schizophrenia, Meniere's Disease, brain tumor, organic brain syndrome secondary to absinthe poisoning or syphilis, and many others. From the age of 35 on, Vincent wrote that he suffered "attacks" that lasted from several hours to a week or longer. During his attacks he was, in his own words, "a madman, a lunatic."

He heard voices, sometimes lost consciousness, felt dazed and disoriented. Between attacks, he was able to write lucid letters to Theo in which he observed himself and his situation. He was able to paint and function in a relatively normal manner. He wrote Theo that "the fields at times are intensely yellow—more yellow than is normal."

An interesting theory about *Starry Night* is that it shows signs of digitalis intoxication. Digitalis is extracted from the flower, foxglove, and was used as a treatment for epilepsy, yet another diagnosis given to van Gogh. The side effects of digitalis include yellow vision (perhaps accounting for his love of yellow and his frequent use of it in his later paintings) and coronal or circular vision, i.e. the seeing of small shining rings. According to this theory, the stars in *Starry Night* were painted that way because that's what van Gogh saw.

In his letters he expressed his longing for a wife—someone he could love and who would love him, for children, for success. But I think that unconsciously all of these were forbidden to him. His mother, during his infancy and childhood because of her depression, conveyed to Vincent that he was not to know or feel loved. His father, because of his religious beliefs, imparted to Vincent the belief that one was a sinner to want praise, recognition, affirmation and success. Vincent unconsciously believed therefore that one should be humble, should strive, but not achieve. "It is only by suffering that one can remain true to oneself as an artist."

Dr. Gachet

Auvers and Dr. Gachet

In May, 1890, he moved to Auvers, a little town an hour's drive northwest of Paris. There were several reasons for this. He would be nearer to Theo and his new wife and son (named Vincent), Vincent was considered to be doing better emotionally, and he would be under the care of Dr. Gachet, who was well known for having treated a number of the Impressionists for their emotional problems. Soon after meeting Dr. Gachet, Vincent wrote to Theo, "I don't know how much good he can do me. I think he is more depressed than I am."

Vincent painted several portraits of Dr. Gachet, which show him to be depressed, and interestingly, also show a vase filled with foxglove in front of him.

Vincent's mood fluctuated from resignation to despair. He painted some idyllic scenes of the countryside, the lark arising, and flowers. The other side of his mental state was expressed in harsh, angular, tormented-appearing paintings of the stone quarry, and close-up views of corn, and flowers—paintings that border on the abstract and are precursors of modern art. In these works one can see van Gogh's influence on artists such as Picasso and Jackson Pollock.

Several more blows occurred to his mental well-being. One of his paintings was sold—about which he wrote, "Success is about the worst thing that can happen to an artist." A favorable review of his work appeared in The Mercure de France, one of the leading art journals of the day. He undoubtedly felt guilty about the success. And finally he argued with Dr. Gachet, because the doctor didn't frame a painting by another artist.

Wheat Fields Under Crows

Vincent's last days

Van Gogh was still trying to attain a loving relationship. He had become friends with Marguerite, the doctor's daughter, which displeased and caused further friction with Dr. Gachet. The strain on Vincent's mind was too great. Near the end, he was concerned about his mental health, writing, "I feel like a cracked pot." Remorseful about the financial burden he was placing on Theo and his family, rejected by the world he so loved and wished to touch, believing that love was never to be his, convinced that his mind was permanently damaged, and enraged at Dr. Gachet, he borrowed a pistol, ostensibly to scare the crows away from his work. A few days later, on July 27, 1890, he went to paint in the fields, then shot himself in the abdomen.

In what is one of his last paintings, *Wheat Fields Under Crows*, we see the premonition of suicide. The crows give an ominous air to the painting. The vanishing point—that point where all lines disappear—which is usually in the background of a painting, is reversed. Here, the point of disappearance is in front of the painting—the point where the artist is standing.

He dragged himself back toward town, was found and taken to his room. His brother, Theo, arrived. It was thought that to move him meant certain death, and there was a chance he would survive if kept quiet and nursed. After two days of agony, he died in his room.

He was buried in Auvers. Theo soon became ill, had a psychotic episode, and died. He was buried in Holland, but later exhumed and buried next to Vincent in Auver.

Summary

Vincent Van Gogh grew up in a home in which his mother, depressed and emotionally unavailable, was unable to provide a healthy amount of nurturing and affirming for him. His father, mainly because of his religious beliefs, was not able to take pride and show satisfaction and pleasure in his son. Therefore, Vincent developed the belief that he was unacceptable and unlovable. Yet he desperately sought throughout his life, to be accepted and to be loved.

With each failure of a relationship—and there were many—he withdrew further and further from contact with others. In his last desolate days, he had only his painting as a way of reaching out and trying to make contact with the world.

If you happen to be traveling from Amsterdam to Brussels, the village of Zundert is just a little way off the highway. As you drive through the main street, which is only 10-15 blocks long, there is a little square—the van Gogh Square—to the left. In back of it is the church where Vincent's father was the minister. The little house where Vincent was born is adjacent to the church.

In the center of the square is a statue of Vincent and his brother Theo. The two of them are with their arms intertwined—side by side as they were in life, and as they are in their graves at Auvers. As I watched, a couple drove up on a motorcycle and stopped to look at the statue. A family arrived in a van, unloaded picnic baskets, and stopped to have lunch on the grass nearby. Another couple stood arm-in-arm for a long time, looking at the statue of Vincent and Theo. I think Vincent would have liked that.

Had we known Vincent van Gogh during his lifetime we probably would have found him to be irascible and emotionally labile—a person difficult to enjoy as a friend. But today his works are viewed and admired throughout the world. His life will continue to be studied not only for its art, but also for its tragedy—for here is the beauty of a tormented, seeking soul.

He has achieved in death what he sought in life. Through his paintings, through his letters, and through his life—at last—he touches people.

Author of Right Brain People in a Left Brain World *and editor of* California Art Therapy Trends, *Evelyn Virshup teaches creativity at Art Center College of Design in Pasadena, and art therapy at California State University, Los Angeles, and has given art therapy workshops internationally. She has hosted and produced over 150 cable TV programs, discussing psychological issues and the use of art with mental health professionals. In 1987, her documentary, Suicide, a Teenage Dilemma, won an EMMY. She is a past president of the Southern California Art Therapy Association.*

Imagination is more important than knowledge.   *Albert Einstein*

Jackson Pollock
Art Versus Alcohol
by Evelyn Virshup, Ph.D., A.T.R.

My interest in Pollock derives from my work with alcoholics and drug abusers. Among the art techniques I used was to have them drag ink-saturated string around on paper, and then, using oil and soft pastels and felt-tipped pens, bring out the images they saw in their drips and splatters. By writing and talking about their images, many of these people were able to understand their conflicts and make peace with their inner monsters. How and to what extent they could organize the chaos confronting them paralleled the way in which they organized the chaos of their lives.

Early in therapy, having just been detoxified, they are often in a state of internal confusion. They create mass confusion on paper with their splatters and splashes, unable to see or form anything.

Later, when they are beginning to function relatively well, they organize the chaos they create and find images more easily. When they describe their artwork, it becomes apparent that they are, metaphorically, talking about themselves and their lives. It becomes apparent that they are as differentiated as their artwork. Their art is a reflection of their inner turmoil.

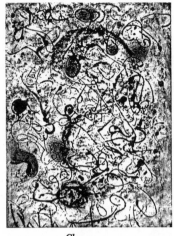

Chaos

Order out of Chaos

It was inevitable that one day I should look at Jackson Pollock's drips and splatters, and wonder what he would have said about them. I felt almost forced to explore his life. I then found that Pollock was an alcoholic; that he had an alcoholic and absent father, and a cold and withholding mother. When he did paint his monsters, he didn't talk about them, but instead, covered them up, creating his famous amorphous drip paintings. He led a flamboyant but ultimately self-destructive life, and finally, drunk, destroyed himself at the age of 44 in an automobile accident.

Almost all of Pollock's critics and biographers have made some allusions to his alcoholism and the influence of Jungian psychology and therapy on his art. But few have mentioned the interaction between his alcoholism and his creative decisions. He and his paintings have not been looked at specifically as the expressions of a disturbed, long-term alcoholic.

We all have memories, moods and responses, which simply are not verbal, which can be expressed only through behavior or emotional reactions. Artists work in these nonverbal ways, making all kinds of unarticulated decisions. The language of art is not always easily translated. Artists themselves frequently have great difficulty finding words to explain their art. Unless artists tell us specifically what their work means to them, and frequently, they are unaware and unable to do that, we never completely understand the significance of their images. Artwork, like a Rorschach inkblot, is a projective screen, where we all bring our own feelings, thoughts and experiences to focus. What we see and interpret from our own and others' art comes from our own personal life experiences.

When we look at Pollock's work in this manner, we see a deeply troubled man.

Pollock's art seems to be a clear mirror of his mind. He created chaos, obscured his images, and failed to confront his demons. When drinking, with little control over his brush and images, his unconscious bubbled forth. Later, when he was on sedatives and the wagon, he gained control, and deliberately concealed his images. When he resumed drinking, the original images returned.

At the time that Pollock, De Kooning, and many other action painters and abstract expressionists were changing the art world in New York, pioneer art therapist Margaret Naumberg was developing her concepts and writing the first book about how art was being used to help people understand themselves. Naumberg demonstrated to the psychoanalytic community through her work that people could reveal and resolve their conflicts through what they drew and painted.

His many therapists might have helped Jackson Pollock use his symbols to help himself in his struggle with alcoholism, but they were not aware in the late thirties and forties of the importance of the process of art and visual metaphors. Although Pollock was in therapy most of his adult life, he was not helped to use his graphic images as metaphors. In his own words, he "chose to veil the images," and no one was able to lift the veil. Like many artists who fear that it will destroy their creativity, Pollock was unwilling to explore the psychological meaning in his work.

I do not wish to disparage Jackson Pollock's contributions. A pioneer, he gave permission to artists throughout the world to develop their own unique expression, away from "schools" of art. However, I do believe we should understand the full dimension all the arts have for all of us, and accord them their rightful place in our educational system, helping us deal with our inner conflicts more effectively, and adding considerable pleasure and understanding to our lives.

Pollock achieved his fame after World War II, when major publications, including Time, Newsweek, and Life Magazine, having refined their color printing processes, went looking for colorful personalities, with interesting human interest angles. They found their men in Pollock, de Kooning, Gorky, Motherwell and others. The magazines reproduced their artwork before the paint was dry. Through this intense focus on their work nationally, New York replaced Paris as the center of the art world and the New York School, Abstract Expressionism and Action Painting came into their own.

The media created myths about Pollock, the western artist, making him bigger than life. He was the first "celebrity" artist, the western frontiersman who was seen walking around New York in cowboy boots and Stetson. A controversial figure, he nightly frequented the Cedar Bar, where sycophants plied him with liquor to watch him behave outrageously, pull doors off hinges, and break windows. Pollock seemed to enjoy the role of the outrageous renegade from the west, always good for a story, a notorious, brawling, risk-taking, self-destructive giant of the art world, succeeding in spite of himself. The apocryphal tale was that Pollock, working fast and literally pouring paint onto canvas, abruptly changed the history of art, and, living dissolutely (as was proper for an artist), died drunk as always, at the wheel of a car.

More to the truth is the story of a vulnerable, creative, and self-destructive man, never able to control his drinking. Never feeling accepted, always needing to be propped up, he was in crisis from the beginning of his life to the end. As we look at his history, we find a lack of stability, familial alcoholism, an absentee father, and a withholding, unempathic mother, incapable of "good-enough" mothering.

His early life

On January 28th, 1912, Paul Jackson Pollock was born in Cody, Wyoming, the youngest of five brothers, to Stella Mae McClure and LeRoy Pollock, a stone mason and cement worker. According to Stella, the to-be-famous artist was born with the cord wrapped around his neck, "black as a stove," weighing 12 1/2 lbs. His mother thought he was stillborn.

Both parents came from Scottish-Irish, sternly religious backgrounds. Neither was known for their warmth or humor. Pollock's father was born LeRoy McCoy, in Eugene, Iowa. LeRoy'a mother died of tuberculosis when he was two, and he was given away by his father to neighbors James and Elizabeth Pollock. He never heard from his father again. LeRoy was rented out to farmers to work the fields, as was the custom. He began his struggle with alcohol as a teenager. Described as a small, stern-looking, silent, withdrawn man, beaten by the depression, fearful, uneasy with people, he was dominated and overshadowed by Stella, his powerful wife.

Stella was the oldest of six, and, as a child, was responsible for her brothers and sisters. She has been described as self-effacing in her relationship with her own children, ready to serve them, but incapable of showing warmth and affection. Said to be more sophisticated than her farming background would suggest, uneducated Stella mistrusted all organized religion and governmental authority. Her artistic activities included weaving floor coverings at age twelve, and doing quilting as an adult. She encouraged doing any kind of art in the home, unique at that time for an extremely poor family with five sons. Even more unusual was her surprise that people would work simply for "moneyed success."

Stella was always seeking more, and restlessly moved the family each time her dreams failed to materialize. In the first nine months of Pollock's life, the family traveled 5000 miles, through eight states; then rested for a year and a half in National City before resuming travels to Phoenix, Chico and finally to Riverside and Los Angeles.

When Jackson was nine, LeRoy Pollock left Stella. He sent checks regularly but appeared rarely. By this time, Jackson, as well as his four older brothers, already drank. He had a reputation for being volatile even as a child, smashing a violin when he couldn't get the right sound out of it. His brothers said that although he was her favorite, his mother had no power over him.

In 1926 his brother, Charles, moved to New York and began studying with Thomas Hart Benton at the Art Students League.

By 1928, when Jackson was sixteen, Stella and her children had moved at least nine times. Possibly because of these frequent moves, Pollock made few friends outside his family. He was described as inarticulate, with a tendency to depression and withdrawal. He was a misfit, said to be uninterested in girls, socially inept, and a poor athlete, unable to fit in.

Family portrait with Jackson, age 5, lower left.

He was expelled from two high schools that year, Riverside High School in Riverside and Manual Arts High School in Los Angeles. Indeed, he was expelled from Manual Arts twice. He wrote his brother that the head of the physical education department and he came to blows. He had been publishing a newsletter complaining that there was too much emphasis on sports and English and not enough on the arts. He reported that they thought he was a "rotten rebel from Russia."

His art teacher, Frederick Schwankovsky, who taught at Manual Arts for thirty two years, encouraged the students to experiment with media. This relieved Jackson of having to be a draftsman in the conventional sense, and he wasn't. One of his brothers suggested, after looking at his artwork, he might do better in plumbing.

"Schwany" took his students to Ojai, where they listened to Krishnamurti. The message Pollock got from Krishnamurti was that it was OK to be an outcast, and he shouldn't strive to fit in, but trust his intuition and bypass the intellect.

In one of the few letters from Pollock to his brother, Charles, in New York, he wrote, "I am doubtful of any talent so whatever I choose to be will be accomplished by long study and work." He added, "People have always frightened and bored me. Consequently I have been within my own shell and have not accomplished anything materially."

After high school and in the summers, he worked with his father on surveying and road construction gangs and continued on his alcoholic path.

Pollock's influences

In 1930, at age 18, he left Los Angeles, joining his brothers, Charles and Frank, to study at the Art Students' League with Thomas Hart Benton. He worked as a janitor, hand-painted neckties and did other survival jobs to keep going.

In what appears to be a family portrait painted that year, Jackson graphically portrayed his perspective of his family, with a grotesque woman dominating all the smaller figures. Benton and his wife, Rita, were strong influences on Pollock, providing formal structure that he hadn't gotten in Los Angeles.

In 1930, the United States art scene was not significant. Anyone important was in Paris: Cassatt, Whistler, Sargent. Benton had studied in Europe also but had turned his back on European painting. Being a mid-westerner, on his return to New York, he assumed an agrarian or populist manner, painting in the social realism style, very acceptable at the time.

Painted Family

Benton was cut from the same cloth as Pollock. Small in stature like LeRoy Pollock, Benton was also an alcoholic from a rural area, distrustful of "city slickers" and art world sophisticates. A far cry from artists in Europe, who painted in suits and ties, he was a drinker, fighter, rebel, and provocateur, and "a sworn enemy of abstract painting." Vulgar, pugnacious and macho, Benton was the role model for a generation of American painters.

Jackson attached himself to him and his wife like a puppy.

For a time, Pollock also worked for Orozco, both modeling and painting on murals for him, and learned Orozco's flattened, highly rhythmic stylization, which may have influenced his later all-over patterning. He also admired the muralist, Rivera, who painted his patrons as villains. An even stronger influence on Jackson was Siqueros, known as El Duco because he used Duco house paint. In 1936, Pollock signed up to study with him on Union Square. Siqueros encouraged experimentation with new materials, spray guns, air brushes, synthetic paints, controlled accidents and the direct and spontaneous application of paint. This atmosphere of experimentation stimulated Pollock's practicality and inventiveness. He was ready to have an eclectic, "matter of fact" unorthodoxy about materials. It also appealed to him because he didn't have to worry about his lack of drawing skills and he could work, like Siqueros, on a large scale.

Jackson learned about surrealism, cubism and Jung initially from John Graham, né Ivan Dombrowski, an erudite Russian émigré, who arrived on the New York art scene from Kiev via Paris. Pollock joined other young artists to hear Graham expound on the concepts of Picasso and Freud as well, and above all, the role of the unconscious in art.

New York In The Thirties

A self-portrait done in dark colors in the fall of 1934 showed a haunted child, emaciated, hollow-eyed, posing before a mirror, depressed and frightened. In the depths of the depression, while he was struggling with his drinking, often hungry and always troubled, he painted *Flame*, a fragmented and thoroughly anxious painting, foreshadowing his later all-over compositions and predicting his radical development. The painting following *Flame* was even more chaotic, covered with fragmented anxious strokes.

At about this time, Pollock was hospitalized after being severely beaten. He had provoked his assailant by attacking him for feeding his dog better than Pollock was eating. He was living with his brothers and their wives, who frequently had to retrieve him from alleys and gutters where he lay drunk at night.

The WPA Federal Arts Project saved him temporarily. In this unusual program created by Roosevelt in the depths of the depression, the government provided salaries of $91.50 a month and art materials to pay starving artists to paint. They were allowed to devote themselves entirely to painting, with the stipulation that every four to eight weeks, they had to submit one painting intended for post

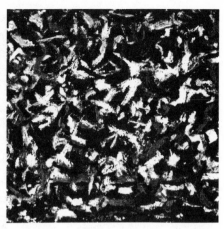

Flame #2, 1934

offices and other government buildings throughout the land. Pollock joined Rothko, Gottlieb, Ad Reinhardt, Arshile Gorky, De Kooning, and Pollock's future wife, Lee Krasner, who all painted in the style of Social Realism, creating clearly-defined people struggling with life. Gorky once referred to their efforts as "Poor art for poor people." As part of this project, Pollock painted about 50 paintings. One of his paintings turned up at a second-hand store on Canal Street in 1943. By the time the project had ended, the paintings, including work done by Alice Neel, Milton Avery, Rothko, Gottlieb and Pollock, sold at auction for 4 cents a pound.

To supplement his income, Pollock and his newly-arrived brother, Sanford, worked at the City and Country School as janitors for $10 a week. A teacher there, Helen Marot, an elderly social reformer and a close friend of Rita Benton, took a great interest in the young Pollock, forming an ongoing and somewhat stabilizing influence in his life.

In 1935 the Bentons moved to Kansas City, leaving Pollock abandoned by this family who had been so supportive of him. That year, he had his first show in a group exhibition, of watercolors, pastels and drawings at the Brooklyn Museum.

Several years later, he painted *Naked Man With Knife*, considered one of the most explicitly violent works in his career. The painting can be seen as an attack by a boy, possibly the artist, about to plunge a knife into his victim, also possibly the artist, who is trying to escape. It is a packed, undulating canvas that strongly reflects the influence of the Mexican muralists and Picasso as well as the violence of his life. Art critics suggest it is Pollock trying to rid himself of Benton's influences. I see it as two sides of Pollock in tremendous internal conflict. Of course, no one asked Pollock what it meant to *him*.

Naked Man with Knife, 1937

Pollock's hospitalizations

Pollock's therapeutic history illustrates the development of psychotherapy in the thirties and forties.

At age 25, Pollock voluntarily hospitalized himself for the first time for alcoholism at Bloomingdale Asylum, a psychiatric institute specializing in the treatment of anxiety disorders, where he saw James Wall, M.D. in 1937. The main treatment was occupational therapy. Wall believed that mothers of alcoholics were aggressive women who dominated their families, and fathers were weak role models. Wall thought that the second most common reason for male patients to seek therapy was conflict over homosexuality. Jackson made hammered copper plates and worked with wood at the hospital to prove his manliness, promised never to drink again and was released in four months. He was remembered at the hospital for his "strong creative urge."

Within six months he had another breakdown and was hospitalized again for his drinking problem, this time at Bellevue Hospital. Like his mother's moving from place to place, he went from therapist to therapist, absorbing the jargon, but not really taking it in. His sisters-in-law, who had to watch over him, felt he didn't really want to be helped, but just wanted to be taken care of. He complained about how incompetent his doctors were but it would seem he got exactly what he wanted. To further describe his impact on others, one of his sisters-in-law reported that she never heard him carry on a logical conversation, and his teacher, Benton, said his mind was absolutely incapable of logical sequences. Since the death of his father in 1933, he had avoided communicating with his mother, and although his brothers continued to support her financially, Pollock never contributed any money to her upkeep. His sisters-in-law felt he was consumed with guilt.

In 1939, after another severe crisis involving his roaming the streets at night drunk, while his brothers and their wives were again out looking for him, Helen Marot suggested that he go to a young Jungian psychoanalyst, Joseph Henderson, fresh from psychiatric training in England.

I interviewed Henderson in San Francisco in 1985 who confirmed Pollock's inability to articulate his feelings. He said Pollock would talk about himself in an impersonal manner, superficially describing aspects of his life. Spontaneously, he brought in drawings he had done, which Henderson felt was to prove his worth as an artist. Art therapy had not yet become a clinical discipline, and it is not clear that Pollock and Henderson used these drawings in an especially therapeutically productive way. However, Pollock did get an extensive course in Jungian symbolism.

Henderson kept no notes, but said his therapy was primarily supportive, not analytic. He saw Pollock as a talented but unknown artist suffering from severe mental disturbances, whose art gave him an avenue for "transcendence." He noted that Pollock was quite agitated at times and then was immobilized and withdrawn. In his periods of violent agitation, Henderson noted that he was incapable of rendering clearly articulated shapes.

Henderson left New York after he had worked with Pollock for eighteen months, with the gift of 83 of Pollock's drawings. He saved them for thirty years, and fourteen years after Pollock's death, after

Lee Krasner showed no interest in acquiring them, sold them to the Maxwell Galleries in San Francisco. They were reproduced in a catalog for a show at the San Francisco Museum of Art in 1971 with the title, *Psychoanalytic Drawings*, the text being notes of a lecture Henderson frequently gave to psychiatric residents. (Outraged, Pollock's widow Lee Krasner sought unsuccessfully to have Henderson's license revoked.) Henderson's selection for the cover of

the book, *Crucifixion*, suggested to him a depiction of self-punishment and death. However, he said he saw the progression of colors upward, from blue to red to yellow, as optimistic.

As Henderson noted, these drawings give remarkable insight into Pollock's psychopathology. Filled with images strongly influenced by Picasso's *Guernica*, which was being shown for the first time in New York, one impulsive jagged drawing looks like a cartoon of a battle. Henderson describes it as

Crucifixion

being done during a period of violent agitation. Another appears like a clown with drunk eyes. There were many agitated renderings of confused human and animal forms, including Picasso's alter ego, the bull.

In one drawing, a large female with jagged teeth denying access to her breast, strikes at an infant's dislocated head. In another picture there are at least two different heads with protruding teeth and a jagged agitated crown. An orange sun, rising or setting, a weapon, a twisted man and animal with jagged teeth, broken bodies exuding pain —all these mirror Pollock's inner world, set free by his acknowledgment of the power of abstract painting, and the willingness to explore his unconscious, in the cubist manner, rather than stay with Benton's conservative regional style.

A human figure in one Picassoid sketch is completely lost in the succeeding sketch, reflecting Pollock's need to dissolve form, to veil the image. By this time he was well on his way to total destruction of all imagery, and of himself, too.

One of the *Psychoanalytic Drawings.*

Pollock's reluctance to discuss the possible significance of his art with Henderson (a stance taken by many artists) was like his later reluctance to expose his imagery. Possibly overwhelmed by the power and violence of his images, he camouflaged them to disguise inadvertent self-revelation, a form of "visual denial."

According to Henderson, Pollock's art began to develop healthier signs during the period of their association. And indeed, although his problems were never resolved, he was able to sustain a high degree of productivity for the next few years. But he still drank. Henderson was not able to deal with that successfully.

1940 was an especially stressful year. Pollock was fired from the WPA for the second time, Helen Marot, who had been a mother substitute, died at age 75, and Henderson, substitute father, left for San Francisco. Two losses in one year took their toll and Pollock's next painting, done at this time, needs little interpreting. Not widely reproduced, this illustration of various ways to self-destruct, including the guillotine, hemlock and hanging, demonstrates the intensity of Pollock's despair.

Pollock then saw Dr. Violet de Laszlo, another Jungian psychoanalyst, for the next two years. Her opinion was that, despite his

29

flamboyant style, he was emotionally inhibited. She wrote a letter to the draft board suggesting his alcoholism would make him unfit for army life. She wrote, "He is a shut in and inarticulate personality of good intelligence but with a great deal of emotional instability, who finds it difficult to form or maintain any kind of relationship." He was declared 4F.

De Laszlo reported that she saw a picture with a figure hanging by a cord. "I took it to be a hint of suicide but I thought it was too delicate a subject to talk about." Forty-five years later, therapists would discuss it.

Ten Ways To Self-Destruct

In reminiscences by Pollock's acquaintances, they said he would react with rage when he couldn't do well, when he couldn't control people. He was said to constantly need stimulation and excitement to fill his empty feelings. According to Krasner, Pollock had severe mood swings. He responded quickly to his impulses. "When he thought of some activity, he'd just go ahead and do it." People remembered him ripping headlights off parked cars, punching his fist through panes of glass, crushing a drinking glass in his hand, and breaking down doors. Krasner said, "Whatever Jackson felt, he felt more intensely than anyone I knew. When he was angry, he was angrier, when he was happy, he was happier...a man of extreme complexity and intensity."

The painting, *Birth*, now at the Tate Gallery in London, is another violent energetic canvas with no center, and with images that defy clear meaning. It was this specific painting that brought him to the attention of the critics. No one else was painting with his kind of energy and force and he was beginning to be noticed.

Lee Krasner

Lee Krasner and Pollock had met originally in 1936 while they were both working in the WPA artists project. After seeing *Birth*, she again sought out the artist who created this powerful canvas. Four

years his senior, she entered his life in 1941 when he was broke, lonely, and in despair. They were in sharp contrast to each other, he inarticulate, avoiding people, she assertive, controlling.

Krasner was a strong, powerful woman. She was considered "aggressively contentious, abrasive and strongly opinionated." (Those terms today might be revised to describe her as "assertive, forceful, persevering, etc.) Since she had many important contacts in the New York art scene, she took over and developed Pollock's career. She was the idealized mother he never had. Her nurturing of him freed up his creative energies, and his style began to change.

Pollock was aware that his drawings had psychological significance. Art critics suggested that he received permission from the surrealists during this period to articulate his

Birth, 1941

unconscious, allowing his inner images to force their way out. Also, de Laszlo encouraged Pollock to accept the "babblings and doodles" of his unconscious as part of his personal identity. The words, "babblings and doodles," failed to convey the power and significance of Pollock's symbols and metaphors and denigrated the content of this revealing artwork.

Shortly thereafter, having met Krasner, de Laszlo terminated her sessions with Pollock. She said, "I could sense she was going to take over and that would exclude me....Lee was very possessive and so she was threatened by anyone else on whom he was dependent.... This was bound to end in antagonism."

Krasner was without doubt the most important figure in his life from then on. But new competition was on the way.

In 1942, the war in Europe brought many artists to New York. Peggy Guggenheim, the largest dealer, collector and art patron of modern art, returned from Europe with her new surrealist painter-husband, Max Ernst, and opened a gallery in Manhattan. Piet Mondrian, one of her advisors, was impressed with the vitality and looseness of Pollock's works. After Guggenheim had disparaged Pollock's work, he said, "I don't understand them but something very important is happening here."

For her part, Guggenheim has been quoted as saying, when she saw him nude, urinating in her fireplace, she knew he was a genius. He frequently demonstrated his genius in that manner, alienating many people. Guggenheim gave Pollock $150 a month initially. Two years later she increased it to $300 a month in return for his total artistic output. Later, she lent him money for the down payment on his house and five acres in Springs, L.I. and, when Pollock was 31, gave him his first one man show in the "Art of This Century Gallery." Pollock had arrived.

The myth begins

In the catalog introduction to his show, art critic James Sweeney began the myth about the artist, affirming Pollock as an instinctive force of nature. "Pollock's talent has fire. It is unpredictable. It is undisciplined," he said. Pollock's torments and struggles were suggested to be on a grander scale than most mortals. Pollock is said not to appreciate these comments.

Clement Greenberg, a friend of Lee Krasner from the WPA days and now one of New York's most influential art critics, also raved about Pollock's contribution, making him the fair-haired boy of the American Art Scene. Greenberg's critical acclaim was responsible for much of Pollock's fame. Pollock was said by Greenberg to be "the strongest painter of his generation, the greatest one since Miro. He was not afraid to look ugly. All profoundly original art looks ugly at first."

In 1942, Guggenheim commissioned him to do a mural for her home. Marcel Duchamps suggested that he paint the mural, 8 feet by 20 feet, on canvas, making it portable. He broke through a wall in his small studio and stretched the canvas out. After brooding and agonizing for a month, he painted the entire mural in one all night session. It consisted of large repetitive rhythmic strokes, in an all-over whirling hieroglyphic pattern, huge totem figures haltingly walking across the canvas, with heads floating about.

The mural finished, his one man show ended, he again lapsed into depression and alcoholism, even as his fame was spreading.

In 1943, Lee Krasner moved in with him on East 8th Street. At this time he painted *Male And Female*, two figures, on the left side mostly female and on the right, mostly male, with clear sexual identity elusive. Another painting, *Wounded Animal*, is reminiscent of prehistoric cave art. One critic said it looked like a dog begging. Upside down, it resembled a drunk. *She Wolf* is perhaps another representation of his angry feelings about the women in his life. It seems that the struggle to separate goes on.

Pollock and Krasner were married in 1945 and lived in the house that Peggy helped them buy in Springs. (Guggenheim declined to attend their small wedding, pleading a previous luncheon date.)

About this time, isolated from his drinking buddies through Krasner's efforts, he began to develop what has been called his "mature style" although there were still recognizable images in some canvases. Pollock named some of his early paintings himself. Other names were collaborative efforts with his friends and neighbors, suggesting that he really didn't deal well with words and lacked confidence. Later, he just numbered his paintings, allowing viewers to project their own meanings onto his works. He said, " I decided to stop adding to the confusion."

The Classical "Drip" Period

In 1947, Pollock stopped drinking. Lee Krasner's general practitioner in East Hampton helped him stop by putting him on phenobarbital and Dilantin, telling him the combination with liquor would kill him. For three years, he abstained. It was in these years, taking pills and not drinking, that Pollock finally developed the style for which he is renowned, where he threw himself into the action of painting, with an unstretched canvas laid flat on the floor, dancing around it, throwing ordinary house paint, producing complex networks of color in which there was no center of focus, no "composition" in the formal sense. He painted in the air and then the paint landed.

Pollock worked in this manner for the next 3 years, from 1947-1950, called by art critics his "Classical Drip Period." He attacked the canvas with a dance whose rhythmic energy translated itself into paint.

On a fateful day in 1950, Hans Namuth made a short film of him working on a huge plate glass, with the camera below watching him throw the paint. Pollock's physician, who had kept him sober by prescribing the sedatives, had died. Namuth was focusing on Pollock as a media star, rather than as an artist. Pollock saw himself as a failure, even though he was being recognized. He was troubled at being seen as "an event" rather than a fine artist, and reacted violently by going off the wagon in grand style. That evening after the film was completed, Pollock took one, then many drinks, and, in a famous, widely reported event, turned over the dining table with 10 roast beef dinners onto his guests.

For the next six years, he drank heavily, alienating many people, while Lee Krasner unsuccessfully attempted to keep him from his drinking buddies. He was famous and "notorious" at the Cedar Bar and other prominent nightclubs, where he created havoc in his tuxedo jacket and paint-stained jeans. Krasner was busy attempting to orchestrate his career as he went about undermining her efforts.

Ruth Fox, his next psychiatrist, confronted his drinking in 1950. She said she wouldn't do therapy with a drunk and put him on

Antabuse, sent him to AA and suggested to Lee Krasner that she was also responsible for the problem. They hadn't heard that approach before and didn't like it. Krasner, however, seems to have absorbed some of the information because she began to withdraw from Pollock and take better care of herself. She had her first solo exhibition in Manhattan several months later.

By 1951, the liquor was again in charge. As drinking loosened his control, he began to find and leave images similar to the those found in his work in the 30's. He still didn't discuss them. By now, Pollock had moved past his pure "splatter" style into his "black" period. Absence of color where it used to be suggests depression and his subject matter confirmed it. Mutilated human figures emerged, and his work had a funereal look about it. He began to find it difficult to paint at all, and since art was his voice, being inarticulate sent him even further into the depths of depression.

Possible Self Portrait, in the '50's

As Pollock deteriorated, Krasner became more invested in her own art. She cut up her old paintings and used them as collage material, reinventing her past! Their relationship deteriorated. In 1956, having broken his ankle when drunk, he stopped painting altogether and began to drink even more heavily. He began an affair with model Ruth Kligman, whom he met at the Cedar Bar. Krasner decided to go without him on what had been planned as their first trip to Europe. Her absence must have felt like abandonment to him.

While Lee was away, Pollock took Kligman and her girlfriend, Edith, for his last drunken drive in the country. Running the car into a tree, he died immediately, together with Edith. Kligman survived and, shortly thereafter, documented her love affair with Pollock in a biography.

Summary

Many in the art world dismiss the concept that fine artists' work can be interpreted in the same manner as "Sunday painters" or art therapy clients. They say artists make intellectual decisions, they are in charge of what appears on the canvas, and they conceal or reveal themselves as they choose. To a great extent, many artists are in charge, but to an even greater extent, their choices are intuitive, and unconsciously motivated.

Pollock talked frequently about needing to "veil the image," which I see as "visual denial," running away from his symbolic language and his personal problems. From my viewpoint as an art therapist, Pollock was painting his inner confusion. We all instinctively try to create order from chaos. It is part of the creative process. By avoiding this process, Pollock denied both himself and his therapists the access to his inner conflicts which his art could have afforded.

Jung wrote that symbol-making is therapeutic insofar as symbols bring to the surface contents of the mind that otherwise remain unconscious. When Pollock's imagery became most clearly defined, he decided to conceal it, consistent with his inability to verbalize his conflicts. His wife said that his abstract paintings began with recognizable imagery, heads, parts of bodies, fantastic creatures. He was acclaimed, however, for obscuring his personal images, for covering up those symbols which could have helped him understand his torment. Critics said that he "transcended" in the drip period with its all-over configurations. I see it as conscious denial.

Overwhelmed by the success of his formless paintings and unable to resolve his conflicts because it was too painful to look inside, he destroyed himself.

Comment by Barry Panter, M.D., Ph.D.

In *How Does Analysis Cure?* Heinz Kohut stated that there are two paths to mental and emotional well being: If the infant and child enjoys the affirming, nurturing empathic mirroring of his feelings, his ideas, his being, from the mother, he learns or "senses" in that pre-verbal world of infancy that his feelings and ideas are worthy; he learns that he has value. The second avenue is via the father. If the child has the presence and acceptance of the idealized father, the child can then merge with and internalize the grandeur and power of the father. Kohut states that if either of these is present, the child will develop into a fairly normal and healthy adult with a cohesive sense of self.

Neither of these paths were open to Pollock. As Dr. Virshup movingly describes, Pollock's mother was incapable of showing warmth and affection. In addition, she was taking care of five young children, and frequently packing everyone up and moving. One can assume that Jackson Pollock received little nurturing and affirmation from her. His father was an alcoholic depressed humorless man. He was not a man one could easily idealize. His absence after Jackson Pollock was nine years old, made for an even greater deficit in the developing personality.

One can speculate that Pollock grew up without the affirmation of an empathic mirroring mother and without a father whom he could idealize. Consequently Pollock never developed a cohesive sense of self. The important relationships in his life can be understood as his desperate attempts to make up for the deficiencies of his childhood and thereby heal himself. His choice of career probably stemmed both from the encouragement of his mother and his older brothers' working as artists, and from seeing his father work with his hands. Pollock may unconsciously have been attempting to merge with an aspect of his father. Unfortunately his heavy drinking was another way in which he could merge with his father.

In the art world, Pollock came in contact with several men who were mentors to him. These include his first art teacher Frederick Schwankovsky and later Benton. Pollock, working with them and becoming a painter, was attempting to merge with the idealized father. Several women provided some mirroring, especially of his painting. Helen Marot, Lee Krasner and Peggy Guggenheim recognized and praised him for his work. It is noteworthy that Pollock seemed to achieve a greater degree of emotional stability, a greater cohesiveness of the self, a greater ability to work, and a lessening of his inner and outer turmoil, when he was in one of these relationships. Some healing of the self was taking place at these times.

One of the consequences of inadequate mirroring is a vulnerability to narcissistic injury, and the reaction of narcissistic rage. Pollock was certainly an angry man. His urinating in public, his frequent fights, can be seen as angry reactions following feelings of humiliation and inferiority. His drinking may have been not only a destructive attempt to merge with his father, but also an attempt to quell the rage that arose in him so frequently.

His paintings and his painting technique are expressive of his inner chaos, the attempt to create a self, and his rage. By externalizing his inner demons onto the canvas, he had the chance to free himself momentarily of them, and possibly to begin to master them. By dripping, "urinating" on the canvas, as he did on the world, he was attacking the canvas. If this had occurred in a man of lesser talent, the work would be simply bizarre. However, Pollock, in his attempts to externalize his inner chaos and his anger on canvas, has given the world great works of art. One need only stand in front of one of his works, especially the larger ones, to feel the power, the energy, the chaos, and the desperation of man.

Scott Carder, a psychoanalyst-psychiatrist in full-time private practice at San Marino Psychiatric Associates in San Marino, California, is a clinical professor of psychiatry at the University of Southern California and a senior instructor at both the Southern California Psychoanalytic Institute and the Los Angeles Psychoanalytic Institute. Dr. Carder has given talks for AIMED on artists, musicians and psychiatric topics. He has published articles and book reviews in psychiatric journals. His special interest lies in the technique and practice of psychoanalysis and its relation to dream theory, to biological interfaces, and to the law.

Linda Carder is a private piano teacher in Pasadena, California, who received her Master's degree in Musicology from California State University, Los Angeles. Arnold Schoenberg was the subject of her thesis. Ms. Carder is a member and regular performer with Tuesday Musical, a music performance group in Southern California. Her interests lie in teaching, performing and studying classical music.

*Mine is a highly susceptible, intense sensuality which must be indulged if
my mind is to create the agonizing labor of calling a non-existent world
into being.* —Richard Wagner

Is Wagner a human being at all? Is he not, rather, a disease?
—*Friedrich Nietzsche*

Richard Wagner
The Symbolic Expression of the Grandiose Self
by Scott Carder, M.D., Ph.D. and Linda Carder, M.A.

The year 1983 marked the one hundredth anniversary of
Wagner's death. As Leonard Bernstein, renowned conductor of the
New York Philharmonic Orchestra, was rehearsing the famous part of
Die Gotterdammerung, known as *Daybreak*, he suddenly broke his
baton in half, and with tears streaming down his face, cried out,
"That is unbearable! How," he agonized, "could such beautiful music
come from the pen of such a corrupt man?"

A love/hate dilemma surrounds the name of this controversial
musician. Wagner's narcissistic personality led his genius down two
opposing paths: the path of a corrupt man on the one hand and that
of a composer of beautiful music on the other. His need to escape
from his developmental shortcomings led to a continuous desire to be
great, in fact, grandiose, which he symbolically expressed in many
ways in his musical dramas.

As the leading composer of German Romantic opera, Wagner is
one of the pivotal figures in the history of nineteenth-century music,
and one of only a few true opera reformers to surface since its birth
at the beginning of the seventeenth century.

As opera developed, composers quickly elevated the music to a position of supreme dominance through the introduction of the aria which then became the "central sun of the operatic system," overshadowing both action and text. Wagner's music drama was an attempt to reform opera by returning to the Greek ideals of unity of the arts, combining poetry, music, and acting into an equal cohesive whole, which he called Gesamtkunstwerke (universal art work).

As the Greeks had used the great myths of their culture, so Wagner turned to the myths of the Germanic or Teutonic races for his subject matter in order to create a feeling of kinship between audience and stage. The myth dealt with universal elements of human life, and presented the thoughts and inner emotions of its central characters. It was the poetry of the people, and he who looks below the surface will find in it the heart of a nation.

Wagner conceived of music as the psychological representation of emotions. He developed the idea of endless melody made up of short thematic ideas called 'leitmotifs' or leading motives, which were psychological expositions bound to people, things, or emotions. They contained a specific meaning and often changed shape as the character developed and displayed various feelings. In an interplay of characters and emotions and in his music drama, the orchestra functioned much like a Greek chorus, setting the mood and telling everything needed to know about a scene, not expressed by dialogue.

In his personal life, Wagner maintained his narcissistic or self-love style by blaming others for his own shortcomings. For deep personal and convenient cultural reasons, he focused much of his "blame of others" upon the Jewish people. (Adolf Hitler treasured the works of Wagner and was especially drawn toward the Aryan supremacy and anti-Semitic themes in Wagner's prose writings. Hitler carried much of what was implicit in Wagner's writings to its horrible conclusion in the holocaust. The Fuhrer often said, "Whoever wants to understand National Socialist Germany must know Wagner." Like the mad King Ludwig before him, Hitler identified with the grandiose heroic style of Wagnerian opera. Both these mad dictators made Wagner and his work their artistic "God.")

Childhood and adult life

Wagner was born in the spring of 1813, in the Jewish quarter of Leipzig, Germany. Three months later Johanna Wagner, his mother, married to Carl Wagner, had a week's rendezvous with Ludwig Geyer, an actor, artist, and family friend. The newborn Richard accompanied her on this unusual trip. Carl Wagner, Richard's legal father, died just six months after the boy's birth and Johanna married Geyer two years later. Ludwig Geyer died when Wagner was eight.

It is likely that Geyer was really Wagner's biological father, and there is evidence that the composer believed that to be true, although he denied it in his autobiography, *Mein Leben*. He was known as Richard Geyer through the age of fourteen. The word 'geyer' means vulture and is a common German-Jewish name. Interestingly, Wagner adopted the vulture as his crest throughout his life, and it was the emblem he chose for the cover of his autobiography. Due to his physical characteristics, his name, and birthplace, Wagner as Richard Geyer was considered Jewish by classmates and townspeople.

Wagner was a child genius, the youngest of nine siblings, over-indulged and extremely close to his mother. Both his mother and sister, Rosalie, encouraged his grandiosity, which was apparent even at that early age. Rosalie was a local stage star, and when the rest of the family moved to follow her stage career, Wagner, then fourteen, stayed behind. Wild and undisciplined, he left school and wandered about, spending some time with his uncle, Adolph Wagner, discussing literature and philosophy. Probably with Adolph's encouragement, he changed his name back to Wagner. He labored over the writing of his first play, *Leubald*, in which the hero seeks

Richard Wagner

vengeance for the murder of his father by murdering several people and then, chased by ghosts of his victims, goes mad. It would seem that Wagner, at fourteen, was struggling with the loss of his stepfather, Geyer.

At age sixteen, Wagner found an idealized love in a leading German actress, Schroder-DeVrient, whom he had seen in the title role of Beethoven's *Fidelio*. Imitating the great Beethoven, who had set the poetry of Goethe's story to music, Wagner decided to compose music to enhance his own drama. With little sense of humility, he felt he started where Beethoven left off and would carry new ideas for melody and harmony into the future.

He enrolled in a university at the age of eighteen as a music student. Here he went from a life style of self-indulgence to one of wild extravagance, as he drank, gambled, and in a brash, grandiose way, challenged some of the best swordsmen of the day. His narcissistic self-centeredness led to his being incapable of making close friends, for he 'talked at' rather than with people, and was intolerant of views differing from his own. His quick temper and tirades of incessant talking alienated so many people that he left the university after six months. Later he was to proclaim, "Life, art, and I, myself were my only teachers."

Throughout his life, experiences with friends and family were turned into components of his art work, for, even more than most artists, his creativity followed the path of his life. He may also have uniquely lived out and practiced some of his artistic ideas as they appeared in his dream life.

Wagner's grandiosity gave him both the reason and the drive to accomplish what his genius allowed, but it also created problems with his artistic creations. His lack of concern for proportion always tended toward the extreme, larger than life and without restraint. The opening night of an early opera, *Rienzi*, for example, continued for five hours, so long that Wagner stopped the clock visible to the auditorium, hoping to dupe his exhausted audience.

Wagner's life, continually stressed by financial problems and the drive to be recognized as a genius, made him withdraw into his grandiose artistic fantasies and escape the blows to his self esteem in the real world. He developed an Olympian attitude, placing himself above all other artists, and frequently demeaning and blaming others for his own shortcomings. By the age of twenty-two, he was well entrenched in his irresponsible pattern of living extravagantly, always pressured by debts, without responsibility or limits in finances or in any other area of his life. He took from family and friends throughout his life and felt no obligation to repay them. When pressed by creditors, he felt contempt and considered them, "the cursed-rabble of the Jews."

His narcissistic personality made it difficult for him to accept the success of others. Expressing contempt and envy for prominent men including Franz Liszt, at age 29, he wrote his mother, "I have felt bound to despise whomever I have seen succeed..."

By then a recognized conductor, Wagner felt it his right to completely revamp the works of others in his own image. Assuming that he alone knew what previous masters like Bach and Beethoven meant to express in their music, Wagner proceeded to alter their works at will. At the same time, he was infuriated with anyone who dared to make changes in his own compositions. Needless to say, Robert Schumann and other music critics of the time were more favorably drawn toward conductors, including Mendelssohn, who were conservative and objective in interpreting the works of past masters. Wagner's envy and inability to take criticism led him to an obsessive hatred of Schumann.

During the course of Wagner's life, scandal and shame followed as he carried on affairs with various married women, often as a house guest under the noses of their unsuspecting husbands. *Tristan and Isolde*, an opera about a great love affair, was written while he was a guest at the home of Matilde and Otto von Wesendonks, immortalizing Wagner's affair with the beautiful Matilde. At the time, the cuckolded husband, Otto, was subsidizing Wagner!

The worst scandal involved Cosima, the daughter of Wagner's friend and ardent supporter, Franz Liszt. Cosima had three children by Wagner while she was still the wife of the famous conductor, Hans von Bulow. Eventually divorcing von Bulow, she renounced her Catholicism to marry Wagner. She dedicated herself to him for the rest of his life through her amazing ability to idealize him, submit to his will, forget his cruelty, and to live for and through his art.

Wagner sold the exclusive rights to publish his works several times to different people. Although his benefactor, King Ludwig of Bavaria, often came to the financial rescue of the ungrateful composer, Wagner ignored Ludwig's legal rights to *The Ring Cycle* and sold it to others for his own profit. After all, "It was only the pursuit of gold by Frenchmen and Jews that Wagner found seriously immoral."

Both *Mein Leben*, his autobiography, and Cosima Wagner's diary were his own "personal myths" in which he freely altered the facts to fit the image he wanted to present to posterity. Cosima's diary reveals Wagner's insecurity and his view of himself as a victim of misfortune at the hands of others. It contains a rather complete dream record for the last sixteen years of his life.

Grandiosity was a striking component in his dreams of royalty, wealth, and power, where he saw himself as the son of a queen or the husband of a princess. The diary also reveals the intensity and dependency in his relationship with Cosima, who was equally dependent upon him. Wagner's dreams betray his constant fear that Cosima would leave him, for she was twenty-four years younger, had deserted one husband already, and was frequently the recipient of his angry, abusive behavior.

Wagner certainly did not treat others fairly, so he had good reason for his doubts and suspicions toward them. He had little concern for others except as objects of self-gratification. Thus the normal, separate, and individual interests of others were seen by Wagner as a criticism of his own thoughts and ideas. Wagner firmly believed in his musical genius, and, in his passionate pursuit of it, any means justified the end.

Wagner's anti-Semitism

Wagner told King Ludwig, "I consider the Jewish race to be the born enemy of pure humanity and all of its nobility. We Germans will be ruined by them." As a true precursor of Nazi madness, he suggested the "final solution" which Adolf Hitler would attempt to carry to its grim and hideous conclusion. Wagner said, "All Jews should burn to death..." In discussions with H. S. Chamberlain, who was to become Hitler's philosophical idol, Wagner developed a sense of racial purity which he then portrayed, thinly veiled behind "Christian doctrine" in his final opera, *Parsifal*. Wagner and Chamberlain decided that Jesus could not possibly have been a Jew, so they contrived to make him a pure Aryan, Nordic figure! Like later Nazi propagandists, they falsified facts and called the result "higher truth!"

(Later, Hitler had a close relationship with Winifred Wagner, the widow of Siegfried, the son of Richard Wagner. Many of Hitler's associates encouraged him to marry her. However, she confided to her physician and her daughter her fear of Hitler's unorthodox approach to love-making, especially after he asked her to whip him!)

Anti-Semitism did not prevent him from seeking out certain Jews to labor on his behalf. In spite of his malicious and demeaning treatment of them, many Jewish musicians and benefactors supported him. For example, Wagner accepted the assistance of Hermann Levi, a great conductor of the Munich opera who was a slavish devotee to Wagnerian opera. Wagner treated him cordially, but drove him to despair by publicly lamenting his miserable fate of having been born a Jew, and taunted him by demanding that Levi convert before he could conduct the premier performance of *Parsifal*.

Frederick Nietzsche, one of the nineteenth century's foremost philosophical thinkers, was once a close friend and admirer of Wagner, but their relationship decayed. As a great dramatist, Wagner was able to both reveal and conceal, which allowed him to make the unacceptable acceptable. The disenchanted Nietzsche feared that others would become intoxicated by the music of this morally degenerate composer and surrender to the subtle message inherent in his works. Nietzsche wrote,

> The last thing I am prepared to do is look on innocently while this decadent man ruins our health and music as well. Is Wagner a person at all

47

or a disease? Everything he touches becomes infected and he has made music sick!

The Ring of the Niebellung

Wagner's mother died in January of 1848. During the following summer, he began work on his famous *"Ring Cycle."* (The longest opera ever written, sixteen hours, it is performed each year in Bayreuth, Germany and Seattle, Washington.) His mother's death probably confronted Wagner with the reality of his own mortality, an almost impossible situation for a narcissist, who by definition has no flaws, especially fatal ones. From this conflict between a fantasized, grandiose immortality on the one hand and the reality of death on the other, *The Ring of the Niebelung* was born.

Based on ancient Teutonic mythology, this music drama tells the story of man's social and political history expressed symbolically through a power versus love conflict. The opera is in four parts: *The Rhinegold; The Valkyrie; Siegfried;* and *The Twilight of the Gods.*

In the introductory drama, *Das Rheingold* (The Rhinegold), he sets the stage for a clash between gods, heroes, giants, and dwarves for domination of the world. He who obtains the ring of gold will rule the world, yet will be plagued by the curse of death. The two main characters are Wotan, chief of the gods and present ruler of the world through an authoritarian government based on law, and Alberich, the leader of the lowly dwarves who conspires to obtain the ring from the maidens, overpower Wotan, and rule the world by ruthlessness.

In part two, *Die Walkure* (The Valkyrie), Wotan fails in his efforts to seize the ring because the first hero he creates, Siegmund, is not free of Wotan's laws. Siegmund is denied the ring because he has broken the laws against incest and adultery. By the end of this drama, Wotan realizes that to obtain the ring from the maidens, he must have a hero free of his rules.

In part three, *Siegfried,* the new free hero created by Wotan forges a magical sword, gains the ring by slaying a dragon, kills the dwarf who raised him, and wins the hand of the fair maiden, Brunnhilde.

The final drama, *Die Gotterdammerung* (The Twilight of the Gods), portrays the death of Siegfried and Brunnhilde and the total destruction of the castle, Valhalla, and the kingdom of the gods.

As *The Ring Cycle* was originally conceived by Wagner, Siegfried was to have been led in triumph to Valhalla by Brunnhilde. Siegfried was the intended hero of the drama. The projection of regenerate man, Siegfried, was to replace the corrupt Wotans, Alberiches, and Mimes of existing society. Siegfried represented Wagner in his youth as well as the middle-aged Wagner's hopes for immortality through a son.

When Wagner first began the drama he was a young revolutionary and follower of Feurbach's optimistic philosophy, but "he eventually came to realize that the 'man of the future' was a figment of the overheated imaginations of idealistic revolutionaries including himself." As he grew older, Wagner shed his youthful optimistic philosophy for the pessimistic ideas of the nineteenth century philosopher, Schopenhauer. The original optimistic ending was cancelled, and Siegfried instead vanishes along with everything else in the ultimate holocaust.

Wotan is Wagner in his maturity at the time of the writing of the drama. Wagner found himself unconsciously allowing Wotan to displace Siegfried as the hero of *The Ring Cycle*. His deep narcissistic fixation would not allow even his own past or future to be superior to his present state!

The third part of *The Ring Cycle*, *Siegfried*, a three act drama, stands as a beautiful example of Wagner's grandiosity. Act I begins in a primeval forest, within a cave containing a forge belonging to the dwarf, Mime, brother of the ruthless Alberiche. The dwarf is complaining about forging swords for Siegfried, the foundling boy he has reared. Siegfried demeans Mime's work and is disgusted with his incompetence. Mime reminds the boy of how he has fed, reared, and cared for him since birth, and he complains that Siegfried is ungrateful. An example of the narcissistic rage of our hero, Siegfried, can be heard in the following comment:

Disgraceful botcher: I wish I'd broken (the swords) across his skull!
...But no sooner do I grasp what he has hammered firmly in my fist than
I crush the rubbish to bits! If I did not find the wretch utterly beneath
contempt, I would smash him to bits himself along with his trinkets, the
stupid old hobgoblin.

Like the Greek god Narcissus, our young Siegfried discovers his
good looks by seeing his reflection in the water. Then in a defiant
self-centered and devaluing way Siegfried continues to tell Mime
how much he hates him. Taking the dwarf by the throat, he demands
to know who his real parents were.

Mime tells him how he found his mother, Sieglinde, who died at
his birth, and as proof Mime produces the pieces of his father's
sword. Siegfried rejects Mime's expressions of love and caring, and
impetuously demands that the dwarf repair the sword so he can leave
and never see Mime again. Siegfried runs off leaving Mime in
despair, faced with a task he cannot accomplish. Mime regrets that
he has not been able to teach Siegfried to love him or to know fear.

Siegfried impatiently decides to make his own sword from the
pieces of his father' s weapon. As he does so, Mime decides that he
must guide Siegfried to the dragon who now guards the gold ring,
then murder Siegfried, take the ring, and himself become ruler of the
world. Act I ends as Siegfried sings his forging song, "Nothung,
Nothung!" and, as he finishes, to Mime's terror, he splits the anvil in
two with one mighty stroke!

As Act II opens, Mime has taken Siegfried to a cavern in the
woods where he has promised to teach him fear by showing him the
dragon. In this scene, Wagner depicts an exchange between the dwarf
and hero which may be reminiscent of repressed feelings about his
Jewish stepfather, Geyer. Through the loss of this previously idealized parent, Wagner developed a vicious anti-Semitism. You can also
see the narcissistic, self-centered rage, omnipotent control, and lack
of regard for the other person.

The libretto reads:

Mime: (when you learn fear) ...then you will
thank me, who guided you, and
bethink you of how much Mime loves you.

Siegfried: (furiously)
You are not to love me! Haven't I told you so?
...How happy I feel
that he is not my father!
...now the loathsome creature has departed,
and I shall never see him anymore!

Wagner never knew his legal father, Carl Wagner, and he feared that Geyer, the Jew, was his true father. He ruminates about this possibility through Siegfried's voice:

What must my father have been like?
Ha!—like me myself, of course!
For had Mime a son anywhere about,
would he not look exactly
like Mime? Just as filthy, senile, and gray,
little and crooked hump-backed and lame,
with drooping ears,
and watery eyes—
Away with the goblin,
I don't want to see him anymore.

Siegfried, our "innocent" hero, kills the dragon and then swiftly murders Mime, his stepfather. Act II ends as the birds lead him to his bride, Brunnhilde, who is also his aunt and half-sister. She sleeps on a rock circled with fire, so that she will be awakened only by a hero who knows no fear.

Act III opens with Wotan (Wagner) calling forth his mother, the earth-goddess, Erda, from a deep sleep underground. He asks how fate can be changed and the destruction of the gods averted? During the exchange, he becomes resigned to the downfall of the gods for he has bequeathed his world to Siegfried, who, free from greed and happy in love, will redeem the world. Here Wagner, in his fantasy, was speaking to his dead mother awakened from her grave beneath the earth. He asks her all-knowing wisdom to reveal his fate. Is it to be death like all those generations who have gone before him?

Passing through the ring of fire, Siegfried discovers the sleeping woman. Confused and excited, he calls for help from *his* mother:

Mother! Mother!
Remember me!

How shall I waken the maid?
...Is this then fearing?
Oh, Mother, Mother,
your fearless child!
A woman lies asleep—
She has taught him to fear!
How shall I put an end to the fear?
... Awake! Awake, holiest of women!

Here the awakening of sexual desire and of idealized love is equated with fear. Love is the vulnerable spot for a narcissistic hero. This desire or need for another person makes the invincible one vulnerable and therefore fearful of the painful loss of the valued object. The incestuous intermingling of mother, step-sister, and erotic lover certainly comes from the depths of Wagner's childhood.

The drama ends as Brunnhilde feels many conflicting emotions: love of Siegfried, joy at awakening, shame and anger at the impending loss of her virginity, and above all a sadness that her lovemaking with Siegfried will mark the end of the gods, the castle Valhalla, and all the world. She resists his advances, but finally she is aroused by his intense love, and they passionately embrace.

The final drama of *The Ring Cycle, Die Gotterdammerung* (The Twilight of the Gods), begins with a lovely daybreak scene, and it ends as the hero, Siegfried, is drugged and then murdered. His lover, Brunnhilde, rides her horse into his funeral fire, which then burns the castle of the gods. The fire returns the world to its basic elements. And the gold ring is returned to the Rhine whose waters rise and cover all. It is the end of the world!

Discussion: the grandiose self, part of a narcissistic personality

The Wagner/Geyer family was flamboyant and theatrical. As a young boy, Richard adored Ludwig Geyer and carried his "step" father's name. His lifelong passionate and dramatic artistic pursuit may have been enhanced by an attempt to identify with, and yet deny, Ludwig Geyer's death which left him "abandoned" when he was but eight.

His relentless anti-Semitism may have been an expression of his self-centered vengefulness. His guilt for harboring these feelings may have been part of the ghosts which plagued his nightly dreams throughout childhood. Throughout many of his operas we find a recurring theme of the absent father, often dead, gone, or else vague and ill-defined. Heroes such as Lohengrin had to hide both name and race in order to work wonders. For Lohengrin, the speaking of his own name destroys the knight's happiness and forces him to leave his home. Lohengrin's self symbol is a swan, while Wagner's was a vulture. (The mad King Ludwig adopted the Lohengrin motif and built the "new swan" (Neuschwanstein) castle. The entire structure is filled with pictures, symbols, and art works of Wagnerian opera, especially that of Lohengrin.)

The *grandiose self* is a part of normal early psychological development. In the normal individual, this original *grandiose self* is gradually integrated into the personality. It is also seen in adults in an extreme unintegrated form in the narcissistic personality. Heinz Kohut initiated the term, *grandiose self,* to stand for an exaggerated sense of self esteem, the outcome of the disturbance of equilibrium of primary narcissism. The original symbiosis of mother and child is inevitably disturbed during normal psychic development, and the heir to that original perfection is this internal psychic structure which Kohut called the *grandiose self.*

Throughout childhood, we have relationships which lay the foundation for our personalities. Just enough *failure* in a relationship which reflects a child's grandiosity and just enough *failure* of merging with an idealized parent *creates healthy separation and a good sense of self.* If too little or too much failure occurs then problems arise in regulating self esteem. In normal development, the child gradually gives up the protective grandiose sense of self and replaces it with a good but limited self concept. For the child or adult with a grandiose self, his love is "boundlessly exhibitionistic with endless yearnings to be perfect and to be admired as such." His aggression has a limitless need for absolute power and omnipotent control. Disappointments lead to an endless wish for punishment and revenge, which Wagner expressed over and over again in his operas.

Otto Kernberg highlights the similarities between destructive self-love or narcissism and the personalities which function on the borderline of psychoses. The main characteristics of a narcissistic personality are: grandiosity, self-centeredness, and a lack of interest in and empathy for others in spite of being eager for admiration and approval. The narcissist is unable to depend on other people and sees an admired person as merely an extension of himself. He has an intense envy of others seen as having things he does not have. He needs to devalue whatever he receives from others in order to avoid experiencing gratitude. Moreover, the narcissist is not able to feel genuine sadness, and when abandoned or disappointed by others, he may show surface sadness but a deeper pervading anger and resentment develops.

The narcissist's enjoyment comes through his grandiose fantasies or from recognition from others. He idealizes some people from whom he expects narcissistic feeding, and he depreciates and treats with contempt those from whom he does not expect anything (often former idols). He is exploitative, parasitic, and feels he has the right to control and possess others and to use them without guilt. There is a cold ruthlessness behind a charming and engaging surface. He needs much tribute and adoration from others, yet has a deep distrust of them and a desire to depreciate their worth.

The self can be considered grandiose and all good only so long as the bad components of one's self are seen as existing in other people or in one's past. By maintaining a sense of grandiosity the person defends himself against awareness of painful feelings such as inadequacy, insecurity, dependence, and loss.

Summary

A brief review will tie together some of the dramatic opera, "Siegfried," with Wagner's life and personality. Both Siegfried, the man of the future, and Wotan, the leader of the gods, represent projections of Wagner's grandiose self, while Alberich and Mime, the dwarves, are components of the denied and projected bad self. Erda, the mother Earth Goddess, and Brunnhilde, his incestuous lover, are selfobjects, reflections of his past early love relationships, especially with his mother and sister/mother, Rosalie.

Siegfried has lost both parents and is reared by Mime, a member of the lower race which inhabits the bowels of the earth, not unlike Wagner, raised by a Jew whose culture was demeaned in 19th century Germany.

Siegfried kills the bad father figure, Mime, shatters the spear of the other demeaned father figure, Wotan and then enters into an incestuous love affair with his sister/aunt, Brunnhilde. Wagner who was haunted by nightmares throughout childhood, possibly achieved relief from his murderous oedipal wishes with this scenario.

Siegfried goes off into the world to slay dragons, aided by his own self-forged sword made of fragments of his deceased father's weapon. In reforging this ancestral sword, Siegfried is Wagner who gathered parts of his past: his musical/legal father, Carl Wagner; his theatrical/artistic stepfather, Ludwig Geyer; and his literary/surrogate father/uncle, Adolf Wagner. From these father figures, Wagner, the fourteen year old composer, proceeded to forge a new identity. He changed his name from Geyer to Wagner, the "tool" of his father who had died so long ago. With this new non-Jewish name, he formed his identity as a musical poet and dramatist, and headed out into the world to pursue his grandiose aspirations.

Wagner endowed his hero, Siegfried, with almost unlimited contempt for the less endowed older men, his father figures, Wotan and Mime. Undoubtedly expressing anger and disappointment Wagner felt for his absent father and stepfather, they also reveal the contempt and depreciation of a cruelly perfectionistic part of his personality toward the imperfect middle-aged and older man that he himself was becoming. The perfectionistic grandiose part of himself was disgusted with and unable to accept the process of becoming older.

Wagner's final acceptance of Siegfried's death may have signified his partial resignation to the passing of his own infantile omnipotence and an acceptance of the ultimate finality of his own death.

Conclusion

The genius of Wagner lay in the fact that he persisted in spite of, and almost because of, conflicts which resulted from his grandiosity and narcissism, and which he was able to express through his art. His creative expression, like that of many artists, was a projection of, as well as an attempt to relieve, his inner emotional stress.

The appeal of Wagner, the musician, and the revulsion toward Wagner, the man, form opposite poles of an ambivalent magnetic field which surrounds his name even today, over one hundred years after his death. Love for his music and hatred for the man and his venomous ideas still create a painful dissonance. It is no wonder that men such as Bernstein and Nietzsche found the seduction of Wagner's music "unbearable!"

Leon E. A. Berman, M.D., is a Lecturer at the Michigan Psychoanalytic Institute, and Clinical Associate Professor of Psychiatry at Wayne State University College of Medicine. His clinical publications include: The Role of Amphetamine in a Case of Hysteria; Sibling Loss and Unconscious Guilt; Primal Scene Significance of a Dream Within a Dream; *and* Rearview-Mirror Dreams. *Publications in applied psychoanalysis have studied* W.S. Gilbert, Max Ernst, *and* The Tale of the Red Shoes. *His international presentations have included studies of* James Bond and Ian Fleming, Gilbert and Sullivan, *and* A Psychoanalytic Inquiry Into the Meaning of Comedy. *Dr. Berman presents the classical psychoanalytic viewpoint in his discussion.*

Birth and death are so closely related that one could not destroy either
without destroying the other. It is extinction that makes creation possible.
—Samuel Butler

An Artist Destroys His Work
Comments on Creativity and Destructiveness
by Leon E. A. Berman, M.D.

The more one studies the subject of creativity, the more complex and bewildering it seems, and the closer one comes to accepting Freud's conclusion that it simply cannot be understood. Attempts to define the creative process have focused on the role of the unconscious and instinctual drives; narcissism; a host of ego activities including conflict, adaptation, sublimation, integration, dissociation, desynthesizing, and regression in the service of the ego; and such diverse affects as awe, wonderment, loneliness, inspiration, and ecstasy. Significant life experiences have been considered as well as innate endowments. Traumatogenic theories of creativity have implicated childhood abuse, loss, illness, and congenital deformity. In the midst of all this attention, the character of the poor artist has been idealized, diagnosed, and defamed. He has been associated with the infant, the child, and the adolescent; the dreamer, the prophet, and the rebel; the neurotic, the impostor, the sociopath, the pervert, the criminal, and the psychotic.

Perhaps no question has been more fascinating and perplexing than the relation between creativity and madness. We are used to thinking of artists as unusual, eccentric characters who step to a different drummer. They seem to stand apart from the rest of society, unconcerned about popular values and the rules of social behavior. We accept this in them; in fact, we come to expect it. We admire and envy them for it—these colorful, eternal children who bring such beauty and joy into our lives. But histories of the lives of many creative artists suggest that they are more than just eccentric: that they show a higher incidence of mental illness than the general population. A number of reports in the recent psychiatric literature have linked creativity with bipolar mood disorders (Andreasen, Jamison, Richards). Is this indeed true, or is it due to the fact that the more pathological examples, such as Van Gogh, receive the greatest publicity? What about great creative artists such as Bach, Rubens, and Saint Saens, who seem to have been healthy, well integrated personalities, who had healthy relationships and led essentially normal lives?

If it is true that there is a significant correlation between creativity and madness, then why is this so? Is it simply that pathological personalities are more attracted to creative fields? Or is there something intrinsic in the creative process that predisposes to emotional illness? Is madness the risk they run, or, like the Faustian bargain, the price they pay for their creativity? However they come by it, is a certain degree of madness a prerequisite for great artistic creativity? If one purposely regresses, relaxes the ego's defenses or dissolves the ego's boundaries, and dips down into the unconscious in order to experience primitive emotions, then it seems reasonable to presume that one is flirting with some form of mental disorder. Certainly many artists have described this to be the case. In some, like Sylvia Plath, their artistic works portray the creative process as a relentless drive toward madness and suicide. Their urge to create is a demon within that must inevitably destroy them.

Yet, this is not the only way in which the artist experiences his creativity. In some it is sustaining, reparative, and even life-saving. Kafka clung to his typewriter as a means of preserving his sanity, and Robert Louis Stevenson's writing helped him bear a painful, chronic physical illness and, in the end, to accept death with remarkable courage and equanimity. While psychoanalysts have important contributions to make to this subject, it must be concluded that we know a great deal more about madness than we do about creativity. We are more familiar with the passions that drive creativity, than we are with the ego functions so vital to the process: the craft that molds passion into art. When it comes to aesthetics or what constitutes "great" art or "genius," these questions are beyond our qualifications.

The psychoanalytic literature is filled with disagreements, generalities, and reductionistic theories. Some state that there is no intrinsic connection between creativity and madness, while others affirm categorically that there is—or must be in the case of "great" works of art. Pathographies of famous artists point to all manner of external occurrences and presumed intrapsychic events that lead to psychopathology and creativity. Yet we are continually vexed by the fact that not all creative artists are mad, and not all mad people are creative. One of the problems in approaching this subject is reductionism: our tendency to speak of the artist and the creative process. In fact, despite the stereotype, there are countless varieties of artists. They are perhaps as different from one another as they are from the general public. And even more importantly, there is not one but many creative processes: different formulas and combinations of factors that can result in creativity. Rubens did his best work while comfortably ensconced at his country estate, surrounded by his loving wife and children; in stark contrast is Caravaggio, who created his greatest masterpieces amid suicidal depressions, paranoid rages, poverty and imprisonment.

In the case I will describe, the artist's creativity was intimately associated with destructiveness. To what extent this is generally true of artists or the creative process, I do not know; but it was certainly a part of this man's formula. When the destructive component was in balance or under sufficient control, he was able to produce excellent works of art; when it was not, he was psychotic and self-destructive, and on two occasions he destroyed all of his work.

Clinical case

John was a 24 year-old artist who was referred to me following a four week hospitalization, which was precipitated by a psychotic episode. I was encouraged to see him because he was considered to be immensely talented and had great promise as a painter.

This particular mode of referral deserves some comment. While I might have decided to see him as a patient in any case, the fact that he came touted as a promising artist and I was encouraged to see him for this reason, raises certain countertransference problems from the outset. He presents as an exception—the "gifted" patient—potentially capable of making a great contribution to society. The therapist in such a case feels an added sense of obligation to help the patient for the sake of posterity. This becomes an unspoken goal of treatment: to see to it that this talented person achieves his potential. The therapist may resent the added burden. Or, he may envy such a patient. He may also be seduced into the narcissistic gratification of contributing to the patient's success, and thus sharing in his greatness.

I saw John three times a week for a period of ten months in psychoanalytic psychotherapy. It ended when he was rehospitalized. While this brief psychotherapy could not yield the data of an extensive analysis, certain characteristics of this patient made it possible to learn a great deal in a short time. Firstly, he was very eager to reveal himself and he had considerable capacity to do so. Secondly, since he was psychotic, he could express unconscious themes in more direct, less disguised forms—often through acting out. While this made for a very interesting study of creativity and destructiveness, or the creative process gone awry, it was also a frustrating and depressing case. I felt there was little I could do but sit by and observe as his destructive impulses put an end to his artistic career, his therapy, and very nearly his life.

In summarizing the case, I will describe the events of his illness, his childhood (which I learned about mainly from his parents), and our work in therapy. While a number of issues came to light and were addressed in therapy, this presentation will concentrate on what was learned about the relationship between creativity and destructiveness in this patient. It should not be construed that such a study was an intended goal or focus of the therapy.

John's earlier life

John was the eldest of two children. His parents were middle class professionals. He recalled a happy, normal childhood, with no serious illnesses or separations. He showed exceptional artistic talent from an early age and was praised and encouraged by his parents. He was an excellent student, winning numerous academic as well as artistic awards. He won scholarships first to college and then to a prestigious art school. His work was highly regarded and he was considered a very promising young painter.

During his last few months before graduating from art school, he became increasingly anxious and depressed. He related the onset of these symptoms to the break-up with his girlfriend, his doubts about the quality, integrity and direction of his artistic work, and his "disillusionment and disgust" with modern society in general. He began using a variety of drugs, including marijuana, LSD, and hallucinogenic mushrooms. He also became increasingly preoccupied with a famous rock group. He would listen for hours to tapes of their music and fantasized joining them.

Following graduation, John left on a trip to another state. He drove a van loaded with his art work, intending to enter competitions and arrange for gallery shows. Some preliminary contacts had been made with galleries and exhibitors who were quite interested in his work. He decided to coordinate his trip with a concert tour of his favorite rock group, planning to attend several of their concerts. He was particularly enamored with one member of the group: an older guitar player and the group's philosophical spokesman. He longed to meet and talk with him and express his love and admiration.

Thus began an odyssey of several weeks, which would include some exalting and frightening experiences. While attending the concerts, intoxicated on drugs, he was so consumed with "insight," a sense of beauty, and love of humanity, that he feared he would "explode." At times, he danced and sang aloud, making such a "spectacle" of himself that he was ejected from the concert. At other times, he tried to climb onto the stage to embrace the guitar player and participate with the group, and had to be forcibly restrained.

Eventually he joined a company of fellow wanderers and went hiking in the mountains, to sketch and commune with nature. During this trip, he experienced two close calls. He fell into a river and was barely rescued by his companions before being swept away by the current. Later, while hiking, he slipped and fell, injuring his leg, and had to be carried back to civilization and treated in a hospital.

When he finally reached his destination, he stayed at the home of a young married couple he knew from college days. In long, intense conversations with them he poured out his feelings about love, beauty, and art, and his anger and disillusionment with the establishment. One night, while alone in his friends' home, he became increasingly agitated and depressed. Then, in a sudden burst of "insight," he realized what he had to do. He coolly and systematically destroyed all of the art work he carried in his van—some fifty drawings and paintings. He then proceeded to destroy the contents of his friends' house: furniture, books, paintings, records, dishes, etc. He even attempted to strip the wallpaper off the walls. When his friends returned they were horrified. They called the police and the patient was taken into custody. His parents were contacted, and they arranged to have him flown home.

Back home with his parents, John was agitated, depressed, threatened suicide, and refused to see a psychiatrist. One night, he destroyed all of his art work that had been stored at his parent's home. He expressed the wish to destroy the contents of their home as well, but didn't act on it. Finally, after much pleading by his parents, he agreed to admit himself to a private psychiatric hospital.

Once in the hospital, the patient became uncooperative, provocative, and threatening, and refused to take medication. He was finally committed to a local state hospital. This was a terrifying experience for John, and he pleaded with his parents to return him to the private hospital. This was done, and he remained there for four weeks, during which time he was docile and cooperative. He was treated with phenothiazines and discharged with a diagnosis of borderline personality with recent psychotic episode.

John begins therapy

John came to see me quite willingly. He was a tall, athletic, handsome 24 year-old, who spoke in a soft, wispy voice, and seemed somewhat effeminate. His general appearance was subdued and despondent. He was very intelligent and, at times, could be warm and charming. He was genuinely concerned about the "crazy" behavior that precipitated his hospitalization, and realized he needed help. At the same time, he felt angry at having been "incarcerated" and treated like a "mad dog." Mostly he was confused about how to reconcile the tumultuous emotions inherent in his artistic work with the "normal" behavior demanded by his parents and society. He was worried and uncertain as to whether he could be the kind of artist he needed to be and still survive in the "real world."

While he regretted having destroyed his art work and recognized the "craziness" in such acts, they still had, for him, a certain rationale. He believed he had reached a critical point in his artistic development. He could either have been content to sell his work as it was, or try to achieve further growth—to strike out in new directions. After much agonizing and soul searching, he decided on the latter course. This required that he break apart the pieces so that they could be rearranged; that he destroy something so that something new could be created; that he desynthesize in order to resynthesize. He likened it to remodeling a clay sculpture or painting over a canvas. The destruction of his friends' home and his impulse to do the same to his parent's home were harder for him to explain. He thought perhaps these homes had come to symbolize the shallow, materialistic, hypocritical aspects of modern society that he so despised.

John's parents remember

John remembered few details of his childhood. Since his parents were anxious to talk to me, and he had no objection, I agreed to see them. They were able to reconstruct a very detailed picture of their unusual son.

John was a difficult and precocious child from infancy. He sat up, walked and talked early, was active and curious, and demanded everyone's attention. He did everything with furious intensity: he laughed hard, cried hard and played hard; he even ate and slept hard. He was stubborn and perfectionistic. If things were not done his way, he would become very frustrated and throw tantrums. He was described as a "spoiled," "bossy" child, who needed to orchestrate and control. Articles in his room had to be arranged just so—and left that way. He would decide how the table would be set, where people would sit in the car and what games would be played. This did not make him very popular with other children. It was recognized early that this child would do best in a private school, and this proved to be a wise decision. He loved school and was an outstanding pupil. He was so curious, creative and energetic, that his teachers referred to him as "the little dynamo."

John showed remarkable artistic talent from early childhood. He would spend hours drawing, coloring, and modeling clay. He worked with characteristic intensity and concentration. Mother would bring him snacks to eat and drink, a steady stream of art supplies, and never-ending praise for his creations. No one had to tell this little artist to fill the whole paper; he came by it naturally. The problem was containing the creative energy once it began to flow. He soon became bored with coloring books because he didn't want to be restricted to staying within the lines. His prodigious output spilled out of his room into other parts of the house. His parents remarked that their home always resembled John's personal gallery.

He also loved to construct things. His room was filled with all types of building toys: erector sets, tinker toys, Lincoln logs, legos, etc. Not content to follow directions, John would compose his own creations, often combining pieces from various sets. He was constantly experimenting. Once he tried frying clay in a pan on the stove. His parents tolerated his "messes," and did their best to contain them within his room.

John seemed to blossom in adolescence. He became more gregarious, was interested in sports and music, and had friends. He continued to be an outstanding student and artist, and won awards and prizes. His parents felt relieved that, in spite of some drug use and other "hippie" behavior characteristic of his generation, their lonely, peculiar little artist seemed to be behaving more normally.

His college years were relatively uneventful. He won scholarships and performed brilliantly, and seemed content in the company of his artist friends. They tended toward a certain amount of drug use and anti-establishment attitudes, but his parents considered this all part of the Bohemian life style. As long as he continued to create such excellent works of art, John's "peculiarities" were tolerated—as they had been from childhood. The one area that concerned his parents was John's relationships with women. While he had a few girlfriends, he never seemed particularly passionate, and his relationships seemed superficial. This they attributed to his immaturity.

John was moderately depressed when he began therapy. He was living with his parents, had no desire to paint, and no plans for the future. He felt as though he were on probation or under observation—like a caged animal. He was gradually able to express his rage, which was primarily directed against his parents. He considered his father a cruel, oppressive tyrant who, while professing love and support, was actually jealous of John's talent, and did everything to undermine him. He wanted John to get a job, conform to the rules of society, and become a dull, materialistic hypocrite like himself.

His feelings toward his mother were more complicated. He was closely attached and dependent on her. She was the one person he could trust and whom he felt understood him. but he was furious with her for deceiving him: for allowing him to be "incarcerated." He struggled to describe how he felt about her. "She's the most beautiful, patient, loving person in the world," he said, "but she scares me."

John's art

He brought in a drawing—the first of many he would show me. It was a bizarre conglomeration of primitive stick-like figures, like a child's drawing. I asked him to associate to the drawing, which he did readily. The tall, sedate, composed figures were female; while the male figures were small, excited, and wildly contorted, like loose-limbed, helpless puppets. It reminded him of the black widow spider, who devours her mate in the sexual act. His mother was such a beautiful, artistic woman, and took such pride and pleasure in his artistic productions. He recalled the excitement of rushing to show her his work and watching her face beam with pleasure. The capacity to thrill her made him feel powerful, but, at the same time, he was frightened of her. She was so exciting, so dazzling, so "loud" that she was "too much" for him. When he showed her a picture he had drawn, her red lips would part, her white teeth would flash, and she would emit a loud exclamation that sent shivers through him.

As therapy progressed, John's depression lifted and his creative energy returned. He resumed painting and brought me examples of his work. His paintings looked wild and chaotic. He applied paint in powerful, intense masses of pure color, often squeezed directly from the tube to the canvas and then smeared with fingers or a palette knife. My impression was that his intent was to arrest, dazzle, seduce and blind the observer. He mentioned being annoyed by frames. He often painted over them— extending the work beyond the boundaries—not wanting to be "boxed in."

He also brought examples of previous work that had been in the possession of relatives and thus had escaped destruction. These were more controlled works that seemed, to me, to be of much higher caliber. I could appreciate how talented a painter he was.

Once he realized that I was not, like his father, determined to get him to behave "normally," a positive working relationship developed. The material of his sessions consisted mainly of his railing against his parents and society, and discussing his art. In long, detailed, metaphysical declamations, he would expound his theories of art, beauty, love, life, and the universe. These included concepts involving grids, six-pointed stars, and the composition of light. His parents, meanwhile, were delighted that he was in therapy and painting again, and strongly encouraged him to continue.

A narcissistic transference developed in which I became an idealized, inspiring, all-powerful mother goddess. He would gaze at me in awe and marvel at my beauty and power. He could feel it filling the room and flowing into him. He was grateful at having "discovered" me; and he was sure that through me he would achieve all his artistic aims.

On a less primitive transference level, I became the adoring mother who would admire his productions, while he became the bossy, controlling child who wanted to control me and the therapy. He wanted to decide what would be discussed, and when I did not go along with this, he was hurt and angry. He would change the radio station and rearrange the magazines in my waiting room. He wanted to hang his paintings in my office. He not only wanted to bring his art work, but his guitar, tapes of his songs, and his philosophical essays.

John would usually wear paint-spattered clothing and shoes to his sessions. In one session I pointed out that he had left a paint smear on my chair, that I didn't like it and didn't want it to happen again. He was appropriately apologetic at first, but with further discussion it became clear that he reacted with genuine surprise, hurt and anger. He really couldn't understand why I should be upset. If his paint touched my chair, wasn't that an artistic act? And if he colors what he touches, isn't that as it should be? In his primitive state of confused, shifting self and object representations, the boundaries between us blurred. At times I became the canvas on which he painted; was his creation; and at other times, he was mine.

As he realized that he couldn't control me, he became angry, withdrawn, and threatened suicide. His thinking grew more bizarre and disorganized. He spoke of there being a limited number of building particles in the universe, and things had to be broken down into their basic elements before new forms could be created. He would have to destroy himself in order to be reborn. It was his destiny to make this sacrifice. He was the Messiah, and his mission on earth was to teach people to love through his art, music and writing. I interpreted that he needed to control me and feel powerful because he was so afraid that I might destroy him.

For a while, therapy seemed to progress

Work in the transference gradually had a settling effect, and John became less delusional and disorganized. We were able to direct the therapy toward bolstering his ego functions: to help him control his impulses and separate fantasy from reality. We talked practically about how he could sufficiently adapt to the realities of life and the demands of society so as to have a stable enough matrix in which to work toward his artistic goals. He worked at detaching himself from his parents and cultivating social relationships. He even got a part time job, which delighted his parents. His art work became more purposeful and less chaotic. He contacted some local galleries and made plans to begin showing his work. He finally decided to move away from home, and his parents arranged for him to rent a small house where he could live and paint.

For a period of about three months, John seemed happy and productive in his work and in his therapy. During this time, we were able to piece together some of the intrapsychic events that precipitated his psychotic episode. He had felt relatively safe for much of his life in the role of the exceptional child-artist. His graduation from art school, and the challenge of his artistic talent being judged on the open market, was very threatening. This was a step in the direction of adulthood and separation from his adoring parents. He was afraid that the outside world would not afford him the love and admiration that they had. He was also afraid to unleash the destructive power of his art on the public. John was trapped between oedipal dangers and pre-oedipal longings. Destroying his art work, such a precious part of himself, was a castrative, suicidal equivalent.

Destruction of the interior of his friends' home, and the subsequent impulse to do the same to his parents' home, was associated with primal scene excitement and rage. This had been building during his journey, and was expressed in his intrusive, exhibitionistic wish to join the rock group. Destruction of the interior of the home was an enactment of a childhood fantasy of what took place in the parents' bedroom: what father's penis did to mother's vagina; and what he had done as an infant to the interior of her body.

Then things took a turn for the worse

The first hint that things were taking a turn for the worse came from the patient's appearance. He began to look thin, tired, and more disheveled than usual. It gradually emerged that he had been painting furiously and barely eating or sleeping. He also confessed that he had resumed smoking pot. He expressed a morbid dissatisfaction with his work and with himself. He brought a "finished" painting consisting of the word "God" scrawled on a canvas. He felt he had "sold out" and abandoned his artistic principles. His thinking once again became disorganized and delusional. There were ominous threats that he had to do something drastic to save himself and humanity. I insisted that he would have to return to the hospital, and when he refused, I called his parents. They tried to convince him, too.

There were lucid moments in which we discussed the crisis he was arranging. I pointed out that it was clear he was intent on destroying himself. His working to the point of exhaustion, not eating or sleeping, smoking pot, and refusing to go into the hospital and take medication, were all designed to push himself over the edge: to precipitate a psychosis or to kill himself. He was very much aware that what he was doing could lose his parents' support, and put an end to our treatment and his career as an artist.

He recognized all this, but felt it was necessary in order to achieve his artistic imperative. His "career," as I called it, his treatment, his health, and even his life were unimportant.

I asked, "Is it possible for you to achieve your artistic goals without destroying yourself?"

He shook his head sadly, and said, "You don't understand." In his complicated, metaphysical terms he struggled to explain. "If I have an idea in my mind, a feeling that I have to get onto canvas, I have to tear it out of me in order to transpose it to the canvas." He pointed out the double meaning of the word execute: "To execute the work I have to execute myself." He spoke of change, growth, metamorphosis: "From caterpillar to butterfly—one dies, one is born." "It's like doing surgery or giving birth: it must occur amid blood, pain, terror and rage."

While we were making arrangements to have him committed, his parents called, frantically, and asked that I come immediately to John's house. The scene I beheld when I arrived is one I'm not likely to forget. John had taken gallons of paint and completely painted the inside of the house: walls, ceilings, floors, furniture, appliances, and windows. Paint had been poured, smeared, and thrown. He had then worked his way outdoors, applying paint to the outside of the house, the sidewalk, bushes, trees and grass. The artist himself was sitting on the front steps, smeared with paint, and calmly playing his guitar. When I approached him, he smiled and said, "Thanks for your help—this is the best I can do."

Discussion

It is not unusual for an artist to destroy his work. One of the most dramatic examples was Richard Gerstel, a Viennese Expressionist, who, following a tragic affair with the wife of Arnold Schoenberg, collected most of his paintings into a pile, set them on fire, and hung himself above the flaming mass. Severe pathology aside, the agonies and frustrations of creative work, along with the narcissistic investment in the product, may give rise to some peculiar attitudes on the part of the creator. Artists have feelings toward their work that may range from disregard, through ambivalence, to hatred and disgust. Some regard their finished work as we regard feces: once produced, they want nothing more to do with it. A writer patient described how she would re-read a page in her typewriter, find it utterly disgusting, rip it out, crumple it into a tight ball, and throw it into the waste basket. When she would see the crumpled balls of paper lying in the basket, she was filled with anxiety and loathing. At times she could "hear them uncrumpling," and would have to rush them out to the garbage. Her unsuccessful creations—her aborted products—had a life of their own. They were like monsters she had given birth to and she had to get rid of them.

My patient, John, destroyed his work as a natural part of the creative process. This relation between creativity and destruction is not original. Similar themes run through various realms of the arts and sciences: old forms must be broken down before new forms can be constructed; desynthesis must pave the way for resynthesis. Living organisms alternate between anabolism and catabolism. The term "psychoanalysis" contains the word "lysis," which means a loosening or dissolution. Our technique relies on regression in order to achieve progression; and includes such concepts as synthesis, reintegration, and reconstruction. Psychoanalysis aims at creating change, and change involves disruption of the status quo. It is succinctly stated in a favorite maxim quoted by Freud: "If you want to make an omelet, you have to break some eggs."

Creativity involves change and change requires disruption. Everything must be made out of something. The painter messes the clean canvas, the writer disturbs the blank page, and the musician breaks silence. The sculptor attacks the block of stone pieces in order to create a new form. Creative movements have had similar effects on society. The best example is the Surrealist movement, led by the painter Max Ernst. Its purpose was to negate, desecrate, and destroy the natural order. One of the Surrealist exhibitions provided a hatchet with which patrons were invited to chop up the works of art being exhibited. Ernst pioneered the technique of collage, in which he cut up pictures from various sources and recombined them into bizarre new forms. The viewer was challenged to suspend his concept of the world and entertain the possibility of a totally new one (Berman, 1987).

This is how my patient, John, rationalized his destructiveness: as a part of the natural and necessary desynthesizing phase of artistic creativity. It was clearly more than this. His tremendous destructive rage invaded his creativity and expressed itself as part of the creative process. For him, the act of artistic creation was suffused with primitive fantasies of violent conception, birth, death, and rebirth. He identified himself with a God-like figure whose duty and right it was to re-fashion the world. He became the divine creator and the world became his canvas. Guilt over his destructive impulses turned his rage inward, and he became a Christ-like martyr who had to sacrifice himself to save mankind.

Where did John come by all this rage and destructiveness? Was he endowed with an innate excess of aggression or some defect in his capacity to bind or modulate aggressive drives? Was his furious creativity, evident from such an early age, an attempt to deal with overwhelming aggression? Certain characteristics of creative children are likely to exacerbate problems of aggression: their pronounced narcissism, greater sensitivity, and vulnerability to frustration (Greenacre, 1957). With this in mind, we will turn to a further discussion of John's childhood.

While there was much that I never had an opportunity to understand about this patient, between his own history and his reactions in the transference, and the considerable data supplied by his parents, I did form what I believe was a fairly clear picture of his childhood. John showed many of the characteristics Greenacre describes in the creatively gifted child: precociousness, supersensitivity, intensity and a need for harmony. He also showed originality and a special capacity to combine elements into new forms. This unusual endowment marked him as exceptional, and caused the people in his environment to act toward him in exceptional ways. Such reactions to a child's giftedness become, in themselves, important formative influences.

A patient, who was a gifted child, recalled an incident from his third year. He received a toy in the mail that was disassembled. His mother was unable to understand the directions and said they would have to wait until his father came home to assemble it. The impatient little boy, as yet unable to read, was able to assemble the toy himself by following the diagrams in the directions. When the parents saw what he had done, they gasped and exclaimed in amazement. This frightened the child. What he had done seemed perfectly natural to him, but the parent's loud reaction made him feel he had done something "terrible." He could recount many such experiences that left him feeling powerful and superior, but also like an evil freak or devil. This is similar to how John felt at his mother's response to his creations.

What about the role of trauma in John's case: was he traumatized? If he was, it was not through any actual situations or events that I could identify. He may indeed have felt traumatized, but he was not, in fact, abused by his parents or the vicissitudes of his life. He suffered no significant illnesses or deformities. There were no actual losses. Perhaps the worst thing that could be said about his parents is that they were overly indulgent. It was hard not to be with such a child. They seemed, on the whole, to be loving, well-meaning parents, who did their best to raise a difficult child; and by no means the dangerous monsters he painted.

John demonstrates something I have observed in other artistically creative patients. They tend to dramatize and mythologize their histories: to distort the people and events of their past through fantasy and exaggerated emotional intensity. What are routine ups and downs of life to most people are charged with intense drama and overwhelming affect. Thus, a sharp criticism from the kindergarten teacher is recalled as a devastating assault and a horrible humiliation, and she is remembered as a terrifying witch; and the winning of a contest is recalled with almost unbearable euphoria and triumph. This reflects the heightened sensitivity and receptivity of creative children, but it also points to a special use of the process of remembering and recollecting. We all distort and embellish our pasts with family romances and personal myths, but this tendency seems to be exaggerated in artistically creative people.

It might be well to bear this in mind when evaluating the traumatogenic theories of creativity. There seems little doubt that artists employ their creativity in attempting to work through trauma; but what constitutes the traumatic experiences of their lives? Were the abuses, illnesses, and losses they describe unusually severe, or were the "normal traumas" of childhood experienced and subsequently remembered that way?

A patient, who was a writer, described the first time she had to get on the school bus as a little girl. The bus seemed "huge," the fumes were "sickening," and it was packed with screaming kids—like "wild animals." She recalled the driver looking down at her "menacingly." The step up seemed "insurmountable—like climbing a mountain." Once on the bus, she gazed out the window at her mother's face, which looked "glazed and distant—like she was in another world." Here is an event that most children experience with varying degrees of anxiety and excitement. But for this patient, a creative writer, it was recalled as an overwhelming trauma. She was a tiny little girl forced into a terrifying situation by an uncaring mother. In the course of analytic work, nothing we could reconstruct of her childhood environment would support this as reality. But we had much evidence to suggest that she tended to "tragedize" her life: to experience herself as the protagonist in an ongoing tale of heroic victories and crushing defeats.

Traumatogenic theories imply a causal relationship between the traumatic situation or event and the creative process. It causes us to question: had Poe not sat beside his dead mother, would he have written Annabel Lee; and had Rousseau not been deformed, would he have painted Boy on Rocks?

I believe the answer is that they may not have created those particular masterpieces, but they very likely would have created something else of equal caliber. Traumatic events don't produce creativity. They serve as the raw material—the framework around which creativity is organized.

Perhaps these two factors, innate creative drive and traumatic life events, interact as a complementary series, with varying degrees of both contributing to the final creative outcome. Some artists may require significant trauma to bring out their latent creativity; others, whose innate creative drive is sufficiently strong, do not. If there are no outstanding traumata, such as the death of a parent or a congenital anomaly, then the normal traumas of life will do. And if this is not sufficient, they may have to create more themselves.

While psychopathology may not be a prerequisite for creativity, some degree of intrapsychic conflict seems a necessary stimulus. Exceptions such as Peter Paul Rubens notwithstanding, most artists are less productive in times of tranquillity. They seem to require a certain level of conflict to stir the pot and get the creative juices flowing. If life does not provide sufficient sturm and drang, they will engineer it themselves. Max Ernst was a good example. His life was continually in turmoil. He went from woman to woman, place to place, movement to movement. If his life threatened to settle into a peaceful state, he could be depended upon to disrupt it.

In his study of creativity and psychopathology, Eissler describes an incident in the life of Schiller, when the famous writer was taken in by a friend at a time of tragic destitution. Schiller could not tolerate such comfortable circumstances. He eventually left, writing to his benefactor: "My heart is contracted and the lights of my imagination are extinguished. I am in need of a crisis. Nature brings about destruction in order to recreate. It may well be that you do not understand me, but I understand myself."

Intrapsychic conflict seems to form the most common ground shared by creativity and madness. Both are fueled by the same instinctual impulses, mediated by the same ego functions, and expressed in the same language of primary process. It may be difficult for us to define those formal elements that mold instinctual conflict into art, but in our everyday clinical work we can readily observe the reverse: the artistry that goes into the formation of dreams, parapraxes, and symptoms.

A patient in analysis described, with difficulty, a long standing masturbatory fantasy. It was a typically obsessional, ritualistic scenario that had haunted him from childhood. During any sexual activity, he was compelled to imagine the same sequence of events involving the same cast of characters. But within the rigid, obligatory outline of the fantasy, he had devised many ingenious variations. The people and events of his life were cleverly woven into different versions of the fantasy, while still preserving its basic theme. It was the magnum opus of his sexuality, and a remarkably rich and creative composition. The patient was ashamed of this fantasy. He abhorred its perversity and boredom, and decried the time and energy he "wasted" on it. During moments when he felt less guilty and more tolerant of himself, he could joke about the fact that his fantasy had sustained a longer continuous run than many Broadway shows. He often remarked that it would make an interesting novel. It would, in fact, have made an excellent novel. Had my patient the inclination and the talent to write, and the willingness to publish, and, most important, the freedom to decide to do it, then his masturbatory fantasy might have become a work of art. This state of affairs is epitomized by Lionel Trilling's incisive comment: that what characterizes the artist is his power to use his neuroticism—"to shape the material of pain we all have."

The outcome of intrapsychic conflict is variable and unpredictable. It may result in neurosis, or creativity, or any combination of the two. In the same artist, conflict may act one moment as a stimulus to creativity and at the next moment as an impediment. How psychoanalysis or psychotherapy affects the creative process may be similarly variable and unpredictable. Treatment may help relieve inhibitions and thus liberate creativity; or, in reducing conflict, it may also reduce the neurotic energy and motivation that drive the creative process. When asked if psychoanalytic therapy might jeopardize creativity in a neurotically-driven artist, a well-known psychoanalyst answered, "Not in the least! It will make him a better artist." Considering the intricate, fluid interrelationship between creativity and neurosis, I would question whether such unqualified optimism is justified.

Joan Fimbel DiGiovanni has been Professor of Psychology at Western New England College since 1973. In 1985, she was a Visiting Scholar on Caravaggio at NYU's Institute of Fine Arts; in 1988, a Visiting Scholar at New York University on Theory and Practice of Biography, and in 1992, she was an NEH Mexican Colonial Art Scholar in Mexico. She has developed a course in the Psychology of Art, and has presented at national and international conferences. She maintains a private practice and audits art history classes.

Ronald R. Lee is a Senior Associate faculty member of the Illinois School of Professional Psychology where he teaches self psychology theory. Previously, he was Professor of Pastoral Psychology at Garrett Theological Seminary. Dr. Lee obtained his Ph.D. from Northwestern University and served as a Fellow in Religion and Psychiatry at the Menninger Foundation. He authored Clients and Clergy (1991) and co-authored Psychotherapy After Kohut (1991). Presently he is a Visiting Scholar to St. Hilda's College, The University of Melbourne, Australia.

I want to keep these sufferings—being without them would ruin my art.—
Edvard Munch

I paint my own reality.   *Frida Kahlo*

The Art and Suffering of Frida Kahlo
by Joan Fimbel DiGiovanni, Ph.D. and Ronald R. Lee, Ph.D.

The life of the Mexican artist Frida Kahlo was suffused with suffering. Frida contracted polio when but six years of age, had a near fatal traffic accident at the age of eighteen, and experienced a traumatic spontaneous abortion when 25 years old. Three years later, she felt betrayed and hurt when her mentor/husband, Diego Rivera, had an affair with her sister. Divorced from Diego at the age of 32 and remarried to him two years later, Frida submerged herself in a conflicted marriage. In the last ten years of her life, Frida Kahlo experienced increased pain in her right foot and leg, which was eventually amputated in 1953. During her life she underwent a total of 35 surgeries and became addicted to pain killers and alcohol.

Frida Kahlo may be an example of a person with a deep sense of despair, emptiness and disconnectedness. Here we view her suffering and art through a broadly conceived self psychology perspective. We examine:

- her suffering and fragmentation,
- her efforts to remain cohesive,
- her use of herself as her own art subject, and
- how art maintained her self-esteem and sense of intactness.

Kahlo's suffering and fragmentation

Frida Kahlo's suffering began during her childhood.

Kahlo did not have a nourishing relationship with her mother, Matilde Calderon, who was a devout Catholic of mixed Spanish and Indian extraction. "The emotional hunger Frida experienced throughout her life can be seen in the earliest known self-portrait, a small pencil drawing on a piece of notebook paper, made for a schoolmate at about age 12," reported Grimberg. Over her head the message reads, "I am sending you my picture so you will remember me."

Her father, Guillermo Kahlo, was a German of Austro-Hungarian descent. Jewish by birth, atheist by persuasion and an epileptic, he was a professional photographer when photography was struggling to gain acceptance as an art form. The children of Guillermo's first marriage were given away. Frida, the third daughter of the second marriage, was obsessed by the fear of abandonment.

At the age of 6 she was diagnosed as having poliomyelitis that permanently restricted the use of her right leg. In 1925, when 18 years of age, Frida was so gravely injured when the bus in which she was traveling collided with a streetcar, she was not expected to live. "They had to put her back together in sections as if they were making a photomontage," said a friend. So great were her parents' shock and grief that neither visited her in the hospital for over a week.

Frida's survival was a miracle. Her spinal column and pelvis were fractured in three places. In addition, her collar-bone and two ribs were broken, her left shoulder dislocated, her right leg fractured in eleven places, and her right foot was crushed. A steel handrail had literally skewered her body in the abdomen and out the vagina. Of this wound, Frida would comment wryly, "I lost my virginity." Thereafter, she never had a day without pain because these severe injuries never fully healed.

Through her interest in painting, Frida, at age fifteen, had already met and flirted with her idol Diego Rivera as he painted his *Creation* frescoes at her school. Then, while convalescing from the accident, Frida resorted to serious painting, using her father's paints and brushes. Soon after this, Frida showed three paintings to Diego and asked his opinion. As Rivera describes the occasion, Frida sought him out when he was painting frescoes on a scaffold at the Ministry of Education and shouted up at him, "Diego, please come down from there! I have something important to discuss with you."

Recognizing Frida's unmistakable artistic talent, Diego visited her home, saw more of her work and agreed to mentor her. This mentoring eventually influenced Frida in dress and behavior as well as painting. As Grimberg says, "It was Rivera who fostered the provocative attitude that helped her overcome her long-standing shyness, suggested she use the retablo format and make her life the iconography of her paintings, and encouraged her to wear Mexican clothing that concealed her short leg and complemented her magnetic beauty." "Rivera," said Gomez Arias, Frida's high school friend and companion in the bus accident, "opened doors for Frida that she would not have opened alone."

Diego Rivera was forty three years of age and already a world-renowned muralist whose works celebrated the Mexican revolution when, on August 21, 1929, Frida Kahlo married him in a match that her parents likened to: "an elephant and a dove. They made an amazing pair, he at three hundred pounds and over six feet, she at one hundred pounds and slightly over five feet. She was delicately featured, he had bug eyes, full lips, and a lumpy face." (Drucker, 1991).

The marriage provided an older partner from whom she sought the good relationship she had experienced with her father and the love she desired but had not received from her mother. Grimberg perceived that "Frida saw a relationship with Rivera as a chance at the reparative experience: thus a chance to have two good parents, plus a husband, in one person." Of her family, only Frida's father, who warned Diego that Frida was a "devil," attended her wedding.

In 1932, while living in Detroit, Frida hemorrhaged, spontaneously aborted a fetus, and then became chronically depressed upon realizing she could not bear the child she had hoped would minimize Rivera's womanizing.

After 1944, Frida wore 28 different orthopedic corsets as a

means of compensating for spinal problems that eventually necessitated nine operations and extensive hospitalizations in 1950. In 1953 her right leg was amputated because of gangrene. By the end of her life, Frida Kahlo's physical condition was so complicated by addiction to pain killers and alcohol that, although her death certificate listed the cause of death as a pulmonary embolism, it was more likely a suicidal drug overdose.

The sufferings of her middle years were exacerbated by her stormy relationship to Diego. He was a known womanizer who considered sex just like urinating—a simple bodily release. Frida once said, "I suffered from two grave accidents in my life. One in which a streetcar knocked me down... The other accident is Diego."

Kahlo's efforts to maintain her sense of cohesiveness

Fragmentation causes us to lose our sense of self as a cohesive person, and to lose other vital ego functions, and is usually accompanied by terror and/or great anxiety.

Frida's life can be seen as a struggle to prevent chronic feelings of fragmentation by resorting to "cohesive functions"— various personal strategies to feel more cohesive. For example, she made her medical experiences more concrete by painting retablos, small altar paintings that were a customary Mexican way to depict accidents, illness or death. As Frida interprets it, "a retablo is a closing of a critical event and [a] continuing with life." These retablos externalized her internal suffering and the tangible focus made her feel more cohesive.

Frida's identification with the Mexican revolution also helped give her life meaning and prevent fragmentation. Entering elementary school, Frida gave her birth date as July 6, 1910. Being older than her classmates, because of the polio, she wanted to appear to be their age;. She also wanted to be born in the year of the outbreak of the Mexican revolution. (Later in life she gave a July 6, 1907 birth date). Frida's life gained meaning by identifying with her Mexican heritage, with the peasant movement, and with the Communist Party, which she joined.

Another source of Frida's self-cohesion was her relationship with her father. Frida's powerful intelligence particularly endeared "Lieber Frida" to her father, and his tender attachment intensified when she was stricken with polio. Guillermo doted on Frida during her illness and convalescence.

The attention Frida received from her clothes, the drama of her art, and as a patient, served to make her feel more cohesive. Frida learned that illnesses could work in her favor—she wrote in her diary, "We like being ill to protect ourselves." As long as she remained ill, "people collected around her and watched over her." Grimberg thought that Frida used her physical symptoms as an adult form of control and attention. We want to add that Frida's need for attention was also an antidote for her tendency to fragment.

The Diego/Frida relationship was a stormy one that had all the features of a complementary emotional bond, where each needed the other as a means of feeling cohesive. When this bond was broken, it severely disrupted their lives, especially Frida's. In 1934, as Frida's hunger for reaffirmation became suffocating, Rivera began to withdraw. Frida, overtaken by fear of abandonment, became more demanding. Wishing to break her control, Rivera withdrew even further. Then he had an affair with Cristina, Frida's young sister, which was discovered through Diego's mural on the National Palace. He rendered Christina in an "ecstasy pose," with glassy eyes looking skyward, which is read as either "orgasmic" or religious.

During a separation and divorce for two years, Frida had an affair with Leon Trotsky. There was a second marriage (December 8, 1940), after which Frida and Diego, at Frida's request, lived peacefully in separate parts of the Casa Azul without sexual involvement.

Because a devotion to Diego organized her life, Frida's attachment had the qualities of an emotional merger. Initially Kahlo surrendered to this merger and, as a martyr, refused to make choices for herself; but during these periods of not being active in the world, she also experienced intense feelings of being abandoned and fragmented. Herrera thought that Diego and Frida needed each other in order to maintain their work; the potential destructiveness of the needed mutual dependence was then contained by their physical separation which gave the emotional space necessary for their art.

Kahlo's search for affirmation from the art community

One of the reasons Frida created paintings was as a means of establishing a self affirming relationship with an appreciative community of artists and art collectors. The paintings, and the responses they evoked, became the means of eventually replacing the initially necessary but stagnant emotional merger with her mentor and husband. A beginning of her quest for self-affirming responses from the art community can be seen after her miscarriage.

To depict this miscarriage, Frida painted herself in Henry Ford Hospital lying naked and hemorrhaging in a hospital bed with the "little Dieguito" floating in the sky along with other symbols of miscarriage. The snail in the painting, Frida once explained, refers to the slowness of the miscarriage which, like a snail, was "soft, covered and at the same time open." According to Herrera, "the half-born baby dropping into a puddle of blood refers to the child that Frida had just miscarried, which made her wish she too were dead." In this painting, Frida lies on an iron hospital bed that seems to be almost floating in space, which is probably how she felt in Detroit. "Like the cold metal bed, the background of the city is filled with hard, man-made objects. Frida is naked, lying in a pool of blood, and her face is expressionless except for one large tear."

Frida's fascination with blood revealed itself in many of her paintings. When her paintings became more sexual in intensity, there was an increase in the blood's flow.

The Henry Ford Hospital painting, although it contains the horror of her loss, was a source of strength. Through it, Frida learned to create, not as a mother, but as an artist: for Frida, her art and friends became her salvation. This hunger to create was not only a search for a self-validating relationship but an effort to liberate herself from the need to use growth-stultifying cohesive strategies. As the art world began to be excited by Frida's work, it responded by mirroring her; that is, others were able to empathically enter her world through her paintings and experience the emotions associated with her suffering. Nourished by this mirroring, she created more art.

Some months later, in *My Birth*, Frida painted how she imagined she was born, showing her mother naked from the waist down with an apparently dead child emerging between her outspread legs. There is no precedent for such a frank and perhaps distasteful image of birth in the history of western art, so to paint this in the 1930s took extraordinary courage and originality. The painting also reflects Kahlo's interest in Aztec iconography because it depicts birth similar to the Goddess Tlazolteotl in the Act of Parturition (ca. 1500)— where a squatting woman in forbidding ritualistic grimace of pain, gives birth to a full-grown man's head. The eyebrows tell us that the baby is also Frida herself.

In this painting Frida not only is born but gives birth herself. A sheet that covers the mother from the waist up and looks like a shroud, makes her spread legs seem all the more naked. "My head is covered," Frida told a friend, "because, coincidentally... [during] the painting of the picture, my mother died." Placed above the bed, pierced by daggers in her heart, the Virgin of Sorrows is not very different from Kahlo's depiction in *The Broken Column*. Frida recalled that she included the Virgin as "part of a memory image" whose invocation symbolizes a tragic occurrence, replacing the traditional representation of the Virgin as the divine intercessor against calamity in an exvotive or religious painting.

The mother, who, like the baby, is dead, represents both Kahlo having the miscarriage and Kahlo's mother giving birth. It is the kind of icon that her devoutly Catholic mother would have hung on her wall. The bed, explained Frida, was the actual bed in which she and her younger sister, Cristina, were born.

My Birth is an odd depiction of a nativity scene as none of the three figures is alive. Jenkins suggests that this painting contained Kahlo's understandings about her relationship with her mother. Because she had never emotionally separated from her mother, Frida thought her individuation would psychologically kill her mother. She felt that her sense of herself as an active functioning person could be

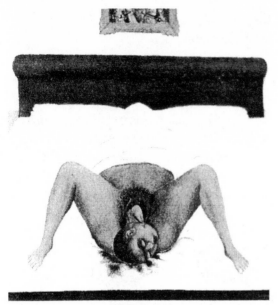

My Birth, 1932

achieved only after her mother died. Indicating the dead woman in the painting, Frida would say, "My Head!" but it was clear that it depicted her mother as well.

Frida's relationship with her mother was not warm and nurturing; it was "dead." Frida had rebelled against her mother's Catholicism and her many conventions. Herrera believes that "although the inevitable battles with the woman she called 'mi Jefe' (my chief) became more intense as both grew older, when her mother died, Frida could not stop crying." This suggests that her emotional merger with Diego repeated a similar earlier emotional merger with her mother. Both included an intense need of another in order to feel an intact sense of self,

Clearly, the figure with its spine as a shattered Ionic pillar in *The Broken Column* is Frida. The bleak, forbidding landscape becomes a potent metaphor for the inner desolation and fragmentation that occurs from the lack of a relationship that affirms the self. The breasts are isolated, full and exposed. She substituted the pillar for her shattered spine, the cracks and instability are reflected in a barren landscape with deep rifts. This painting portrays an extraordinarily beautiful body unclothed to the waist, covered —like that of San Sebastian—by small nails that pierce the skin. The cloth, also reminiscent of the loin-cloth of Christ, veils her sex and covers her body, which appears completely fragmented. "The nails are reminiscent of the Madonna of sorrows, and the presence of a column that splits open the body suggests symbolically a phallus of steel."

She wrote,

I paint self-portraits because I am so often alone.. Because I am the subject I know best.

By painting herself as a martyr transcending pain, Frida formed an icon of herself for others to admire or pity.

Kahlo's art as a subjective experience of fragmentation and a search for cohesion

Frida made herself the subject of her art. She portrayed her suffering in her art—in 1954 she told

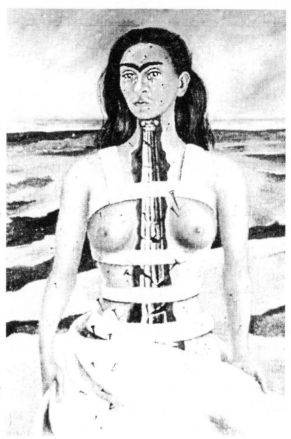

The Broken Column, 1944

a friend, "My painting carries within it the message of pain." What makes her art so special, however, is her concrete depiction of the subjective experience of fragmentation. For example, In *Without Hope*, Frida is spewing out her internal organs onto a ladder over a bed. According to Herrera, "The miscarried child thus becomes her sacrifice placed upon the cross-easel between a pale moon and a blood red sun." She also says, "Psychological and physical pain are intertwined in a weeping self-portrait of rejection in love and a spinal spasm." There was a time when Frida spent three months in a nearly vertical position, with sacks of sand attached to her feet to straighten out her spinal column. This experience may be reflected in the painting.

Frida's paintings were affected by her frequent mood swings from euphoria to deep depression, and her periods of paranoia. She had extensive knowledge of medical terminology and hospital routines, continually used analgesics for pain, and had multiple surgical interventions. Frida's close encounters with death so terrified and immobilized her that, when in pain or ill, she feared she would die. She began to call death "la pelona," which means "the bald or stupid woman," as a way of coping with her fear. "I tease and laugh at death," she shared with a friend, "so it won't get the better of me."

Kahlo's work resonated in a society that didn't shy away from death as a part of life. There are streets in Mexico with names such as *Ravine of the Dead* and, in November, all of Latin America celebrates *Dia de los Muertos* (day of the dead) with people dressed up as skeletons, skulls, and dark hooded figures, all representing death.

Frida's periods of starvation, her frequent bouts of self-destructive behavior, her frenzied search for love all her life, and her endless ritualistic pilgrimages to medical centers, clinics and hospitals, point to a personality with severe primitive infantile emotional needs. Dr. Eloesser, Frida's physician, thought that because Frida sought surgery for invented symptoms or exaggerated ailments, she needed psychotherapy. Frida tried psychoanalysis, perhaps the first woman in Mexico to do so, but as her type of personality was not understood and was considered untreatable then, her psychoanalysis was an heroic exploration into the frontiers of psychotherapy. Although Dr. Eloesser diagnosed scoliosis, a deformation of Frida's spine, as early as 1930, he

Without Hope, 1945

viewed most of Kahlo's illnesses in the last decade of her life as tragic manipulations to get people, particularly her husband Diego, to accede to her whims. After Frida was admitted to Saint Luke's Hospital in the early fifties, Dr. Eloesser diagnosed her condition as osteomyelitis complicated by a nervous exhaustion that needed rest and abstinence from alcohol. A general exhaustion may have contributed to Kahlo's outbreak of tropical ulcers and to gangrene that necessitated amputating her right leg in 1953.

Frida's horrendous medical history has been depicted in her paintings, diary and letters. Her biographer Herrera thinks that she used illness to make herself into a tragic victim and a heroic sufferer. At considerable risk, she may have chosen unnecessary operations to develop more self-cohesion and to experience feelings of "being alive." As a surgical patient, she reduced feelings of disconnectedness, through the admiration, sympathy, and, most importantly, the ministrations of her husband, Diego Rivera. Rivera tried to wean Frida off daily pain medications, which included Demerol, morphine, and other addictive drugs, by substituting a fifth of brandy or two fifths of vodka daily. One of her doctors said that Frida's health so often depended on her feelings about Rivera that when he was away and she felt abandoned by him, there was a crisis.

This pattern of using various strategies to feel cohesive must have had childhood origins. While Frida was recovering from polio, her father involved himself in helping to restore his favorite daughter to health. Her father, and sometimes Diego, provided her with an experience of cohesiveness that would otherwise have been missing. When this form of cohesiveness was absent or insufficient, she resorted to drugs and alcohol. Many of Frida's paintings center on the conflicting forces of her identity and relationship with Diego.

Grimberg believes that Kahlo's art did not exist until July 1932 when she spontaneously aborted a desperately wanted pregnancy, and, in effect, gave birth to her own personal style. As he pointed out, "She kept on her shelf a jar containing a fetus—her still-born child." In her paintings the "Latina" artistic idiom is both naturalistic and mythic. Her art centered on her feelings, on her need to paint her pain and anguish. Art historian Mulvey wrote that, "Kahlo's painting seems to move through a process of stripping away layers, that of the actual skin over a wound, that of the mask of beauty over the reality of pain." Her powerful personality appears to have over-shadowed her work, which came to be seen as a depiction of her sickly body mutilated by painful operations.

She had three spontaneous abortions, a fact that Rivera confirmed. She said "Painting completed my life, I lost three children." Although she compensated for her loss with paintings, she grieved all her life for a child, and the inability to have one provided a spur to her artistic work. What she created empowered her to go on living. Her paintings, which took the place of an imaginary friend, were an attempt to obtain mirroring and affirmation from those who responded positively to her art.

Christian imagery, especially the theatrically bloody martyrdoms that hung in Mexican churches, pervaded Frida's paintings. Kahlo freely used religious imagery in her retablos that, as visual adaptations of her own life, helped her in a concrete way to feel more cohesive. Like the patron Saint of Suffering, San Jude, she surrounded herself with her personal iconography of snails, skeletons, and rainfalls of milk. The Virgin of Guadeloupe over the bed is in the Catholic tradition; her corset floats in the air attached to her by thin ribbons of blood. The swallow, as her special emblem, resembling as it did the way her eyebrows appeared to be joined between the eyes, flutters around. In one painting, the bird is even merged with her eyebrows. "Blood is a constant unifying element in Kahlo's paintings, a symbol of her physical and psychological pain," wrote Drucker, "which was a basic organizing principle in her life."

In an age of "celebrity" artists as much as art, at her first solo show in Mexico in 1953, a year before she died, Frida was carried in on a stretcher in native dress. She transformed the event into theater. Her paintings depicted her fragmented self, cracked open, weeping beside an extracted heart, hemorrhaging during a miscarriage, anesthetized on a hospital trolley, sleeping with a skeleton, and always—even beside her pets or husband—she looks fearfully alone. The nearly two hundred works that she produced between 1926 and 1954 bring us face to face with Frida, both the legend and the reality and, through her, to face unexplored parts of ourselves.

The fierce candor with which she recorded her loves, losses, ill-nesses, childlessness, and abiding passion for her husband was rec-ognized by Rivera, who wrote:, "Frida is the only example in the his-tory of art of an artist who tore open her chest and heart to reveal the biological truth of her feelings... She was a superior painter and the greatest proof of the renaissance of the art of Mexico."

Grimberg believed that "Kahlo's late still-life paintings repre-sent not only the... passage of time, but Kahlo's regressive state and her desperate and ambiguous hunger for life."

On the morning of July 13, 1954 Frida Kahlo was found dead in her bedroom; the evidence painted a picture of suicide. In her last diary entry, Frida thanked those to whom she felt closest during the past year, and she drew her last self-portrait: nude, with her leg replaced by a stump, and a shower of arrows flying at her. "I await joyful my departure, and I hope never to come back again. Frida." Her journal's last drawing was of a black angel rising into the sky.

Frida's death came six days after her 47th birthday. It reflected the conflict that gave shape to her life. Grimberg believed that "Frida Kahlo lived afraid she would not be able to survive the loss of love. Kahlo spent much of her life attempting to fill this insatiable hunger. She only partially succeeded. She chose to starve rather than to set-tle for what she did not want to eat."

Summary

Kahlo, the sufferer, became Kahlo, the voyeur of her own suf-fering. She wanted to be pitied for the misadventures of Diego, for her physical disabilities, and for a thousand troubles she dramatized to make sure that people responded to her sympathetically.

In recent years, Frida has become a cult figure as Mexico's greatest woman artist, and, in the opinion of many, Mexico's greatest artist. Frida's former home is now a sanctuary and a monument that bears testimony to a life and an art that pleads for resurrection, rebirth, and a miracle. To Mexican-Americans, Frida is a political heroine; she demonstrated her love for la Raza (the people) in her life and in her paintings. She portrayed the feelings of a victim in a modern society that easily lends itself to victimization. She addressed herself directly, intimately and viscerally to all women, giving esthetic form to the drama of her biological experience. She created an art object of her own scarred and crippled body. For women throughout the world, and especially for women artists, Frida is an example of perseverance, endurance and generativity.

Unconventional and willful, strong and independent, Frida was a role model for women at a time and in a country where this was suspect. Her personality and very existence, the focus of her art, have been transformed into iconography. She was the "Grande Dama" of suffering. Being a patient was part of her theatrical self-presentation; it went with her clothes, it went with her exotic personal image, it went with the drama of her art.

The repetitious painting of self-portraits may have exorcized pain by externalizing it as a replica of herself. It is possible to see these self-portraits as means of attempted externalization of the agony she could not bear. Her work stimulated pain in her viewers. To look at her self-portraits is to experience her anguish. Toward the end of her life, Kahlo began to hand out photographs of herself to her friends.

Frida Kahlo

Was her constant self-portraiture also a way of assuring herself that she existed?

94

In summary, Frida's life was dominated and shaped by chronic feelings of fragmentation which evoked a pervasive fear of being unloved and forgotten. She painted as an attempt to create a life-sustaining mirroring and affirming relationship with her art community, and so that people would remember her. She made the subjective state of her suffering the subject of her art. Of the two problems, the physical suffering and the absence of a structured sense of emotional nourishment of the self, the latter was the more serious.

Anne E Rice, MA, Jennifer M. McLeod, Suzanne May Garber, and Daniel F. Eckert are thanked for their assistance in preparing the manuscript.

Susan E. Backes is a psychiatrist, formerly on the faculties of Baylor College of Medicine and Louisiana State University, and currently in the private practice of psychiatry in Houston, Texas. Active in the Director's Circle of the Houston Grand Opera, love of music led to her research into the psychological lives of great composers, and their music. Dr. Backes has participated in national and international conferences on the subject.

In a moment of grace, we can grasp eternity in the palm of our hand.
                                                    —*Marcel Marceau*

Gioachino Rossini
Creativity at the Mid-life Transition
by Susan E. Backes, M.D.

With 1992 marking the 200th birthday of Gioachino Rossini, we
have seen a renewed interest in his operas, some neglected since his
death in 1868. Certainly recognized by most people as the composer
of *The Barber of Seville*, and *William Tell*, Rossini is widely appreciated by opera fans.

Rossini's personality is full of paradox: vigor and incredible productivity followed by lethargy, a passionate zest for life followed by
desolation, wit and charm alternating with isolation and sullenness.
An even larger paradox was created by his premature retirement from
opera composition at age thirty-seven, after thirty-nine operas. How
to explain why someone who lived to age seventy-six ceased to create the art he so loved? Ill health, depression, childlessness, laziness
and artistic inertia have all been suggested. To understand this
conundrum, one must look into Rossini's life and the context in
which it occurred.

The importance of opera to nineteenth century society in Italy
cannot be overestimated. Even small towns with populations under
thirty thousand had lavish opera houses easily rivaling those in
France. Usually, some man of importance in the town would hire a

librettist and a composer to write an opera. This self-styled impresario would then hire singers and begin rehearsals. The townspeople would intently follow the goings-on of the opera, delighting in the usually scandalous behavior of the singers—often, the singers were thought to have lax morals and considered one notch above courtesans.

La Scala in Milan was the ultimate in opera houses and the focus of attention in Italian society. Attendance at opening night and the nights that followed was imperative for those who mattered. Other cities, including Venice and Naples, had several theaters, each with its own season; so opera was available throughout the year. Inside the theaters were privately owned or rented boxes, described as "two hundred miniature salons, sufficient to contain all that is of worth and value in Milanese society" (Till). Unlike behavior at contemporary theatres, all forms of social behavior took place in the nineteenth century theatre boxes, including loud talking, card-playing and love-making. Silence occurred only during the opening night arias or, at subsequent performances, during a particularly memorable part of an act. Lobbies were alive with gambling tables, a major source of funding for opera in the golden age.

The political atmosphere of Italy

In late eighteenth and early nineteenth century Italy, the political atmosphere was one of the factors responsible for opera's popularity. With little or no political freedom or involvement in democratic process, people became concerned with social matters. Italy was a political patchwork of twelve different states, with governments varying from papal to monarchy to republican autonomy. The opera houses in the various states competed with each other and reflected the states' chauvinism.

Harsh rules and strict censorship governed the opera houses, and punishment for broken rules could be extremely severe. Librettos were judged, and often rejected as unsuitable, on religious, moral and political grounds. With so much censorship inhibiting creative writing, audiences were ready for new operas by the time Rossini arrived on the scene.

The birth of a genius

Even his birthday gave a hint that Rossini was someone special. Gioachino Rossini was born in a leap year, February 29, 1792, in Pesaro, a small port town on the east coast of Italy. His father, Giussepe, was the town trumpeter in Lugo where he met his mother, Anna, a moderately talented opera singer. In 1798, they began touring together. Vivazza, as Rossini's father was called, played in the orchestra, and accompanied her while she sang baggage arias, so named because they were generic selections inserted into any opera when an aria was required.

While the elder Rossinis were touring, Anna's mother cared for the boy, Gioachino. Various authors have described the "little Adonis" as a difficult, precocious child who was undisciplined and mischievous. It was evident, however, that the young Rossini had an interest in and a talent for music. His voice was also extraordinary, but his loving mother refused the suggested offer to surgically preserve it as a castrato. At about age ten, Rossini began to accompany Anna and Vivazza with the touring opera. His behavior was more appropriate by that time but his extreme attachment to his mother was evident.

In 1804, the family moved to Bologna, where Gioachino studied music at the Liceo Musicale and earned money as a choir soprano and harpsichord player. It was through contacts made during this period that Rossini's composing began. His first opera composition came as a result of his musical genius. When a composer refused a request by a lady friend for some opera music, Rossini attended the opera and wrote the music from memory at home that evening. The composer was angry, but so impressed that he commissioned young Rossini to compose another opera. This became *Demetrio e Polibio*, and was followed in a few years by *La Cambiale di Matrimonio*, performed in 1810 in Venice.

Tancredi was the opera that, in 1813, opened at La Fenice in Venice and made Rossini internationally famous. The most familiar aria, *Di tanti palpiti*, dubbed the "rice aria," reportedly was written in the time it took for his dinner rice to boil. The aria became known by most everyone in Venice and later throughout Europe, and was sung repeatedly. Following *Tancredi*, a few weeks later, he completed and produced another success, *L'Italiani in Algeri*, with what seemed to be boundless energy and creative drive.

For Italy, the year 1815 was an important one politically. The country was still quite divided but French rule had encouraged republicanism. In Naples, Bourbon rule had again been established and opera flourished under its beneficence. The Teatro San Carlo, richly endowed, had as its impresario Domenico Barbaia, who convinced Rossini to come to Naples, with a contract for composing two operas per year for the two Naples opera houses.

In Naples, Rossini composed *Elisabetta, Regina d'Inghilterra*, for Barbaia's mistress, the famous Spanish contralto, Isabella Colbran. The opera was a huge success. It is not certain when the love affair between Colbran and Rossini began, but apparently she transferred her affections from Barbaia to Rossini with little fanfare. Between 1815 and 1823, Rossini wrote ten more operas for Colbran, mostly in the opera seria convention. Comic operas (opera buffa) were generally performed at another Naples opera house.

The Barber of Seville

After the huge success of *Elisabetta*, Rossini set his sights on Rome and signed a contract for an opera to be performed at Teatro Argentina. A month before the scheduled opening, Rossini still had no libretto to work with. Cesare Sterbini was hired and "adapted" a libretto from a popular play by Beaumarchais, the theme of an earlier work by Paisiello, and one of his most popular operas. Recycled librettos were not unusual in the days before copyright laws. Audiences seemed to like familiar stories with new music. In frantic haste, within three and a half weeks, *The Barber of Seville* was written by Rossini and staged.

Biographers and musicologists agree that this is Rossini's best and certainly his most famous opera. It is considered best not because it has the best music or greatest dramatic skill, but because it has the best libretto (Till, 1983). Its roots are from commedia del-l'arte, the popular theatre of historical Italy, steeped in character roles and conventional plot twists. Essentially, it is the story of handsome Count Almaviva's romantic pursuit of the pretty Rosina who is also desired by her music teacher, Don Basilio and her jealous guardian, Dr. Bartolo. The count is helped in his disguise and pursuit by the barber Figaro, the general right-hand man of Dr. Bartolo.

In a psychoanalytic interpretation of *The Barber of Seville*, Daniel Schwartz proposes a love triangle in which Rossini is represented by the successful Count Almaviva and his father is the old Dr. Bartolo who keeps his love object as secluded as possible, just as, in real life, did Vivazza. There is also a similarity between the character Figaro and Rossini's father. That Figaro represents a potential castration threat is suggested by his occupation of which he boasts so much. Supposedly Rossini overcomes his castration anxiety by making Figaro his ally. The father image, then, is split into Figaro, a potent and good figure, and Bartolo as the bad and impotent figure.

Sixteen operas in twelve years

The next twelve or thirteen years brought Rossini triumphant success, with sixteen operas produced in Naples for Barbaia. Though he had his share of unpopular responses, most of the operas were well received and carried him to phenomenal popularity. Two notable operas following *The Barber of Seville* were the opera buffa *La Gazzetta* and the opera seria *Otello*, both first performed in 1816. Rossini's *Otello* was never well received even though its music was thought to be elegant. Written half a century before Verdi's opera of the same name, it remains overshadowed by the latter.

Rossini returned to Rome for the successful production of *La Cenerentola*, from the French fairy tale of Cinderella, with a libretto written by Cartoni that was finally approved by the censors. This dazzling success was followed by *La Gazza Ladra* (The Thieving Magpie), a tragic tale done in an opera semiseria motif with comedic characters and a rustic setting.

By June of 1819, Rossini was back home in Naples, writing *La Donna Del Lago*, from Walter Scott's poem. Another production at La

Scala required a journey back to Milan. Although Rossini was just twenty-seven, he was tired of travel and already considered retiring before he reached thirty. During the four years which followed, he composed only four operas, but was becoming known all over Italy. Further expansion came with Barbaia's contract in 1821 to provide productions for the Vienna state opera.

After leaving Naples, Rossini and Isabella Colbran stopped off in her villa at Castenaso and were married. Unfortunately, the marriage was the beginning of the end for Rossini and Colbran. Her career was already beginning to wane, and it was rumored that Rossini had married her for her wealth and fame rather than for love. Meanwhile, Vienna was about to experience Rossini mania during the three month opera season. While there, Rossini made a point of scheduling a meeting with Beethoven.

International fame at age twenty nine

Between 1821 and 1827 Rossini was an international celebrity. Wherever he went, crowds followed and he was feted by high society. "His wit, his good temper, his beautiful manners..." (Toye) were spoken of often, as was his appreciation of fine cuisine. In those years, some thirty of his operas were performed throughout Europe, rewarding him with fame and wealth.

By autumn of 1823, Rossini had started work on *Semiramide* which opened at La Fenice in Venice. This opera marks the high point of Rossini's "bel canto" style. It also marks the end of Rossini's Italian period—it was his last Italian opera. He settled in Paris with Isabella where he directed the Theatre-Italien.

During rehearsals for a new opera in Paris, early in 1827, Rossini was told that his mother was gravely ill with an aneurysm. Although he wanted to go to her side in Bologna, physicians advised against it, fearing that the stress of his visit would be harmful. She died shortly thereafter, leaving Rossini guilt- and grief-stricken. Although immediate effects of his loss were not visible, at one curtain call at a successful performance, Rossini was heard to say, "Ah, but she is dead!" His greatest admirer, his source of tremendous support was gone.

Rossini's last opera

Rossini made one more attempt at comedy with *Le Comte Ory*, which attained clear success. He then set to work on the long-promised serious French opera which would become *William Tell*. This is considered by many to be his ultimate masterpiece. It certainly was an important opera, and, unbeknownst at the time, it was Rossini's very last. The estimate of time spent composing *William Tell* is thought to be almost a year, in sharp contrast to the three days for completion of his first opera and the twenty-four days for *Barber of Seville*. The opera was postponed many times so that Rossini could be satisfied with the contract. He now required a full salary for life for the promise of five operas to be delivered within a space of ten years. At that time, he may have unconsciously known that he would no longer be productive. He also exerted tremendous pressure to have the artistic control he needed to produce his masterpiece.

The story of William Tell, the Swiss national hero, is adapted from Schiller's play about Swiss countrymen and women who struggle to escape the tyranny of Austrian rule, personified by Gessler. Jemmy, Tell's son, is the soul of the story. In a scene known around the world, Gessler forces William to shoot an arrow into the apple on his son's head.

Rossini never wrote another opera. Why did he cease what had been a prodigious operatic output at the age of 37, at what might be considered the height of his powers? There are several theories.

Rossini himself claimed he retired because of the negative political atmosphere and that artistically he felt out of step with the diminishing of "bel canto" style.

In July, 1830, revolution was underway in Paris. Charles X was dethroned, and Louis Phillipe, the "bourgeois monarch," took over. Opera was simultaneously revolutionized, the most notable change being the inclusion of themes of romanticism and liberalism. Even though in musical expression Rossini was considered a romantic, he turned away from librettos that glorified ignoble people and their behavior. Moreover, Rossini felt that opera was transforming in ways that betrayed his principles: in particular, the decline of "bel canto."

This decline he attributed to the disappearance of the castrati and their teachers (Osborne, 1986).

His physical ill health was certainly a factor. He developed symptoms of an undiagnosed illness that required him to rest much of the time, and for which he traveled to spas for recuperation, and he developed urethritis and nephritis, probably venereal in origin.

His psychological ill health was a more important factor.

Rossini's retirement may have been triggered by his mother's death, and his inability to have a mature internalized image of her due to his intense ambivalence. *William Tell*, his last great opera, may represent a renunciation of genitality, a theme that had been stated more humorously in *Le Comte Ory*. Schwartz theorizes that Rossini's basic identification in William Tell was with the child Jemmy who, as the only undisturbed and confident character in the whole story, represented the security of a non-competitive, pre-Oedipal role, which, with his mother's death, disappeared forever.

In 1830, Rossini and Isabella Colbran separated after many years of unhappiness. Meanwhile, Rossini entered into litigation over his contract, keeping him in Paris for five years. In 1832, he met Olympe Pelissier, a well-known French courtesan, who became his mistress, nursemaid and eventually his second wife.

Ten years of depression

The next ten years were filled with depression, increasingly severe anxiety attacks and obsessional preoccupations. More illness, the destruction of the Theatre Italien by fire, and his father's death intensified his depression. A move to Florence worsened the situation. Obsessions and delusions of being despised and, worse, unimportant to the world, became severe. Olympe encouraged him to move back to Paris, where, as the phobias and obsessions worsened, life became more and more regimented. For a time, Rossini had the peculiar compulsion of having to imagine the major third with any musical note that he heard. Servants were hired just to keep street musicians from playing, so that Rossini would not have to suffer the compulsion.

Finale

In time, Rossini improved. Although anxiety remained and phobias never disappeared, the rigid obsessive routines became comforting and kept life organized. By 1857, he was able to write again. He began some of the 186 musical compositions which together form *Sins of My Old Age*. During this time, the "samedi soirs" of the last ten years of his life began. These were social and musical gatherings hosted by the Rossinis in their Paris apartment. The guest lists were an impressive array of talented composers and performers, including Saint-Saens, Meyerbeer, Verdi, and Franz Liszt.

In 1863, at age seventy-one, Rossini wrote *Petite Messe Solenelle* and, in 1867, a great composition for the Paris Exhibition. The next year, following surgery for rectal carcinoma, he died. Over four thousand people attended the funeral in Paris and memorial concerts were held throughout the world.

Caricature of Rossini observing his seventy-fifth birthday.

Bruce Burrows, in his editorial preface to the commemorative review in The Opera Quarterly, says, "...surely knowing or not knowing the reasons has no bearing upon our enjoyment of the composer's music. We can only marvel at and be grateful for the accomplishments of the years prior to his sudden cessation of operatic activity."

Comment by Dr. Panter:

I would like to offer two additional perspectives on why there was such an abrupt drop in Rossini's output after the age of thirty-seven.

Dr. Backes tells us that he was intensely attached to his mother, that she died when he was 37, and that he composed little after this. From a self psychology perspective, Rossini basked in the relationship with his mother. Being a singer herself, she provided mirroring and affirmation of his musical ability. One could speculate that not only did he bask in her adoration, but that it was essential for the cohesion of his Self. When she died, this mirroring selfobject, so necessary for his functioning, was no longer present. (A selfobject is a person or thing that provides a function for the individual. In Rossini's case, the function was to maintain his self esteem and identity as a composer.)

He tried, in his relationship with Colbran and later with Olympe Pelissier, to replace the needed selfobject. To some extent, they were useful to him, but not to a degree sufficient to enable him to continue his meteoric career. Rossini's creativity, his energy, his phenomenal output as a composer, were rooted in the preoedipal bond, the support, the nurturance and affirmation that he received from his mother. As Dr. Backes wrote, Rossini was not able to internalize his mother, and thus take over and provide these functions for himself. When she died, his strength ebbed, his overflowing creativity diminished, and he decompensated into ill health and depression. Olympe became the nursing mother of the depressed needy child. His attempts to have cities and opera companies support him can be seen as attempts to coerce fate to provide the unconditional love that he desired and needed.

Elliot Jaques, in his article, *Death and the Mid-Life Crisis*, describes two types of creativity: lyrical and sculpted. Lyrical creativity occurs in adolescence and young adulthood. "The creativity of the twenties and the early thirties tends to be hot-from-the-fire creativity. It is intense and spontaneous, and comes out ready-made. The spontaneous effusions of Mozart, Keats, Shelley, Rimbaud (and one might add, Rossini) are the prototype. The conscious production is rapid, the pace of creation often being dictated by the limits of the artist's capacity physically to record the words or music he is expressing."

Rossini gives us an example of this lyrical effortless flow of creativity. When asked how to compose an overture, he replied, "Wait until the evening of the day before opening night. Nothing is a better goad to inspiration than necessity, than the presence of a copyist waiting for your work. I composed the overture to *La Gazza Ladra* on the day of the premiere, right under the roof of La Scala, where I was imprisoned by the manager, watched over by four stagehands who had orders to hand my manuscript pages, one by one, to the copyist waiting below to transcribe them. In case there weren't any music sheets forthcoming, they had orders to throw me out the window."

With mid-life comes the beginning of physical decline, and the awareness of one's mortality. This brings a note of sadness and denial or resignation to the personality. The creativity that occurs as the personality adapts to these events and the conscious or unconscious awareness of the approach of death is different in character. It is sculpted creativity. No longer is every perception and impulse quickly transformed into art. The inspiration is followed by a longer incubation, by the working and reworking of the impulse, and finally by the work itself, which imparts the awareness of sadness, resignation and intimations of death. This is seen in the works of Beethoven, the later Michelangelo, Goethe and Brahms.

Jaques writes that the age near 37 is pivotal regarding the type of creativity seen. At about this age, that of the mid-life crisis or transition, there are three possible courses for creativity: "The creative career may simply come to an end, either in a drying-up of creative work, or in actual death; the creative capacity may begin to show and express itself for the first time; or a decisive change in the quality and content of creativeness may take place." He also reports that a survey of the lives of great artists reveals a very high death rate between the ages of 35 and 39. This group includes Mozart, Raphael, Chopin, Rimbaud, Purcell, Baudelaire, Watteau, van Gogh, Sylvia Plath at a slightly earlier age, and many others.

Very few artists are able to make the transition from lyrical to sculpted creativity. Among this select group is Michelangelo, although after the dazzling masterpieces of his early adult life (including *David*, at age 29), he produced little between the ages of 40 and 55. His creative career resumed with the *Last Judgment* and the Sistine Chapel ceiling in later life. Marc Chagall also traversed the mid-life blockade and continued into sculpted creativity. Bach is an example of the emergence of creativity after mid-life. Until the age of 38, he was an organist. He then took on the cantorship at Leipzig, which required that he compose. He then went on to his magnificent and prolific life as a composer. Gauguin is another example of the start of a creative career at mid-life. Until the age of 35, he was a married man with five children who made his living as a stock broker. At 35, he abandoned his wife and children, and began to devote himself solely to art.

Rossini is an example of the drying-up of creative work. If one utilizes Jaques' formulations, it appears that Rossini was not able to accept the inevitability of physical decline and subsequent death that occurs with mid-life. The energy, optimism, and lyricism of his youth faded. He was not able to make the transition to sculpted creativity. He did attempt to make the creative transition. The few works he composed after the age of 37 are mostly religious pieces, and include at least one that is considered a major work—the *Stabat Mater*. They have a mood of sadness and resignation about them, in sharp contrast to the gaiety and lightness of his earlier works.

Perhaps Rossini himself knew his limitations when he said, "J'étais né pour l'Opera Buffa, tu le sais bien." (I was *born* for comic Opera, you realize.)

Whatever the reason for Rossini's musical decline, the loss was forcefully expressed by Richard Wagner, who met the 62-year-old Rossini in Paris. In a celebrated conversation, Wagner is quoted as saying, "You have created music for all times and that is the best. Oh, why did you throw away your pen when you were only 37? It is a crime."

Dea Adria Mallin, Associate Professor of English at the Community College of Philadelphia for the past 24 years, is a freelance writer with articles published in The Washington Post, The Philadelphia Inquirer, The Boston Globe, and many magazines. Listed in Who's Who in America, and Who's Who in Writers, Editors, and Poets, and a Phi Beta Kappa, Ms. Mallin is the Philadelphia Field Representative of Earthwatch, and participates in many of their expeditions.

A poet is an unhappy being whose heart is torn by secret sufferings, but whose lips are so strangely formed that when the sighs and the cries escape, they sound like beautiful music. —Soren Kierkegaard

Edgar Allan Poe
Descent into Madness
by Dea Adria Mallin, M.A.

Do you remember Poe? The frisson, the thrill, the terror? The sensation of being sucked in—to the teller, the tale, the maelstrom, the grave...? With a mere re-reading of the frenzied lines of *The Bells*, Poe's world comes shuddering forward.

Yet Ralph Waldo Emerson looked down upon Poe's shaking of the bells and dubbed Poe derisively, "the jingle man." T. S. Eliot said Poe's intellect was that of a highly gifted person—before puberty. For James Russell Lowell, Poe was "three-fifths genius and two-fifths fudge."

Now contrast the literary response in America to that in France where the poet Baudelaire made his morning prayers to God—and to Edgar Allan Poe. Joseph Conrad praised Poe's story, *Manuscript Found in a Bottle*, for its art and realism, ranking the story over Coleridge's *Rime of the Ancient Mariner*. "A very fine piece of work— about as fine as anything of that kind can be—and so authentic in detail that it must have been told by a sailor of a somber and poetical genius in the invention of the fantastic," said Conrad.

For all that he was misunderstood and distorted, condescended to, or, by the French, venerated, Poe did and does cast a spell. Freud said that the pleasure we derive from reading comes from the release of narcissistic tension. Edgar Allan Poe gives us that release at its most perverse—walking literary tightropes of obsession, compulsion, fantasy, and nightmare. Uncomfortable with these feelings, America has preferred thinking Poe was mad. Yet, to whom do these obsessions and nightmares belong? To Poe only, who dreamed them? Or to us too, who come back to be haunted by them—to feel that wild uncontrolled glee, that despair, that divided self—time and time again? What we do not wish to acknowledge in ourselves, we call "mad" in others.

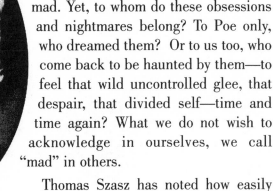

Edgar Allan Poe, 1848

Thomas Szasz has noted how easily being "poor and unwanted" (two categories fully applicable to the adult Poe), with swings between depression and elation, can predispose a person to being cast by society as mentally ill.

We pursue here through the details of Poe's life and his writing, not a madman, but a brilliant young boy for whom a series of tragic and unfortunate events destined him to re-enact his early trauma and to re-traumatize himself. On a wild ride between having life cheat him and having ruined some of his own best chances, at the end—at age forty—he became defeated and intensely self-destructive, and he died wretchedly in 1849.

Poe is probably the saddest figure on the American literature landscape. For the most part, Poe made a very good pre-Freudian attempt to understand what he termed his "imp of the perverse"—his self-destructiveness—to face it down, and to establish some kind of a loving framework, as he actually succeeded in doing with his wife and mother-in-law. This is not to say that Poe knew who he was or why he felt or didn't feel, or why he could act or be paralyzed by inaction—but he surely wanted to know.

Contrast these two 19th century males:

Chief Sitting Bull met with a group of United States senators at the Standing Rock Sioux reservation in 1863. Wanting to be reassured that the senators understood just how important a chief he was, he said, repeatedly: *"Do you know who I am?"* For the senators, the answer was "Not really," yet Chief Sitting Bull knew exactly who he was. His problem was an external one, a clash of cultures and politics, without.

Edgar Allan Poe asked the same question: *"Do you know who I am?"* But it was not rhetorical. It was a cri du coeur, a cry from the heart. Can't anyone tell me who I am, or why I am haunted by certain images and half-memories, or why I have an imp of the perverse goading me to do things I shouldn't. "My terror," said Poe to a friend, "is not of Germany (meaning the Gothic literary tradition), but of the soul."

Poe, then, was the first American writer to dare to lay bare the inner conflicts of the alienated, the orphaned, and the outcast, predicting 20th century Alienated Man. Though he yearned to understand these tensions and conflicts, his narrator in the *Black Cat* speaks for Poe about the hope of ever understanding. Anticipating Freud, the narrator says:

Hereafter, perhaps, some intellect may well be found which will reduce my phantasm to the commonplace, some intellect more calm, more logical, and far less excitable than my own, which will perceive in the circumstances I detail with awe, nothing more than an ordinary succession of very natural causes and effects.

Poe used the power of words to enter the world of powerless people. If he could not control his life, at least he could control his art—and an audience. And if, instead of reducing the pain of his internal landscape, Poe wanted to heighten it to an ecstasy of feeling, he had but to do as Joseph Conrad believed a writer must do: "In the destructive element," commanded Conrad, "immerse."

Thus we have Poe using art as an attempt to give order and control to his internal chaos. Poe's area of sanity is his art. The characters, utterances, and situations may be mad, but in the act of ordering them, Poe is not.

Let's go now to the details of his life and examine the interplay between his tales and poems and the unfortunate circumstances that destined him to re-enact his early traumas.

Eliza Poe

Poe's entire literary output could be said to center on a single traumatic event which occurred when Edgar was nearly three years old. His mother, Eliza Poe, died of consumption, her three children surrounding her in her literal bed of poverty.

Eliza Poe was lovely in face and body with large luminous dark eyes, dark hair, and an exquisite voice. But with all that, her life had been star-crossed by death and loss. Her father died when she was two, her mother when nine. She became an itinerant actress, marrying at fifteen, then becoming widowed, and marrying David Poe Jr. several months later. David, destined for a career as a lawyer, fell in love with Eliza on the stage and, though untalented, joined her acting troupe and married her. Soon overwhelmed by the responsibility for a wife with two children, and a third on the way, David simply disappeared when Edgar was eight months old.

Orphaned, widowed, deserted, Eliza Poe now became consumptive. Her three young children watched, in the same bed with her, for several months as their mother suffocated, choked, and bled from the mouth. These would be powerful images for any adult; they were overwhelming for the child Edgar, who would be haunted by his love for his mother and the images of her dying, and his separation from her—evermore.

Eliza, Poe's mother

Losing his mother at three, Poe was then separated from his two siblings, to live in material comfort with his foster parents, the Allans.

John Allan

While Poe's life may have been woman-dominated, the

inescapable figure was John Allan—his foster father, and not a good match with Poe. It is the souring and demise of this relationship that led to Poe's recurrent literary theme of paternal revenge—to set aright the narcissistic injuries of youth. Later, with other men, Poe tended mostly to argue, re-enacting his drama of estrangement from John Allan with male authority figures throughout his life.

When John Allan agreed reluctantly, after having once refused, to allow his wife, Fanny, to rescue Eliza Poe's little son Edgar from orphandom, Allan was a thirty-two-year-old merchant in Richmond, Virginia. "157 lbs. of good hard flesh," he described himself. He had a hook nose, small keen eyes, shaggy eyebrows, and reminded one contemporary of a hawk.

His business brokered everything from marble tombstone to frying pans. And though he took the orphan in and gave him a genteel life, good furniture and sweets, it would seem that Edgar's feelings and spirit were not provided for.

In being John Allan's ward, Edgar became totally dependent on the care and generosity of a man who despised dependence. In fact, John Allan felt he had been cheated of care and generosity in life, himself. He had left his family in Scotland as a teenager to come to America where he worked for his very successful uncle in Richmond. The uncle was a taskmaster, and apparently, Allan was resentful of the uncle for denying him an academic education and keeping him instead "tight to business."

Allan's resentment was even greater because the uncle, a beneficent bachelor, had adopted four orphans and supported four more—and had given several of them the advantage of "a better and more expensive education than I ever had—although (as nephew) I had stronger claims."

John Allan's sense of deprivation thus distorted his code of independence from "Stand on your own two feet" to "Why should you get what I didn't?"

As an employer, Allan was didactic, frequently dispensing his "wisdom" and requiring of others what he required of himself: obedience, industry, and self-control. "The mind," he said, "is like a garden judiciously laid out. Neglect permits thorns and weeds to arise, which greatly hurts the fruits."

So industrious was Allan that he filled in some of his gaps in culture and literature, buying himself a piano and a flute, and reading and quoting Shakespeare. "God," he wrote, "what I would not give if I had Shakespeare's talent for writing!" Yet when Allan tried to keep his own journal, he could do no more than enter "Warm weather for the season," or, "Nothing done in horticulture yet."

Imagine the resentful John Allan having a young man in his house—not his own blood, but more like the orphans his uncle had once helped—who possessed real writing talent—and who would get to go on to the University of Virginia for a classical education!

Edgar was well schooled both in England for five years and then back in Richmond, though he recalled those days as lonely. In Richmond, those who knew him remembered Poe as "blatantly competitive" and locally famous for swimming six miles under a hot June sun against a strong tide—and then walking all the way back to Richmond. Young Edgar was considered daring and ambitious, and he led others with his strong desire to excel and to command.

In this, he was like many other orphans in whom a feeling of non-existence and the need to master changeable surroundings often produce a will to power.

By his teens, Edgar had not yet been adopted by the Allans, though the promise had been held out to him. His sister had been adopted, and even John Allan's uncle had officially adopted a teenage son. Edgar noticed. In England, as a youngster, he'd signed his name Edgar Allan. Back in the States, it was Edgar Allan Poe, though he still signed letters as Edgar A.—showing hope of being a full-fledged son to John Allan.

Edgar called Fanny "Ma"—but with her constant complaints of ill-health and unavailability, he eventually sought replacements for her. At fourteen, he was infatuated with the thirty-year-old mother of a classmate, and went to her when he was unhappy for consoling. She herself was a depressive, and suffered, she told Edgar, "from a death-like sickness." At thirty-one, she died insane.

Edgar went often to her grave, and it was at this point of grieving for a surrogate mother that he began to clash with John Allan. The foster father saw him, at sixteen, as transformed into "sulky and ill-tempered." Allan interpreted this mood as sheer thanklessness.

In fact, John Allan was the only father Edgar had ever known, and the young Poe still wanted his approval desperately. In adolescence, Poe tested him, as adolescents will do. But Allan wasn't a man to be tested.

The University of Virginia

When Poe entered the University of Virginia, his guardian's heart was already turned against him. Allan had once thought Edgar a darling child. Now he thought him merely an ungrateful one. And having a businessman's temperament, he apparently wrote off both his losses and the young man. To punish Edgar, John Allan sent him off to the University of Virginia with insufficient funds.

Edgar, at sixteen, was three years younger than the other freshmen, and not chronologically or temperamentally suited to the year-old school's atmosphere of high stakes gambling, carousing with women, pistol shooting, and drunkenness. This violent atmosphere unnerved Edgar, and he wrote home of his "great consternation" and hopes of doing well "if I don't get too frightened."

He participated in the student drinking, but unlike his classmates, drank in a joyless fashion. "He would always," said his classmates, "seize the glass and without the least apparent pleasure, swallow the contents, never pausing until the last drop passed his lips." One glass, it was reported, was all he could take.

Poe's drinking had its beginnings in his infancy, when an elderly nursemaid fed the Poe children freely with bread soaked in gin, or gave them laudanum (opium dissolved in alcohol) to quiet them when they were restless. Moreover, in the Allan household, when Edgar was four years old, he was encouraged to stand on the dining room table in stockinged feet to toast the health of guests with a glass of sweetened wine. When he had finished the wine, he would recite the most moving and lengthy passages of English poetry. Perhaps two strains of Poe's DNA came together in this scene: from his mother, who at fifteen was lauded for knowing perfectly the lines from 300 different stage roles, came memory and theatricality—and, from his biological father, the susceptibility to alcohol.

At the university, Poe drank and gambled to fit in, and these would be both his immediate and long-term undoing. But in spite of the general view of Poe as morbid and neurasthenic, it is important to note that Poe was, in fact, an excellent student, a good debater, and an exceptional athlete, able to complete a running broad jump of 20 feet.

His schoolmates also knew that he was dependent upon the bounty bestowed on a foster son, and his ambiguous social position led Poe to feel a sense of isolation. In *Alone,* an introspective poem about his youth, Poe delineated his alienated position:

> "From childhood's hour I have not been
> As others were—I have not seen
> As others saw—I could not bring
> My passions from a common spring.
> From the same source, I have not taken
> My sorrow—I could not awaken
> My heart to joy at the same tone —
> And all I loved—I loved alone."

At sixteen, from a sensitive boy, one could expect an identity crisis, but overall, Poe's future looked promising—that is, until a crisis over money and power changed the relationship between Poe and his foster father.

Sent to the University of Virginia with insufficient funds, Edgar was virtually forced to gamble to try to pay his essential university expenses of books and tuition. He ran up over $2,000 worth of debt, and John Allan refused to pay off the debt. He decided, despite Poe's academic brilliance, to cut him off entirely.

Four years later, Poe's letter of recrimination to his father shows an embittered catalogue detailing every slight by one of the richest men in all Virginia:

> "I will boldly say that it was wholly and entirely your own mistaken par-
> simony that caused all the difficulties in which I was involved while at
> Charlottesville. The expenses of the institution at the lowest estimate

were $350 per annum. [Most students needed at least $500.] You sent me there with $110. Of this, $50 were to be paid immediately for board—$60 for attendance upon 2 professors —and you even then did not miss the opportunity for abusing me because I did not attend 3. Then $15 more were to be paid for room-rent—remember that all this was to be paid in advance, with $110.—$12 more for a bed—and $12 more for room furniture. I had, of course, the mortification of running in debt for public property—against the known rules of the institution, and was immediately regarded in the light of a beggar. You will remember that in a week after my arrival, I wrote to you for some more money, and for books. You replied in terms of the utmost abuse—if I had been the vilest wretch on earth, you could not have been more abusive than you were because I could not contrive to pay $150 with $110."

Allan's motives? Perhaps a testing of Edgar's self-sufficiency, but more likely a combination of the following: jealousy of his wife's preference for Edgar, a desire to punish Edgar for supporting Fanny over Allan's adultery and illegitimate child, resentfulness of Edgar's intellectual and artistic success, and an unconscious wish to see Edgar fail so that he could not emerge from college as superior to the merchant, John Allan.

John Allan cuts Edgar off

Whatever the motive, he cut Edgar off. All at once, Poe's career at the university was cruelly terminated, he was expelled from Allan's household, and he was heavily in debt. Though he was reared for the aristocratic life, he was suddenly thrust into the business world— with only a writer's pen—not a good prospect in the South.

At a high moment, he wrote to Allan:

Neglected, I will be doubly ambitious and the world shall hear of the son you have thought unworthy of your notice.

But mostly, Poe was despondent and destitute. In a state of starvation, with no clothes and no means of eating or getting from place to place, he wrote to John Allan: "I am perishing—absolutely perishing for want of aid. For God's sake, pity me and save me from destruction."

No answer from the hard-hearted Allan. Soon after, when Allan was seriously ill, Poe visited Allan's bedroom. As soon as he entered,

Allan raised his cane, and threatened to strike him if he came within reach, then ordered Edgar out.

Cursed instead of blessed by the father and driven from the family home, Edgar passed out of Allan's life forever, and Allan, who died six months later, set him adrift by leaving him absolutely nothing in the will. Taught the habits and tastes of a Virginia gentleman by Allan, Poe was denied by Allan any means to support them.

Poe antagonized publishers and writers

Now Poe began to re-animate the drama of fatherly disapproval and desertion, time and time again, with his male employers and his literary peers.

In his first magazine job, his publisher felt paternal solicitude for Poe, but, seeing that alcohol was destroying him, he was rigid about Poe not drinking. Poe drank. Poe was dismissed.

His second publisher made Poe a drudge, giving him only $10 a week and no opportunity to advance. Displacing, perhaps, his anger at his publisher, Poe began to write caustic reviews of other writers—the kind that later got him the name "Tomahawk." About James Fenimore Cooper, Poe was all vitriol:

"A flashy succession of ill-conceived and miserably executed literary productions, each more silly than its predecessor...causing the public to suspect a radical taint in the intellect, an absolute and irreparable leprosy."

Poe jeered at New England writers as "arrogant bumpkins" and bludgeoned James Russell Lowell as "a ranting abolitionist who deserves a good using up," (explaining, or perhaps in response to, Lowell's derogation of Poe.)

And so it went—with his editors, publishers, with powerful literary figures in the Northern establishment, even benefactors. If Poe didn't choose destructive fathers, he turned the males in his life into them, returning himself to the familiarity of the agitated state of dependence on their good will.

Poe marries

Penniless, Poe was taken into the house of his real father's widowed sister, Maria Clemm, where he lived with Maria and her young daughter Virginia. At the age of 24—the precise age of his mother's death—he pleaded passionately for the hand of the fourteen-year-old Virginia Clemm—and recreated the original idealized script of a doting mother and a little sister. The newlyweds, along with Maria Clemm, made up a menage à trois, and despite chronic financial difficulties, theirs was a happy existence.

Maria Clemm, Poe's mother-in-law

Much has been made of Poe at twenty-four marrying his fourteen-year-old cousin whom he affectionately called "Sissy" while he called Mrs. Clemm "my own darling mother" and "my dear Muddy."

On one side of the argument about sexual coziness is the shared opinion of psychiatrist Marie Bonaparte and literary critic Joseph Wood Krutch that the marriage was never consummated, that Poe was impotent, and that his sexual energy was transmuted into artistic energy. Others believe that in time, this was a full marriage.

Either way, Poe's anxieties were largely relieved as he replaced those from whom he had long been separated with a mother and a sister-wife who both adored him. The selfobject tie was, it appears, exquisitely mended. In fact, shortly after the marriage, Poe wrote one of his rare positive letters to a friend:

> "My health is better than for years past, my mind is fully occupied, my pecuniary difficulties have vanished, I have a fair prospect of future success—in a word, all is right."

Poe's work life and love life were both full, and he wrote the bulk of his stories and poems during this period. While he was hardworking, he would relax in the evening by reciting poetry to the family, taking long walks, and working in his flower garden. During the four years before Virginia became ill, there was stability in the Poe household. Poe gave over much of his magazine editor's salary at *The Southern Literary Messenger* to Virginia's education, and she was becoming an accomplished singer and musician.

Says biographer Jeffrey Meyers, "Everyone who saw her was won by her, and Poe delighted in her round face and plump figure, so opposite his own." With her, he was playful, affectionate and witty. Meyers counters the notion that Virginia's prolonged illness made sexual relations impossible after she reached maturity—reminding that there were four healthy years from age sixteen to twenty when there was the probability of a consummated marriage.

Poe's wife, Virginia

In 1842, an eerie coincidence that was to rock Poe's life took place. Virginia, undernourished because of their poverty and subsistence on bread and molasses, was singing and playing the piano when she suddenly began to hemorrhage. Blood gushed from her mouth, as it had so many years earlier from Eliza Poe, and though she partially recovered, she would sink and sink again for the next four years, finally dying at the same age as Poe's own mother.

A visitor recalls Poe fanning her as she could hardly breathe, the low ceiling of the poor room nearly touching her head. Poe would not allow a word about her dying—the mention of it drove him wild. His old publisher recalls Poe's "rapturous worship of his wife. Virginia's slightest cough caused him a shudder and a heart-chill that was visible."

Each time Virginia would flutter on the edge of death and then return, Poe relived his old wound and added to his terror of loss and sensation of breathlessness. There was also the question of boundaries:

122

would he, should he die if she died, so bound up were they as one?

Poe's heroines die

Let's see how this works itself into his writing. Poe's literary heroines are typically affected with mysterious diseases, much as his mother's coughing and spitting and pallor must have been mysterious as they lay in the same bed; much as, later, his foster mother's endless coughing and assorted maladies must have seemed mysterious. The heroines waste away before the lover's eyes, their bodies drained of a life energy that neither hero nor heroine can halt. Yet Poe's women are not exactly allowed to die. They return from the tomb, as a grieving child might yearn for the magical return of the lost idealized beloved parent.

Signalling Poe's return to the Oedipal dream is the mellifluous sound in the naming of his heroines. A *la* or a *li* sound recurs—resonating off the syllables of his mother's name, Eliza. Thus we have: Ulalume, Annabel Lee, Lenore, Helen, Morella, Ligeia.

Not only names, but the titles of Poe's poetry reveal his longing for the selfobject: *A Dream within a Dream; The Happiest Day and the Happiest Hour; Romance; Fairy Land; The Sleeper, The Valley of Unrest; Silence; Dreamland; A Valentine; To My Mother; Alone.*

Recurring images of Poe's mother's death and burial get worked into the tales in a fascination with—and often a confusion between— the womb and the tomb. While most of the heroes of American literature are out engaging the wide open prairies and conquering and opening up the wilderness, Poe's heroes are going inward and into limited space. The protagonists of the tales and poems are always within something: a single room, a series of rooms, dark pits, damp caves, coffins, under the floorboards, inside a wall. Even in the vast and limitless ocean, Poe brilliantly manages to enclose his characters inside a maelstrom or whirlpool. In *Descent into the Maelstrom*, the reader feels as if a projectionist in a movie house were running a birthing film backwards, and the baby is being sucked back into the womb—only without an umbilical cord to breathe. In *The Pit and the Pendulum*, the walls actually move in towards the narrator. In *The*

Cask of Amontillado, the seven rooms of the underground get progressively smaller and lower.

At its most extreme, the closing in of space is actual entombment, a constant in Poe's stories. Madeline Usher is buried alive, Berenice is buried alive, Morella is buried, Lady Rowena is buried, Ligeia is buried, Lenore is buried, Annabel Lee is buried. These are the mother-wife in her two aspects: the ideal and beautiful maiden doomed to die at an early age, and the revenant whose flesh has been ravaged by the Conqueror Worm. In the stories, there is a confusion between womb and tomb, between love and death, and the women are often loved better in death.

In life there was always, to be sure, the question of what to do with a real woman. From a distance, especially that of death, a woman can be idealized and adored. Close up, on a wedding night, for example, a woman could make demands. Quite possibly, the obligatory entombment of women in Poe's narratives is a metaphor for Poe's repression of his sexuality plus his desire for physical re-union with the lost mother.

In fact, coupling, when it does occur in Poe's stories, can be grotesque. Think of the twins, Roderick and Madeline Usher, in *The Fall of the House of Usher*. Roderick manages to bury Madeline while she is still alive, and she comes back to him from the tomb, rattling her chains.

> There was blood upon her white robes. For a moment she remained trembling and reeling to and fro. Then with a low moaning cry fell heavily inward upon the person of her brother, and in her violent and now final death agonies, bore him to the floor—a corpse.

Here is the incestuous embrace and the love/sex/death confusion.

Love, on its prettiest side in Poe, is idealized love and longing. The poem *Annabel Lee* has many of the features of Poe's male-female geography:

- The female is utterly devoted to the narrator who gains a semblance of control and cohesion: ("And this maiden she lived with no other thought than to love and be loved by me.")
- The love is pre-sexual. ("She was a child and I was a child.")

There will be lots of this to follow in American literature—think of J. D. Salinger whose good characters are either killed before puberty or go crazy, like Holden Caulfield, because of sexual impulses.

- Love incites a powerful male to wild jealousy, and the girl gets stolen by a rival ("her high-born kinsman"). Then she has to die.
- There is a too-early walling up of the female—here, in a sepulchre.
- Coupling occurs, but only in a dream state. Annabel Lee's eyes (orbs) are the sexual focus, and the lovers lie imaginatively in the tomb together:

So all the night tide, I lie down by the side
of my darling, my darling, my life and my bride
in her sepulchre there by the sea,
in her tomb by the side of the sea.

Poe, in writing, is not good at transferring his longing for his mother, the original love object, to the substitutes that life offers. Instead, he is haunted by the original love-object in his memory's storage bank—which is both forbidden and incestuous—his secret of secrets—and, though dead, the only image genuinely desired. In his longing, Poe anticipated Freud, though what we know today about mothers and sons was considered absolutely mad in Poe's time. Poe's stories explore the connections between love and guilt, and love and hate, and yet there is not a single Poe tale that is a love story, without a posthumous heroine.

Says Poe:

I could not love except where Death
was mingling his with Beauty's breath.

So the love stories are always doomed to reduce by the end to one—to the narrator—who must inevitably confront the reality of the loss. (Interestingly, the title of Poe's story, *The Colloquy of Monos and Una,* indicates a dialogue—colloquy. However, the names of the participants are Monos and Una—the Greek masculine for the pronoun "one" and the Latin feminine for the pronoun "one.")

Berenice is Poe's first story with a love-obsessed but monomaniacal narrator—a successful artistic device. In the story, the narrator, Egeus, has a fiancée, Berenice, who is also his cousin—that is, part of his mother's blood. Egeus and Berenice are locked in a pathological symbiosis, and as their wedding day approaches, she ceases to be a dream to him and becomes a reality. Immediately, Poe shrinks her into corpse-like emaciation while the narrator fixates on her perfect white teeth. He calls them her "ideas," but more, he sees them as permanent objects having the ability to transcend death while the body decays.

Though Egeus reports to the reader that Berenice has now died in an epileptic seizure and been buried just prior to the wedding, a servant tells Egeus and the reader that Berenice's grave has been violated, and she's been buried alive. The servant then tactlessly points to Egeus's hand with a spade in it, to his muddy garments clotted with blood and gore, the human nailmarks in his hand—plus instruments of dental surgery and a box out of which spill thirty-two perfect small white teeth. The narrator-bridegroom, then, is the murderer of his own bride. Since teeth—the gate to the orifice of the mouth—appear in so many other stories, we must wonder at the fear of the bridegroom of his unmentioned wedding night, and perhaps a fear of vagina dentata—the vagina with teeth. Extracting Berenice's teeth would not be so much the symbol of transcending death and triumphing over its decay, but a way of avoiding sexual terror.

Other tales of sexual repression and displacement abound in the stories of women. In *The Black Cat*, "cat" equals "pussy" equals "wife"—and both, by physically loving the narrator, cause him such anxiety that he murders one of each and walls them up together just as (Poe's narrator states outright) the monks walled up their victims. Experiencing relief that the white-breasted cat and the wife of his bosom are both gone, the narrator is discovered and condemned to be hanged—impotent by order of the police.

Then there is *Murders in the Rue Morgue*—in which a nubile young woman is savagely dismembered and stuffed up a chimney with her head (did he mean maidenhead?) torn off.

Or the tales of *Morella and Ligeia*—in which the woman is an idealized all-knowing master of esoterica who promises to teach the narrator her secrets and to initiate him. Then, just as the initiation approaches, this first love sickens and dies and is replaced by a second female, who is detested. But then the first comes back and fills the body of the second. Even if the desired and adored first love is back, she's still dead, and so the stories end where they began—in a lost love and an isolated and usually impotent narrator.

This may prove that when you write a story, you can't always get what you want, but sometimes you can get what you need. For Poe, with women, it's the ecstatic state. And the route to the ecstasy and agitation can be either his own disguised sexual longing and terror— or his never-ending remembrance and mournfulness (to borrow Poe biographer Kenneth Silverman's book subtitle) over the loss of the original beloved.

Poe's men

It is only in the imaginative world of writing that Poe can gain control over male authority figures, expose them or ridicule them, give them their come-uppance, even murder them. It is little wonder, in the light of his treatment at the hands of John Allan, that male authority figures do not do well in Poe's tales. In life, he was betrayed, tortured, and triumphed over; in imaginative life, Poe took his full measure of revenge.

Interestingly, many of the male protagonists are men whose manhood still finds them in their fathers' houses. Roderick Usher lives in the Usher mansion; Egeus still lives in his father's house. These men, can be found, symbolically, in the library, presumably seeking knowledge and wisdom—that which should be inherited and passed from fathers to sons.

Poe's anger against his foster father, turned inward in life, turns outward in the tales, but always, it is done aslant. There is never a mention of a father in the stories. In fact, there are no parents in Poe's writings. No mother. No father. All is on a symbolic level. Sonhood and fatherhood are far too dangerous for Poe to specify. Yet these themes recur:

127

- Rivalry for power between two males.
- Displacement of sexual energy.
- Tension between powerful feeling and denial of that feeling.
- Secrecy.

In a political parody called *The Man Who Was Used Up,* Poe undoes a male authority figure.

The tale recounts the efforts of the narrator to learn all about "that truly fine-looking fellow, Brevet Brigadier General John ABC Smith, whom all applaud as a remarkable man, a very remarkable man, indeed one of the most remarkable men of the age."

The narrator hears about the general's virtues: "Great Man!" everyone says. But when the narrator pays the Brigadier General a visit, he makes a startling discovery. The American hero, whose physical appearance as a brigadier general has been exemplary, is found at his toilette—and Poe's angry buffoonery takes off. The Great Man, the Indian killer, is nothing but a shapeless squeaky-voiced mass of matter on the floor. His valet provides him with one prosthetic leg, then another, then an arm, then another arm, then a set of teeth, a false palate, shoulders, a chest, a wig, and finally, the well known physique of the general has taken shape. This is a savage portrait of authority—especially the kind Americans deify—who is nothing more, according to Poe, than a mouthpiece, a puppet.

In 1848, after Virginia's death and a year before his own, Poe wrote a retaliation story called *Hop Frog.* Hop Frog is a dwarf—symbol of the smallness and powerlessness of childhood. Like Poe, the protagonist is touchy and explosive. He is a court jester, doubly plagued by being both a dwarf and a cripple—psychic states for Poe.

Hop Frog and his companion Tripetta, also a dwarf, have been kidnapped from their homes and sent to the King as a present. Like Poe, they are displaced and dishonored and not even allowed their baptismal names. The king, a sadistic practical joker, knows that Hop Frog can't tolerate drink—"it excited the poor cripple almost to madness," says the narrator—but commands and forces the dwarf to drink. Tripetta intervenes, and the King dashes wine in her face. When the King orders Hop Frog to come up with a novel sport for his masquerade ball, Hop Frog gets him and his ministers to consent to be coated with tar and flax to look like escaped orangutans and frighten the guests—which they happily do. Hop Frog then hoists them to the ceiling, while a hideous grating sound comes from "the fang-like teeth of the dwarf—who ground them and gnashed them as he foamed at the mouth and glared—with an expression of maniacal rage." Hop Frog torches their combustible costumes and cremates them, leaving a "fetid, black, hideous, and indistinguishable mass."

So there! The wrongs have been avenged and the coupled Hop Frog and Tripetta run off, presumably to "get a life." The teeth and foaming mouth—possibly displaced organs of sexual prowess—are the engines of power and destruction in this story.

In a less than successful humorous tale called *Loss of Breath; A Tale Neither Out Nor In,* the narrator is one Mr. Lackobreath, who loses his breath in the middle of a tirade with his new wife. No breath means no voice which means no ability to verbally affirm his existence. For Poe, remember, the energy of words often replaces sexual energy. So Mr. Lackobreath—thought to be dead—is hung, mutilated, dissected, and buried alive. As such, he is incommunicado and utterly impotent. In the coffin, however, he sees Mr. Windenough (Lackobreath/Windenough!) who—we now discover—was having an affair, an "iniquity," with Lackobreath's new bride. And that, on the morning after the wedding, was the source of the tirade and the reason for Mr. Lackobreath's problem.

The vital force of speech and breath appears here to have been substituted for seminal fluid! Mr. L. then grabs his sexual rival's proboscis (get it?) to get his loss back. He demands apology and gets it.

Triumph. But still, as the subtitle reports, the hero is neither in nor out.

In *The Tell-Tale Heart,* the narrator is a young man who gains a gleeful sense of his own power when he turns anger outward and terrorizes, then murders, an older man. Undetected, the narrator makes sure he gets found out and punished for his Oedipal misdeed.

How do we know it's Oedipal? In part by the young man's constant denials. First, he denies knowing why he wants to kill off the old man: "Object there was none. Passion there was none." Then, there are false protestations: "I loved the old man." "He had never wronged me." "For his gold, I had no desire." Looking at the narrator's murderous impulses, we may surmise that the object *is* to get rid of the old man whom he hates and to get his gold, money being equated with power.

Oedipal also is the narrator's obsession with the old man's eye—the watchful, all-knowing eye of authority, perhaps analogous to the ever watchful surveillance of Poe's foster father, John Allan.

Poe's choice of diction also points to an Oedipal sexual rivalry, although no woman appears in the story. When the young man accomplishes his surveillance of the old man in the middle of the night, he stares down the old man by thrusting his head in the doorway. "I thrust it in," he repeats several times.

As the story progresses, whatever power the old man had, the young man now reverses, until, shrieking in triumph, he rushes in at night and kills the old man by pulling the bed over him. A bed is a most unusual weapon. But psychologically, it is the locus of his argument with this authority figure. The murder is followed by the dismembering of the corpse—first the head, then arms, then legs. All appendages that are socially mentionable. Then he buries the parts under the bedroom floorboards, and when a neighbor alerts the police, although the crime is perfect, the narrator gives himself away with guilt. With the police—more watchful eye-surveillance-authority types—the narrator, who thought he had control, cannot even control his flow of words. The power is returned to the authority figures who will reduce the narrator to the impotence and nothingness of death.

In *The Cask of Amontillado,* written four years before his death, Poe writes a tale with all of the vengefulness but, seemingly, none of the guilt of *The Tell-Tale Heart.* Not only is revenge taken against a powerful male, but it is apparently taken with fifty years of impunity. This tale is very popular with all readers who have ever felt deeply wronged or even slighted by another. It is a boy's wish for omnipotence, combined with the fantasy of how nice life could be if only Daddy would go away...

The story begins with the narrator, Montresor, providing the motive for murder: "The thousand injuries of Fortunato I had borne as best I could, but when he ventured upon insult, I vowed revenge." We are not told the specific insult, nor even its nature. The repayment for the insult, however, is not a simple return of insult from Montresor to Fortunato. It is no less a leap than "immolation"—a design born of narcissistic rage.

The setting for the act is the supreme madness of carnival season—the make-merry season, the carnal season. And we must wonder—since the narrator is not dressed for carnival while Fortunato is—whether the narrator doesn't bear some sexual envy.

The narrator tricks Fortunato into coming to his underground vaults to check the quality of some amontillado. Partially into the catacombs, Montresor reveals his deep motive of jealousy. He tells Fortunato, "You are rich, respected, admired, beloved. You are happy—as I once was." Here is a self that needs repair.

The narrator's family motto, translated from the Latin, is "No one who harms me shall go unpunished." In the tale, Montresor succeeds in his revenge, reversing power by walling up Fortunato alive and restoring to himself something he feels should have been his.

But did he really get the triumph Poe believes he got?

Fortunato's last words from behind the death-dealing wall still affirm life: "We will have many a rich laugh about this back at the palazzo. Will they not be awaiting us, Lady Fortunato and the rest? Over our wine?"

What each of the two men does with the fluids of life is interesting. Montresor stores his wine in vaults, while Fortunato uses his wine in social intercourse. Montresor, in murdering Fortunato, has buried male sexuality and the life-force without having given birth to his own.

Fifty years later, in needing to unburden his soul to the reader, we may surmise that Montresor has been thinking at each waking moment of the murder. The narrator, now a man near 80, is on the bitterest side of disappointment and "deadened" by his encounter with revenge. Despite his insistence on the superior virtue of his clever-ness—and in selfobject theory, the utilization of revenge as a cohe-sive function—the fact is that Montresor's obsessed life has not had one trace of the life force of Fortunato (whose last sound is the jingle of his bells)—nor one trace of growth.

One last note on paternal revenge. If the son succeeds in killing the father, exactly who will the son grow up to be? Note here that Poe, in his life, fathered no one...

The two years of life left to Poe after Virginia's death were the closest he came to madness.

When Poe was connected in life to Virginia and Muddy, he achieved both cohesion and growth. It is during those years that the bulk of his creative output occurred—including the hideous revenge tales that came out, not in life, but in his art, where he could effec-tively re-organize.

After Virginia's death

After Virginia's death, Poe became frantic in his need to con-nect again, and courted several women simultaneously, experiencing leaps from hope to hopelessness, to alcoholic descents, to renewed hope of love, to despair.

One acquaintance noted that Poe was truly attractive to women: "His remarkable personal beauty, the fascination of his manners and conversation, and his chivalrous deference and devotion to women gave him a dangerous power over the sex." Add that Poe was a tal-ented poet and an emotional wreck—probably an irresistible combi-nation to a certain type of woman who is esthetic, sentimental and maternal.

Not unexpectedly, Poe's courtship involved a recycling not only of his feelings but of the actual words of his love letters, just as he recycled his love poems to different women. Poe's multiple courtships seem to preclude the possibility of his commitment to any single woman. Perhaps his loyalty to Virginia's memory led to guilt about remarriage and to destructive behavior during the courtships.

He grew overwrought and insecure as he drew close, calling each woman, "my sister." With Fanny Osgood, he used the operatic gesture of falling on his knees and pleading hopelessly for her consent to marriage. To Helen Whitman, he wrote eight-page love letters:

> "I would have fallen at your feet in as pure, as real a worship as was ever offered to Idol or God. I grow faint with the luxury of your voice and blind with the voluptuous lustre of your eyes."

Here are Poe's eyes/mouth/voice sexual substitutions. And by the end of his letter, there is a confusion between sex, love, and death, as Poe vows that Helen would be as attractive to him dead as alive:

> "If you died, then at least would I clasp your dear hand in death and willingly, of joyfully, joyfully, joyfully go down with you into the night of the grave."

A perfect liebestod.

Always pursuing but getting no closer to cohesion or the comfort of marriage, Poe half-heartedly tries to commit suicide by taking laudanum. The most popular portrait of Poe is the one taken a few days after his attempted suicide, with the tilted head, asymmetrical features, and contorted expression showing a ravaged Poe.

Perhaps it is the hopelessness of having the love or even the friendship of a redemptive woman from among the living (since he cannot reclaim either his mother or Virginia from among the dead) that leads him to the dissolution of drink.

There is a long list of American writers who drink compulsively, but Poe stated that his desperate need for stimulants was "to compensate for and recover essential things that had been lost—love, wealth, social status, and literary reputation."

With considerable insight, he observed the following about his drinking: "It has never been in the pursuit of pleasure that I have imperiled life, reputation, and reason. It has been the desperate attempt to escape from torturing memories, unsupportable loneliness, and a dread of impending doom."

Poe may also, in his last year, have felt the need to punish himself—an irrational but powerful guilt—for the premature death not

133

only of his beloved mother but his beloved wife. Poe's quest for unity with his beloved dead is doomed, and his last days are shrouded in mystery and bad luck. Bearing up under a chronic fever, Poe is on his way to New York on business and stops in Baltimore to drink with acquaintances, having abstained successfully for the three months prior. He collapses into unconsciousness and hallucination, with no one to rescue him for one week and he dies there in the hospital. A sad end—with no loved one even notified that he was in the hospital.

In many ways, life let him down. He was pathetically underpaid, and death trailed love too closely in his lifetime. In other ways, Poe ruined his own chances. And yet, some of those very behaviors actually helped Poe to keep a certain kind of control, as he remained always in familiar psychic territory:

He kept himself an outsider, an outcast, an orphan.

He kept himself dependent.

He married a girl who not only died (as if she were one of his creations) but supplied him with her loving and supportive housekeeping mother.

And he turned every man with any power over him into John Allan.

With only a short period of connectedness in his life, Poe established a psychological world in which, much of the time, he was able to write. If Poe's writing allows the reader that exquisite release of tension in the psyche, then it is all the more poignant that, in the end, his writing could not afford Poe the restoration of his own equilibrium.

Kay Goebel is a clinical psychologist in private practice in Oklahoma City, Clinical Professor in the Department of Psychiatry at the Oklahoma University Health Sciences Center, and served as a research therapist for the National Institute of Mental Health. Currently Chair of the State Arts Council of Oklahoma and Vice-President of the Arts Council of Oklahoma City, she is also a member of the Board of the Cultural Coalition and Vice-Chair of the Department of Commerce Futures Task Force for Cultural Affairs. She has presented frequently at the Creativity and Madness Conferences, discussing Michelangelo, Raphael, El Greco, Frederick Remington, and Charles Russell.

Art is a form of therapy. Sometimes I wonder how all those who do not write, compose, or paint can escape the madness, the melancholia, the panic-fear inherent in the human situation. —*Graham Greene*

Michelangelo's Creativity
The Conquest of Adversity
by Kay Goebel, Ph.D.

During his lifetime, Michelangelo Buonarroti became known as *Michelangelo, the Divine.* The accolade seems appropriate since many consider him the greatest artistic genius who ever lived. His life spanned nearly 90 years of the Italian High Renaissance as he became an outstanding sculptor, painter, and architect.

His work not only shows his great talents but also reflects internal struggles and the resolutions he found in his creative works. With his compassion, insight, and great technical skill, he reaches across the centuries to touch the hearts and minds of those who view his work today. He took themes and fantasies common to many, and expressed them with wisdom, courage, and passion.

A great deal is known abut Michelangelo through almost 500 letters he wrote to friends and family, and over 800 written to him. Two biographies were written during his lifetime. Giorgio Vasari, a biographer of Renaissance artists, was a close friend of Michelangelo for the last 15 years of his life. Ascansio Condivi, a young assistant, published his biography when Michelangelo was 78, of which it is thought Michelangelo dictated much. There are also many poems and sonnets that reflect his dreams, disappointments, and inner life, and we have records of dialogues with his friends, his contracts, and other civic records.

Michelangelo was born March 5, 1475, in a small village about fifty miles from Florence, the second of five sons. At his birth, he was sent to live with a wet nurse, the wife and daughter of stone masons in Carrera, the site of some of the finest marble quarries in Italy.

Michelangelo said to his biographer, Vasari, "Giorgio, if I am good for anything, it is because I was born in the good mountains of Arezzo and suckled among chisels and hammers of stonecutters." This early experience may have helped shape Michelangelo's interest in becoming a sculptor. Throughout his life he would return to Carrera to find marble for his work and even though he achieved great acclaim for his painting and architecture, he always considered himself first and foremost a sculptor.

In *Michelangelo, A Study of His Life and Images*, psychoanalyst Robert Liebert suggests that Michelangelo's relationship to stone was based on his infant experiences with the stonemason's wife. He proposes that Michelangelo could not abandon the hope of recovering that idealized early reunion with his mother figure, and that his sculptures were futile attempts to change the stone mothers into something more nurturing. Two thirds of Michelangelo's statues were never finished because, Liebert believes, completing a work would revive separation anxieties. In the last 15 years of his life, Michelangelo turned to one theme in his sculpture, the union of the son and mother in the Pietas, the stone carvings involving the Virgin Mary and Jesus.

A troubled childhood

After Michelangelo was returned to his family at around age two, his mother had three more sons. When he was six years old, she died at age twenty six. Thereafter, he had no significant woman in his life until he was past age sixty. There are indications that he was a man with a prolonged and profound sense of deprivation of maternal care. In all his writing, Michelangelo never mentioned the death of his mother, yet the theme of the mother prevailed throughout his life, portrayed most often in works of the Madonna and Child or the Virgin Mary with Jesus. In the works with the Madonna and Child, the mother figure often seems emotionally distant. In some, she is turned away from the older child, looking at another, smaller, child. Only in his sculptures of Mary and the dead Christ is there a feeling of closeness and the appearance of attention.

Pitti Tondo

After his mother's death, Michelangelo endured inconsistent care and abrupt changes and losses. His grieving father was left to raise five small sons alone, a daunting task to which he appears to have been particularly ill suited. In his father's letters throughout the years, we find a man filled with vanity and self-pity, indifferent to the needs of others. Petty and quarrelsome, he never achieved any success of his own. In his twenties, Michelangelo took over as head of the family and, during the last thirty years of his father's life, was his main support. Despite this, in their letters, Michelangelo reflects feelings of never having gained his father's approval.

Michelangelo transferred his need for parenting to powerful and caring males for their support and protection. However, another major theme emerged from this dynamic. In Michelangelo's life and art, he appeared often to feel obligated to this male, and forced to do what he wanted.

139

Michelangelo seems to have felt bound and burdened by the troubled relationship he had with his father, and sculpted several statues of slaves that may reflect these feelings, including the *Dying Slave* and the *Rebellious Slave*, done as part of the tomb for Pope Julius II. Another series for this tomb are the four *Boboli Slaves* which, partially finished, show figures straining to break free from the stone.

Finally, in one of the last letters Michelangelo's father wrote to him before he died, he acknowledged Michelangelo's worth.

Resilience

Despite Michelangelo's internal struggles and burdens, he achieved heights of artistic greatness matched by few if any other individuals.

Several authors have looked at the ability of individuals to overcome troubled backgrounds and ongoing hardship, and survive and thrive. Steven Wolin, M.D., and Sybil Wolin, Ph.D. have a special interest in resilience, which they define as the ability to sustain hardship and to gain strength in the process. In their book, *The Resilient Self, How Survivors of Troubled Families Rise Above Adversity*, they identify seven strengths that are found in survivors:

> Research shows that children of disturbed or incompetent parents learn to watch out for themselves and grow strong in the process. Young survivors figure out how to locate allies outside the family, find pleasure in fantasy games, or build self-esteem by winning recognition in school. Over time, the capacity to rise above adversity by developing skills such as these expands and ripens into lasting strengths or aspects of the survivor's self that we call *resiliencies*. There are seven:
>
> *Insight:* The habit of asking tough questions and giving honest answers.
>
> *Independence:* Drawing boundaries between yourself and troubled parents: keeping emotional and physical distance while satisfying the demands of your conscience.
>
> *Relationships:* Intimate and fulfilling ties to other people that balance a mature regard for your own needs with empathy and the capacity to give to someone else.
>
> *Initiative:* Taking charge of problems: exerting control: a taste for stretching and testing yourself in demanding tasks.

Creativity: Imposing order, beauty, and purpose on the chaos of your troubling experiences and painful feelings.

Humor: Finding the comic in the tragic.

Morality: An informed conscience that extends your wish for a good personal life to all of humankind.

James Anthony, M.D., a psychoanalyst, has found from his research on children with disturbed parents, that the children who developed the ability to think independently and see themselves with their own separate identity fared best. He termed them *children of steel.* They developed inner strength to withstand adversity and thrive. They achieved a sense of independence and put distance between themselves and their disturbed or troubled parents. They expanded their contacts and increased their resources from others in their world.

Judith Wallerstein, Ph.D., studying the impact of divorce on children, also found that children who learned to take command of their lives and get away from the domination of a sick parent or parents did the best.

From this perspective, Michelangelo's life of conflicts and internal struggles is a great example of the use of creativity to help one work toward resolving internal struggles and overcoming adversity. He showed many signs of being one of these independent young people who was able to take charge of his life at an early age. Countless times he was faced with seemingly insurmountable hurdles, only to overcome them. He was very determined and when he set his mind to accomplish a task, he was often successful in carrying it out. He was capable of defying authority and making decisions based on his own insight and sense of self. He inspires not only from his art but also from the model he set for facing and growing through the crises and struggles that are presented by life.

Despite his artistic successes, he continued to encounter many rivalries and intrigues rife in the courts and art circles of his day, repeating another emotional link to his past, when sibling rivalry and rejection by parents had occurred. The portrayal of the outsider, the *uncared-for* child, is another repetitive theme, that, contrasts with the strong, powerful, and courageous male that was also a part of his self image.

Resisting his father's opposition to his desire to pursue an artistic career, Michelangelo left grammar school at age 13 to become an apprentice in a painter's studio. Some accounts state that Michelangelo was beaten by his father and his uncles for it. Nevertheless, at age 14, Michelangelo began studying sculpture at a school in the Medici Gardens.

He draws the attention of Lorenzo de Medici

At this time, the wealthy Medicis were the most prominent family in Florence and the surrounding area, and great patrons of the arts. While studying in the sculpture garden, Michelangelo drew the attention of Lorenzo de Medici, the powerful ruling prince of Florence. Lorenzo invited Michelangelo to live and work in his palace, which Michelangelo did for the next two years, later saying that this was the happiest time in his life.

Evident here is another of Michelangelo's traits that enabled him to succeed in life and art: capturing the attention and support of strong paternal figures who could help him accomplish his goals. However, turning to males for nurture and support also seems to have caused Michelangelo highly ambivalent feelings toward other men. His homosexual feelings, often a part of his creative work, were part of a lifelong struggle.

Michelangelo's second known work, the Battle of the Centaurs, done while at the Medici Gardens, is a bas-relief of nude males.

The High Renaissance was in full bloom in Florence, and Lorenzo and his friends' interest in Neoplatonic philosophy and Greek and Roman antiquity and its tolerance for homosexuality had a major influence on the direction of Michelangelo's artistic endeavors. The Neoplatonic view was that the perfect human body was a reflection of the ideal self. The nude male so frequently used in Michelangelo's sculpture and painting thus reflected two aspects of Michelangelo's personality. One was his desire to become his ideal self—through his magnificent creation, he could become the perfect male. A second was his search for love and affection from a male, partly to compensate for the deprivations of his formative years. In his life and his art, as he searched for either a young male lover, or a protective man, he became one of the grand masters of all time at portraying the nude male.

Savanarola

When Michelangelo was 17, Lorenzo de Medici died and he returned to his father's home. Radical reformers, led by the monk, Fra Savanarola, who saw the Medicis as a force of evil, took control of Florence. Savanarola's aim was to reform the church and the public morals. He outlawed what he defined as sin and tried to turn Florence into a model Christian community. The futility of this became clear three and a half years later when Savanarola was hung and burned in the Piazza della Signoria in Florence. Michelangelo's oldest brother was a monk with Savanarola, and some of Savanarola's hell-fire made an impact on him and his homosexual inclinations, reflected in the damnation and guilt of later works such as the *Last Judgment* in the Sistine Chapel.

Rome: Bacchus, and the Pieta

Now Michelangelo was without a protector and in July, 1496, when he was twenty one years old, he went to Rome. The next five years were very difficult for Michelangelo as he worked under very adverse conditions. Again, however, he was able to find support and assistance in pursuing his career, this time from Cardinal Riaro, a member of the clergy who was interested in the arts, and in whose palace he lived for a while. One of his major achievements while in Rome was a statue he created of a nude male, Bacchus. It reflects a sense of pagan sexuality and carefree spirit. Later he sculpted one of his most famous works, the Pieta of St. Peter's, depicting the sacred and holy. The Rome Pieta may reflect Michelangelo's feelings that in death there is reunion with the mother. Many have noted that the Virgin is too young to reflect Mary's actual age at the time of Christ's death. Psychoanalyst Jerome Oremland offers an interesting theory

143

La Pieta

about the Virgin's youth based on Michelangelo's early childhood. Since his two mothering figures, the wet nurse and his own mother, were lost to him while they were young, the Virgin could represent Michelangelo's unconscious hope that in death one can return to the idealized mother. The Virgin does look to be a young woman about the age of Michelangelo's mother when she died.

What was this young man like at this time in his life?

His biographer, Condivi, wrote,

> He was of good complexion, muscular, healthy by his natural constitution and his habitual continence in food and sex. He was of middle height, broad shouldered, slender body, with an oval face and a flattened nose which had been broken in a boyhood fight. At times he could be very optimistic; at other times he would experience great melancholy and sadness. Sometimes Michelangelo was suspicious and withdrawn in relationships, especially in his younger years. He could be quick tempered, sarcastic, blunt and capable of violent rages. However, with those he trusted, he was humorous and a good companion, a gentle and generous man. He was often surprised to learn he was considered difficult. He had a number of friends and repaid them with affection.

This capacity to form intimate and rewarding relationships with others is another indication of resilience. By engaging the interest of

144

others, these people find allies and supportive people, as did Michelangelo, repeatedly throughout his life.

His confidence and optimism showed in the great scope of his artistic ambitions and his willingness to take on the most challenging and seemingly insurmountable tasks. What often caused Michelangelo trouble was his inability to recognize he only had a certain amount of time and energy. He would often over-commit himself and create situations where, despite his enormous output, he was forever under demand, and kept failing himself and his patrons.

Florence: David

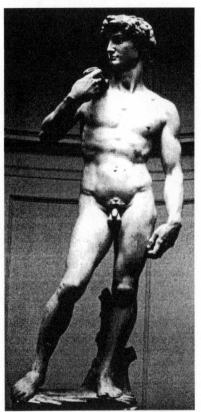

David

In 1501, Michelangelo moved to Florence, where he signed a contract for 15 large statues for the Piccolomini Chapel. Then, in an example of how he caused himself grief, six months later, he signed a contract for the *David* statue. The Piccolomini contract was ignored, and *David* was completed in 1504 after 3 years of work. One of Michelangelo's major masterpieces, *David* is the personification of the neoplatonic ideal, the powerful and perfect male.

By now, Michelangelo was known as the greatest sculptor of the Renaissance. Michelangelo made an interesting choice when he picked David as his subject. David slaying the giant Goliath is one of the best known stories ever told of the young and strong man overcoming the older and more powerful male. David went on to become famous as a shrewd and ambitious king, one of the greatest leaders of his people and a man of God. In some aspects, this is a model that Michelangelo followed in his life. He, too, was ready to pitch battles against supposedly stronger forces as he endeavored to carry on with his life's work.

Four Madonnas and Child

During these years he also did four well known works of the Madonna and Child. The first of these is the Doni Tondo, Michelangelo's only painted Madonna, now in the Uffizi Gallery in Florence. Between the years 1503-1505, Michelangelo sculpted three more Madonnas: the Bruge Madonna at the Notre Dame in Bruge, the Pitti Tondo, which is at the Bargello museum in Florence, and the Taddei Tondo. In all three, there is the theme of the detached mother. The Taddei Tondo, in London at the Royal Academy of Arts, shows an attempt at resolution of one of his primary childhood conflicts—the frightened child seeks comfort from an emotionally unavailable mother.

By 1504, Michelangelo had completed David, the Bruge, Tondi and Pitti Madonna sculptures, and the Doni Tondo painting. Then he contracted for twelve larger than life statues for the Florence Cathedral. With the fifteen Piccolomini statues still to deliver and a copy of the David in bronze to finish, he had enough work to last for several years. At this point, he took on another project so large, it commanded all his creative energies, and all other projects had to be postponed or cancelled.

Competing with da Vinci

Leonardo da Vinci was an older and well recognized artist at this time. The Florence city fathers had asked him and Michelangelo to decorate the Grand Council Hall in the Palazzo del Signoria in Florence with two huge murals. Leonardo da Vinci had many qualities that Michelangelo lacked. Leonardo was handsome, admired for his great intellect, poise, and refined manners. He had the physical and social graces and the ability to be very charming and popular. With this commission, Michelangelo would now have the chance to prove he could excel in Leonardo's chosen field, painting. The preliminary drawings, called cartoons, were the focus of the art world of the time. Artists from all around the region came to watch these two masters at work, Raphael among them. However, neither painting was ever completed. Leonardo used a technique that caused his painting to run and to ruin, and before Michelangelo could finish his fresco, Pope Julius II summoned him to Rome.

In Michelangelo's time, the Roman Catholic Popes were men of power, influence, and wealth. Pope Julius II was tough and shrewd, and had plans to make Rome a site of power to glorify his papacy. To make Rome the grandest city in the world, he needed artists. He commanded Michelangelo to come to Rome in 1505.

Michelangelo was now about to enter the most difficult years of his life, but was also on the verge of becoming the *Divine Michelangelo*.

Julius' tomb

Julius' first task for Michelangelo was the design and production of his tomb. The original plans were so grand that it was decided a new cathedral would have to be built to hold it and thus new plans were begun for the reconstruction for St. Peter's, for which Julius hired the architect, Bramante. Both Julius and Michelangelo were carried away with their grandiose fantasies. The plan Michelangelo developed would have required him to create more work in five years than he did in seventy.

Julius' tomb became a major burden in Michelangelo's life and a much reduced version was not completed until forty years later. Part of the problem was that Julius lost interest in his tomb and began giving more attention to Raphael and the paintings he was doing for the papal apartments. Julius stopped seeing Michelangelo and giving him money. Michelangelo became very upset and returned to Florence.

For several months a power struggle went on between them. Michelangelo's strength and independence was evident in his willingness to defy the Pope. Eventually Julius agreed to some of his requests and then demanded his return to Rome. Seven months later Michelangelo was back in Rome.

Painting the Sistine Chapel

In 1508, Pope Julius assigned Michelangelo a new project that has been called by many his grandest masterpiece—the painting of the ceiling of the Sistine Chapel. Michelangelo tried every way he could to avoid doing this painting. He said he was a sculptor, not a painter, which was true. His only experience with fresco had been one year when he was an apprentice years ago in Florence. To add to his difficulties with the project he was convinced the architect, Bramante, was behind the Pope's demands. Both Michelangelo and Bramante were vying for Julius' attention and money. Michelangelo thought Bramante wanted to discredit him and promote himself and his friend, Raphael. It certainly would appear that Michelangelo's lack of experience and interest, the great area of the ceiling, and the technical problems would result in Michelangelo having a colossal failure. At the same time Raphael would be painting the frescoes in the Pope's apartments and would have close contact with him. Raphael had become known for his perfect painting techniques and was a handsome man of charm and talent. It appeared he would have successes that would make Michelangelo's failure even more evident. Michelangelo even tried to talk the Pope into giving the project to Raphael. This angered the Pope who insisted even more strongly that Michelangelo begin. Michelangelo's words at the time were:

> I accord how on this date, the 10th of May, 1508, I, Michelangelo, sculptor, have received from the Holiness of our Lord, Pope Julius II, 500 ducats on the account of the painting of the vault of the Sistine Chapel on which I begin to work.

It is not to be supposed that Michelangelo created his work alone. On the contrary, he organized a sophisticated assembly of craftsmen to do much of the labor and preliminary work. In the beginning of the Sistine project, Michelangelo had five assistant workers but he soon found himself painting over their work. Thereafter he worked on the ceiling alone, on a scaffold, painting over his head. He said:

> I strain more than any man who ever lived and with great exhaustion, and yet I have the patience to arrive at the desired goal.

Wolin and Wolin, in discussing the strength of initiative in the resilient self, say:

> Initiative (is) the determination to assert yourself and master your environment... In adults, the gratification and self-esteem associated with completing jobs become a lifelong attraction to generating projects that stretch the self and promote a cycle of growth.

This kind of initiative, they write, combines several traits such as assertiveness and the ability to assess and solve problems. These survivors take command of their lives and reap the reward of seeing results due to their efforts. The Wolins continue:

> By setting goals, by persisting despite frustration, by claiming success where they can, resilient survivors forge lasting strength... To the extent you take hold of life rather than letting life take hold of you, you are resilient.

As Michelangelo continued to paint, his enthusiasm and inspiration grew. The original contract had called for twelve figures. Four years later he completed the project, eventually painting over 5800 square feet with over 300 figures.

The subject of the ceiling is the world in the beginning of time. There are three zones. One shows the Biblical ancestors of Christ, the second shows the sibyls and the Old Testament prophets, and the center zone shows nine episodes from Genesis. Michelangelo was expressing the Renaissance belief that life is a journey from existence as man to the soul's eventual spiritual communion with God.

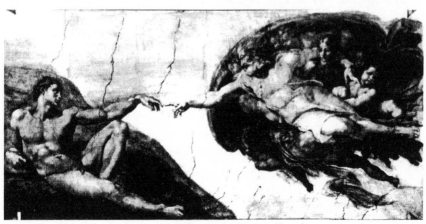

Section of Ceiling of the Sistine Chapel

149

Of the many remarkable scenes in the ceiling, the most notable is the center panel depicting the creation of Adam. In this scene Michelangelo's familiar themes can be found: the overpowering God, the creator, his own ability to create man from stone, and his feeling of being under the dominion of the overpowering paternal figure. The Virgin Mary is there, but the child in the painting is being ignored by her, and held very tentatively.

Even though Michelangelo at times described himself as under the dominion of a strong male, he had the ability to stand up to any authority who provoked him. For example, while Michelangelo was working, Julius often came to the chapel, climbed the scaffold and watched Michelangelo work. One day he asked when Michelangelo would finish. Michelangelo replied, "When I can." The Pope became angry and struck Michelangelo with his staff and shouted, "When I can, when I can!"

Michelangelo became angry in return, rushed home and began packing for Florence. The Pope sent a messenger with apologies and 500 gold ducats and Michelangelo returned to work. Despite the problems and struggles, Michelangelo continued, and his final creation was truly superb. Liebert described the ceiling as "a fantastic world of imagination of a man who has penetrated the mysteries of human existence."

The Sistine ceiling was unveiled October 31, 1512, when Michelangelo was 37 years old. The work drew admiration and praise, but a month later, he wrote his father, "Be satisfied you have bread to eat and can live in peace with Christ and not as poorly as I do here, for I lead a miserable existence. I live wearied by stupendous labors and beset by 1000 anxieties. And thus I have lived 15 years now, and never an hour's happiness have I had, and all of this I've done in order to help you, though you have never either recognized or believed it... God forgive us all. I am prepared to do the same as long as I live, provided I am able."

As Michelangelo became wealthy, he continued to be generous with his family and to give them guidance and support. Despite this, despite fame, fortune, and intimate connections with the most powerful people in Rome and Florence, he still remained in this ambivalent bondage to his father.

More work on Julius' tomb

In 1513, shortly after the completion of the Sistine ceiling, Pope Julius died, to be followed by Pope Leo X, the second son of Lorenzo de Medici. Despite their differences, there had been affection between Michelangelo and Julius. Affected by grief and loss, Michelangelo worked steadily on the delayed Julius tomb project for the next three years and finished much of the architecture at the base of the tomb.

The statue of Moses

During this time, he also created three of his most outstanding statues, the *Dying Slave* and the *Rebellious Slave* which can be seen in the Louvre in Paris, and *Moses*, the most famous of the three, which has often been called his single greatest sculpture. Freud wrote after seeing this statue:

Moses

> No piece of statuary has made a stronger impression than this... Michelangelo has added something new and more human to the figure of Moses so that the giant figure with its tremendous physical power becomes a concrete expression of the high mental achievement that is possible in

151

man, that of struggling successfully against an inward passion for the sake of a cause to which he has devoted himself.

In 1516, events caused work on Julius' tomb to be put aside and to remain a still unfinished burden.

As Pope Leo took power, he is reported to have said, "God has given us the papacy, let us enjoy it," and he did. Leo supported artists, scholars, musicians, and architects. He continued with Julius' plan to beautify Rome. After Bramante's death, he made Raphael the chief architect of St. Peter's. Money and gifted artists filled the city with activity and of course, Leo wanted to use Michelangelo to enhance his papacy. He insisted that Michelangelo abandon the Julius tomb again, and instead, design the facade for the church of San Lorenzo in Florence.

Michelangelo becomes an architect

When Leo decided this, Michelangelo had no experience in architecture. One may wonder why he would take it on. Maybe it was the challenge of a new field. Resilient people often seek out challenges to gain the sense of accomplishment and enhanced self-confidence that comes from mastering new areas. He rapidly went from novice to developing a grand architectural design. However, the project ended with nothing being built.

From 1519 until 1534, when he left Florence for the last time, Michelangelo's art was distinguished by the integration of art and architecture.

Michelangelo's next project was the Medici tombs in the same church of San Lorenzo. The Pope's brother and nephew had both died a few years before, and Pope Leo decided to build a new sacristy at San Lorenzo as a memorial.

In many ways, this was the turning point of Michelangelo's life. In 1520, he was 45 years old. He felt old and had a haunting premonition of death. Leonardo de Vinci died in 1519 at age 67, and Raphael died in 1520 at the age of 37. Now Michelangelo alone remained of the three major Renaissance artists.

In 1521, Pope Leo died. Under his rule, Rome had become the

most cultured city in the world, but he left huge debt. In 1523, Cardinal Giulio Medici became Pope Clement VII. Clement was sensitive and understanding of Michelangelo. He wanted Michelangelo to continue the Medici tomb. However, the heirs of Julius were insisting that their tomb be finished.

More work on Julius' tomb

As part of the Julius tomb project, Michelangelo carved the *Boboli Slaves*, powerful statues that show men struggling to break free from the stone. None of them were completed, giving the feeling of being trapped in the stone. Michelangelo was depressed during these years, saying, "Worries hardly let me live, let alone work." These slaves may reflect his feelings over his enslavement to the tomb.

The New Sacristy in the Medici tomb

Leaving the Julius tomb still unfinished, Michelangelo returned to the Medici tomb. One of the major achievements during this period of his life was the New Sacristy in the Medici tombs, his first architectural project. In it he placed seven statues. On two walls are groupings of three figures; both have the Duke in the center, with a nude male and female reclining at his feet. In the two female figures, it is evident that Michelangelo had difficulty in portraying the female form. The women look like masculine figures with breasts that appear to be harsh and ill formed afterthoughts attached to the body. At the end of the Sacristy is a statue of Madonna and Child. Both Dukes face toward this symbol of life and hope.

It was a very difficult period in his life. His favorite brother, Buonarto, died in 1527. Of the five brothers, Buonarto was the only one married with children. Michelangelo was especially fond of him and his children, and was a life-long support to them. Then Michelangelo's father died in 1531. Michelangelo was so overcome with grief that his friends feared for his life. The statues of the tomb convey his feelings of death and sorrow. The hopeful tone is the turning of the Dukes to the Madonna and Child, the symbol of eternity. Michelangelo never finished this work or the other projects planned for this Sacristy.

Another complication that added greatly to his difficulties was the political life in Florence during this period. In 1531, Pope Clement installed his illegitimate son, Alessandro, as ruler of Florence. Alessandro, described as a monster by some of his contemporaries, particularly hated Michelangelo. Condivi wrote, "There is no doubt but for the Pope's protection, Michelangelo would have been killed."

To Rome, and new friends

In 1531, Michelangelo's health gave way from the stress and worry that he was encountering. By 1532, he began spending more and more time in Rome, and in 1534, at age 57, he left Florence for the last time, ending his 45 year relationship with the Medici family. Two days later, Pope Clement died.

The Rome that Michelangelo moved to had been through a very difficult period. It had been sacked, pillaged, and looted, in 1527, by the rampaging, unpaid soldiers of Charles V. Two outbreaks of the plague had killed or dispersed two thirds of the population. Doubt was cast on the Renaissance belief that man was in control of his destiny.

Michelangelo felt old, tired, and disappointed, in his life and in himself. The loss of his brother and father left him feeling abandoned and alone. Then, in 1532, Michelangelo met 22 year old Tommaso de Cavalieri, a handsome, and cultured Roman nobleman, who became the passion of his life. In Tommaso, Michelangelo may have seen the idealized version of himself that he had created in his handsome statues of males. Many sonnets, letters, and drawings express his strong passion for Tommaso.

Michelangelo also had friendships with other young men, and wrote some love poems to them but most were for Tommaso. These poems, published 60 years after Michelangelo's death, were presented as having been written to a woman, so as not to hurt his reputation. The poems reveal sexual longing but, despite speculation, there is no evidence that Michelangelo ever had a sexual relationship with him, or indeed, anyone.

Tommaso married several years later and had children, but he and Michelangelo remained friends for the rest of Michelangelo's life.

In Michelangelo's earlier years he had put art above everything in his life, including friendships and relationships with his family. Now the loss of his family, his advancing years, and his disappointments in his work caused Michelangelo to turn to friendships as a crucial part of his life.

Vittoria Colonna

In 1536, when Michelangelo was 61 years old, a very important person entered his life and became a major influence. Vittoria Colonna was 47 years old when she and Michelangelo met. They remained friends until her death 11 years later. A widowed noblewoman, she was a very pious intellectual. Through his friendship with her, Michelangelo resolved some of the internal struggle he had been having between the Neoplatonic and Christian philosophies. He looked to her as his spiritual guide, enjoying both the intellectual companionship and their mutual respect. During these years Michelangelo came to have a deep belief in Christ as the Redeemer, identifying with Christ's suffering. Through his relationship with Vittoria, Michelangelo developed a theme that dominated his life for his last 17 years, the Passion of Christ and the union of Christ and the Virgin.

In 1533, still another Pope became dominant in Michelangelo's life—Pope Paul III. His sister had been the mistress of the Borgia Pope Alexander VI. However, Pope Paul had a reputation as a man of good morals, willing to support the arts.

By now Michelangelo had become a wealthy man and enjoyed living well (although he was never extravagant). He had a fine home, a large studio, was not as driven by his work, and had reached a time in his life when he desired independence and peace.

To entice Michelangelo to work for him, Pope Paul cut the size of the still unfinished Julius tomb project. In September 1535, the Pope put forth a statement proclaiming Michelangelo to be the world's foremost sculptor, painter, and architect. Michelangelo was put in charge of the arts at the Vatican and given a lifetime income of 1200 gold ducats. The Pope's next command to Michelangelo was that he paint the *Last Judgment* on the altar wall of the Sistine Chapel. Michelangelo initially refused but Pope Paul said he had waited 30 years for Michelangelo to work for him and he commanded that he do it now.

In 1536, as Michelangelo painted *the Last Judgment*, the Counter Reformation was happening. Some considered Michelangelo's painting to be pagan, the nude males receiving special criticism. One church official, Cardinal Beggio de Cesna, declared the painting more fitting for a bath house than a church. Michelangelo paid him back by putting Beggio in the picture in a scene of deepest hell, portraying him horned and wearing nothing but a serpent. The *Last Judgment* was unveiled Christmas Day, 1541. During the following years, various Popes ordered draperies over the genitals of 36 of the figures.

In the *Last Judgment*, there are three main figures: Christ, the Virgin, and St. Bartholomew. St. Bartholomew is holding his flayed skin, on which appears to be Michelangelo's self-portrait. Psychoanalysts Richard and Edith Sterba believe that Bartholomew represents Michelangelo. In this painting, Bartholomew is being reproached for his attack on the mother of God. His knife is pointed at her and at Christ. There is tension between Bartholomew and Christ, the omnipotent male. By now all Michelangelo's father figures had left him through death. Michelangelo may have had guilt both over his feelings of anger at being abandoned, and his feelings of homosexuality. His fear of punishment may go back to the preaching of Savanarola he heard in Florence as a youth. Along with this fear is the strong hope for forgiveness and salvation, the central theme of the *Last Judgment*.

After finishing this painting Michelangelo wrote,

I am a poor fellow and of little worth, plodding along in all that God has assigned me in order to prolong my life as long as I can.

Pope Paul still insisted on Michelangelo's services. Within a few months, he had Michelangelo working on two frescos for the Pauline

Chapel. They were the *Conversion of St. Paul* and the *Crucifixion of Peter.* These two frescoes kept Michelangelo occupied for seven years. Meanwhile, Paul had Michelangelo working on the fortification of Rome and the new Farnese family palace.

In addition, he was now the chief architect of St. Peter's and he was redesigning the piazza and palaces of the Capitolene Hill.

The tomb of Julius is finished

At last, Michelangelo completed the tomb of Julius in 1545, although the final product was a small fraction of the original plan. He wrote,

> I lost the whole of my youth chained to the tomb, contending, as far as I was able, against the demands of Popes Leo and Clement. An excessive honesty which went unrecognized has been my ruin.

The last eight years of Paul's reign was a time of severe personal losses, great sadness and external conflicts. Michelangelo had serious illnesses, Vittoria Colonna died, as did two friends and a younger brother. Michelangelo tried to resolve his grief and despair in his work. In the Crucifixion fresco, Peter is a powerful figure who looks at the world with defiance, in contrast to the Christian myth that Peter accepted his martyrdom with humility. This Peter does not meekly accept death, possibly reflecting Michelangelo's own attitude. As he became increasingly aware of his own death, he began the Florentine Pieta for his own tomb.

During the decade of the 1540's until his death, Michelangelo worked on his two most important architectural contributions, the Basilica of St. Peter and the continuing plans for the Capitolene Hill.

Despite his great successes and prestige, the harassment and conflicts over his work never stopped. This was especially true for St. Peter's. In 1551, when Julius III became Pope, Michelangelo's critics persuaded the Pope to call a meeting of all those working on St. Peter's. One of the opposing cardinals charged that Michelangelo had made no provision for light into the church from the side apses. Michelangelo explained there would be a window in the vaulting. "You never told us anything about that," said the cardinal.

Michelangelo replied,

> I am not obliged to tell your Lordship or anyone else what I do or intend to do. Your business is to provide the money and to see that it is not stolen. The building is my affair.

Other architects worked on the church but the Dome was Michelangelo's. He also designed the great gate to the city of Rome, the Porta Pia. At age 85, he still supervised the work of St. Peter's on horseback.

His last sculptures

Michelangelo worked on three sculptures in the last years of his life. They were all Pietas, the union of the dead Christ with the Virgin Mary. Michelangelo began the Florentine Pieta shortly after the death of Vittoria Collona. In this group, he created a scene of union between Christ and his mother. While working on this statue, Michelangelo purposely mutilated it. Some scholars have speculated that this could be an expression of rage at the mother. Nicodemus, the male figure in the group, is supposed to be Michelangelo's self portrait.

It could be that these last Pietas were Michelangelo's effort to come to terms with the fears he had about his own death together with fantasies of recapturing the closeness he had experienced from his own mother, or his wet nurse foster mother. He told Vasari at this time, "I have reached the 24th hour of my day. No project arises that does not have the figure of death graven upon it."

In his last work, the Rondanini Pieta, the unfinished Christ is fused with an incomplete Mary. It has the appearance of modern sculpture. This was his final image; in the fusion of son and mother, the boundaries are eliminated.

There is a dramatic contrast between the earlier rejecting Virgins, and the warm encircling Virgins in these stone Pietas. On February 12, 1564, he spent all day on the Rondanini Pieta. Six days later, he died. In his will, he left his soul to God, his body to the earth, and his goods to his nearest relatives.

Summary

As noted earlier, creativity is one of the strengths of a resilient self which Michelangelo demonstrates repeatedly. Wolin and Wolin quote psychoanalyst Hanna Segal on this subject:

> All creation is really a re-creation of a once loved and once whole, but now lost and ruined, object, a ruined internal world and self. It is when the world within us is destroyed, when it is dead and loveless, when our loved ones are in fragments and we ourselves in helpless despair, it is then that we must recreate our world anew, reassemble the pieces, infuse life into dead fragments, recreate life.

Wolin and Wolin state:

> By imposing the discipline of creativity on their despair, resilient survivors heal an injured self... Resilience is not a suit of armor or a magical ability to walk between the raindrops. Nor is it the capacity to bounce back from every blow. Resilience is the will to accept the discipline of an art form in order to shape your pain into 'something else.'

Michelangelo's extraordinary talent, and his ability to use his creative abilities to express and work at resolving his internal struggles, gave the world some of the most moving and powerful artistic images ever created. That he possessed several qualities found in the resilient self enabled him to continue to accept tremendous new challenges and gain repeated success. His wisdom and the courage he displayed as he struggled with common human themes engage those who view his work today. His work continues through the centuries to represent some of the most glorious achievements of man.

Mary Lou Panter, R.N. is the co-founder and co-director of the American Institute of Medical Education. She has given presentations on Bruegel, Rembrandt, and Saints and Symbols at the Creativity and Madness Conferences. In addition to her interest in art history, she is a painter of water colors and oils. She served for a year in the pediatric department of The Hospital Ship HOPE in Sri Lanka. She also has been a teacher in elementary school art programs.

I have chosen to paint our own age because that is what I understand best,
because it is more alive, and because I am painting for living people.

—Frederic Bazille, painter

Pieter Bruegel, the Elder
An Artist and His Times
by Mary Lou Panter, R.N.

Pieter Bruegel the Elder, sometimes referred to as Peasant Bruegel, is considered the greatest and most original Flemish artist and draftsman of the 16 th century. He is such a national hero in 20th century Belgium that three different cities jealously claim to be his birthplace. Bruegel's art offers us a psychological view through the eyes of the artist, into the interior of the troubled world of Flanders during the Northern Renaissance. His paintings and drawings reveal the unconscious undercurrents of his time. In the dramas of his works he portrays broad themes of the universal human experience, viewed especially from the point of view of the peasant or common man. Through his amazing inventiveness and his impressive range of subject matter, Pieter Bruegel was able to blend Biblical themes, fantasy, allegories, landscapes and dream worlds with reality to create his personal philosophy, which he expressed in his art.

Following his death, the Habsburg royal family collected and sent much of his art to Vienna where we can see it today. There are 100-150 drawings, and approximately forty-five paintings which survive, one third of which are in the Kunsthistorisches and Albertina Museums in Vienna. The oils are one of the jewels of the

Kunsthistorisches, and the drawings are prized by the Albertina. They reflect the anxieties, inner turmoil, hardships and uncertainties of a society whose social and religious belief systems were crumbling.

Bruegel was born about 1525, making him a contemporary of Michelangelo. Very little is known of his personal life. There are only five documented events plus Karel van Mander's *Schilde-Boecke*—the book of the lives of Flemish painters, that give us information about his private affairs. The documented facts are:

• He was accepted as a Master into Antwerp's Painters' Guild in 1551, when he was 25 years old. At this time he dropped the "h" from his name, making it Bruegel instead of Brueghel.

• Two letters, dated 1561 and 1565, by an Italian geographer in Bologna to the famous Antwerp cartographer, Abraham Ortellis, inquired after the health of their mutual friend, Pieter Bruegel, whom the geographer remembered with affection during Bruegel's journey to Italy in 1550 or 1551.

• A record of Bruegel's marriage to Mayken Coecke van Alst appeared in a church record in Brussels in 1563. Mayken was the daughter of Brussels painter Pieter Coecke van Alst, Bruegel's master, and Maria Verhulst Bessermers, a prominent painter also influential in the development of Bruegel's art. After the marriage, he moved to Brussels and in the remaining 6 years of his life painted many of his best known masterpieces.

More apocryphal is the story that while living in Antwerp, before his marriage, he kept house for a while with a servant girl whom he would have married, but for the fact that she was in the habit of lying, a trait Bruegel greatly disliked. It is said that he made a contract with her that he would cut a notch in a stick for every lie she told. Should the stick be covered with notches, the marriage would be off. And so it was.

Karol Van Mander's *Schilde-Boecke, The Book of Painters*, published in 1604, 35 years after Bruegel's death, gives us information about his private affairs in an intriguing twelve hundred word account of his life. The author, K. Van Mander, was dean of the

Harlem painters' guild. He chronicled the lives of three dozen Flemish and Dutch artists, in a manner quite similar to Vasari who chronicled the lives of the Italian Renaissance artists. The *Schilde-Boecke* is a fanciful, significant book, mixing gossipy anecdotes with facts. His account of Bruegel's life begins enthusiastically:

> In a wonderful manner, nature found and laid hold of the man who in his turn was to take hold of nature so magnificently. In the obscure village of Brabant, she chose from among the peasants, as a delineator of peasants, the witty and gifted Pieter Bruegel. She made of him a painter to the lasting glory of our Netherlands.

According to van Mander, Bruegel learned his craft from van Alst, whose daughter, Mayken, Bruegel first carried in his arms as an infant, and later took into his arms as his wife. After van Alst died in 1550, Bruegel settled in Antwerp and worked as a printmaker for H. Cock in the Four Winds Print Shop. In 1551, at age 25, he made the traditional artist's pilgrimage to Italy to see the works of the Italian Renaissance Masters. His path took him south from Antwerp to Lyon to Geneva, over the Alps, into Italy as far as Sicily. After visiting Sicily, he went to Naples where he made sketches for his famous painting, *The Harbor Of Naples*. Finished in 1563, it is the earliest seascape with ships, done in oils. The following year he was in Rome, the city of the aging Michelangelo and his Sistine Chapel ceiling, which filled the painter with inspiration. Bruegel later adapted Michelangelo's style of *Mannerism* for several of his subjects, including *The Peasant Wedding* and *Magpie on The Gallows*. While in Rome he completed the pen and ink drawing of *Ripa Grande on the River Tiber*, and worked with Clovio, a noted miniaturist whom Vasari called "A Little Michelangelo."

Bruegel did not hurry back to Flanders but wandered through the Alps as far as Innsbrook. By the time he returned to Antwerp, his mind was filled less with Rome, and more with the mountains and valleys he had traversed on his return journey.

As van Mander recorded,

> When he traveled thru the Alps, he swallowed all the mountains and rocks, and spat them out after his return onto his canvases and panels.

January—Hunters in the Snow

The landscape drawings made during his travels formed the basis of his printmaking partnership with H. Cock, then the leading publisher in Antwerp. The prints launched a long and important association of the two men.

After the style of Hieronymous Bosch

Cock's Print Shop also made engravings after the style of Bosch, the 15th century Flemish artist, whose fantastic and frightening scenes of hell and sinners were still popular in Antwerp, and whose wastelands and demons have had their effect on nearly all the terrifying and surrealistic art since his time, from Bruegel's *The Witches Sabbath* and Goya's *Capriccios* down to Dali and Picasso. Philip II of Spain, although an enemy of the Flemish, was fascinated by Flemish art and had countless paintings brought to Spain where there are many works of Hieronymous Bosch as well as other Flemish masters in the Prado in Madrid. (Another major transplant from Flanders to Spain was a Flemish peasant dance, which quickly took root and flourished. It is now known throughout the world by the Spanish word for Flemish—*Flamenco*.)

164

Bruegel did a series of Bosch-like diabolical scenes for H. Cock. Many of these were based on the seven deadly sins, Anger, Sloth, Lust, Gluttony, Avarice, Pride and Envy. Painted in 1562, *Dulle Grete or Mad Meg's* central female figure is a personification of the sin of Covetousness. Dulle Grete, the old hag, is even ready to enter hell because of her obsession.

Detail from Dulle Grete

Peasant Wedding

About this time in Antwerp, Bruegel did a great deal of work for the merchant Franckart, described as a "noble and upright man," who found pleasure in Bruegel's company and met with him nearly every day. Bruegel often went with him to the country to see the peasant fairs and weddings. Disguised as peasants, they brought gifts, as did the other guests, claiming relationship or kinship with the bride or groom. Bruegel delighted in observing the humorous and outrageous behavior of the peasants, as they ate, drank, caroused and made love. *Peasant Wedding* is one of Bruegel's most famous paintings, considered to be the most straightforward and natural rendering of everyday life in 16th century Flanders. The figure in black seated on the right end of the table is thought to be a self-portrait of the artist.

Peasant Wedding

The Seasons

Bruegel created a group of five paintings called the *Months* or *Seasons*, considered to be the finest landscape paintings of the age. In *January—Hunters in the Snow*, we see the influence of his trip to Italy crossing the Alps. Bruegel conveys the mood of a bitter northern winter brooding over the world, dwarfing the lives of the dark figures inhabiting it. This moving view of peasants and snowbound scenery is admired for the complete truthfulness of its atmosphere.

Bruegel, the political and religious commentator

Little as we know about the man, we know a great deal about his world, and can infer from his paintings how he felt about it. One of the 16th century's chief political and religious commentators, Bruegel editorialized with his brush and sermonized with his colors. While many of his paintings seem to be a simple recording of the world in which he lived, they often contain biting criticism and censure, and give a picture of a man outraged by the political and religious climate and happenings of the time.

Shortly before his birth, in 1517, Martin Luther's edicts challenged the Roman Catholic Church and established the Protestant

Reformation. In 1520, Charles V, grandson of Ferdinand and Isabel of Spain, was the Catholic King of Spain, the Holy Roman Emperor, and the ruler of the Low Countries. The Low Countries consisted of 17 small provinces known as the Netherlands. During Bruegel's lifetime, Dutch nationalism arose and Protestantism was established. Together they combined to defy the religious and political authority of the Catholic Kings of Spain, the powerful Habsburg Dynasty, and the Roman Catholic Church. The conflict which followed is known as the 80 year war and was decisive in European history. It resulted in the separation of the 17 northern provinces, becoming the country known today as Holland—free, democratic, and mostly Protestant. The remaining provinces became modern Belgium and remained in Catholic hands. With the emergence of Holland as a separate state, the Catholic kings of Spain suffered a major blow. The 80 year war, the conflict between Catholic and Protestant, and between Spain and the Netherlands, the inquisition (torment that racked the Netherlands)—these shaped Bruegel's maturity and are the subjects of many of his finest and most powerful statements.

Charles, the Fifth was born in Ghent and raised in Brussels. A Catholic king, part of the Habsburg line and empire, he was sympathetic to the Protestants of the Low Countries. Weary of trying to resolve the political and religious differences, he abdicated the throne to his son, Philip, who had been born, raised, and lived in Madrid.

To the Netherlanders, Flemish-born Charles, powerful and tolerant, had seemed a revered part of their world, but Philip was a foreigner, who stayed in Madrid, and cruelly tried to eradicate Protestantism from the Low Countries. Within a decade, he had driven thousands of Netherland leaders who had been loyal to his father into open rebellion, and created a bitter national resentment against himself and Spain.

Several of Bruegel's paintings refer to precise contemporary political events, although they are disguised by their Biblical settings. The height of terror was reached following a Flemish armed rebellion against the rule of Philip. The Netherlands were invaded by

Spanish troops led by the Duke of Alba, who re-introduced the Inquisition where large scale arrests, tortures and executions were frequent. They spared neither the young or old, male or female, but slaughtered without mercy great numbers of young children as well. The rich were spared because they bribed the troops; the poor were hanged.

With the introduction of a figure in black who is thought to represent the Duke of Alba, Bruegel's painting, *The Massacre of the Innocents* is a savage indictment of these events.

The Massacre of the Innocents

The sin of pride

The *Tower Of Babel*, modeled after the Roman Coliseum, shows Bruegel's awareness of architecture. In the 16th century, the biblical story of man's calamitous attempt to reach heaven was a favorite symbol of the sin of pride. The painting can be understood as a warning to Philip, with his grandiose plans of unifying the Netherlands.

Tower of Babel

The man behind the brush

Many other paintings show the man behind the brush. For example, *Fight Between Carnival and Lent* shows carousing peasants, not an unusual event. The 16th century Flemish world seemed to indulge in an inordinate amount of carousing. Indeed, they were noted for tipsy brawling. An Italian visitor of the time noted that people of the Netherlands would gladly walk 40 miles to go to a drinking party. But mixed with Bruegel's carousing peasants is a moral—the contrast between religion and hedonistic abandon. The leading theme came from a folktale which depicts the pleasures of Mardi Gras and the piety of Lent. A man with a huge stomach standing on a barrel impersonates King Carnival, representing the Lutheran movement, while Lent, a gaunt old figure sitting on a go-cart drawn by a monk and a nun, symbolized the Catholic Church.

In a similar picture of peasant life, *Peasant Dance*, peasants boisterously dance, kiss, quarrel, and drink. The occasion of these excessive festivities is a kermass or Saints' Day. However, a church that stands empty, and a picture of the Madonna that is ignored, are Bruegel's comments on the sins of lust, anger, gluttony and hypocrisy.

Similarly, the theme of *The Procession to Calvary* and *Carrying The Cross*, Bruegel's largest and most elaborately detailed work, is the condemnation of Christian hypocrisy. It outwardly displays piety, but there is no commitment to holy deeds. The callousness of the crowd is part of the theme and expresses the people's indifference to

The Blue Cloak

the fate of Christ, as well as their enjoyment of the outing, as if it were one of the day's popular amusements—a good outdoor execution!

Another painting, *The Netherlandish Proverbs* or the *Blue Cloak*, is a lighter display of Bruegel's knowledge and interest in Flemish folklore. Each motif depicts a proverb. More than 100 have been identified. In the proverb represented in the *Blue Cloak*, which deals with infidelity, the woman who gladly welcomes favors here and there must hang a blue coat around her husband signifying her unfaithfulness.

Children's Games, on the other hand, is a delightful, wholly original and straightforward work with no known symbolism. Instead, it is an encyclopedia of games indispensable to anyone interested in the recreation of childhood through the ages.

Other notable paintings

The Sermon of St. John the Baptist: By 1550, the Habsburgs attempt to stamp out Protestant heresy had sent many martyrs to the stake. Calvinist sympathizers, forbidden to meet in the cities, gathered in the countryside to hear "hedge sermons." Bruegel's painting of John, the Baptist, preaching, portrays such an assembly. A further parallel was that St. John was put to death as were many Calvinists for heresy.

The Cripples

Bruegel's beginning illness may have contributed to his interest in subjects with medical aspects. His portrait, the *Cripples,* was so accurate that French physician, Dr. Torrilton, believes he must have had some medical training. He claims many of Bruegel's cripples are easy to diagnose. Their afflictions range from spastic paraplegia—seen in the center cripple (with bells on his boots)—to advanced locomotor ataxia, a result of syphilis, and includes maladies that waste and curl the legs. Equally accurate are the various kinds of orthopedic aids shown.

The Blind Leading the Blind illustrates a Biblical proverb "...if the blind lead the blind, both shall fall into the ditch." This can be understood as an expression of the blindness of mankind in pursuing worldly aims despite Christ's teachings. This painting is also remarkable in its accurate clinical depictions. The victims suffer from five different eye diseases, from the patient with the white film over his eyes, known as leucoma, to one with atrophy of the eyeball from per-

The Blind Leading the Blind

manently neglected glaucoma. Flemish doctors of the time believed eye trouble was caused by leakage of toxic vapor from the stomach to the brain. Their counsel to patients with eye problems was to have someone blow gently in the eye with a breath sweetened with cloves.

During the last nine years of his life, Bruegel married, fathered 2 sons, and completed 25 paintings. He was given a grant by the Council in Brussels in 1569 to fund him, which may have been a gesture of help to an already ailing man. He was to die later the same year with the diagnosis of stomach problems, possibly cancer. He bequeathed to his wife *Magpie on the Gallows*, which symbolized the gossips expected to be present at his funeral. The dancing peasants under the trees are possibly a wry comment on the world's ignoring his significance as an artist, social and political commentator and his death.

Bruegel died in September 1569 at about the age of 45-49. He was buried in Notre Dame de la Chapelle in Brussels. When his young wife died 9 years later, his mother-in-law cared for and began the artistic training of his two sons: Pieter Brueghel, the Younger, born in 1564, and Jan Brueghel, born in 1568, less than a year before his father's death. With the birth of his grandchildren, an artistic dynasty continued and lasted until the 18th century.

His son, Pieter, the Younger, also known as *Hell Brueghel* because he had a predilection for painting scenes of Hell and Damnation, was an excellent copyist of his father's works. His son Jan, known as *Velvet Brueghel*, because of his predilection for painting flowers and softer scenes, was a friend of Peter Paul Rubens, a great admirer and owner of 12 oils by Bruegel the Elder. Jan honored his parents' memory by placing an epitaph on their tombstone while Rubens adorned it with a painting of Christ giving the keys of the kingdom to Peter.

Even though he was called Peasant Bruegel, the great intellectual range of his paintings and the quality of his friends and patrons suggests that he was not just a gifted bumpkin, but a worldly and cultivated man. The famous map maker, Abraham Ortilis, who was both Bruegel's friend and a collector of his works, gave a memorable eulogy in which he called Bruegel "the most perfect artist of the century."

Since 1900, there have been many interpretations of the meanings of Bruegel's paintings and of his philosophy and private life. One of the most persistent and seemingly frustrated of all Bruegel scholars, Fritz Grossman, wrote:

> The man has been thought to be a peasant and a townsman, an orthodox Catholic and a Protestant, a libertine and a humanist, a laughing and pessimistic philosopher. Bruegel appeared as a follower of H. Bosch, and continued in the Flemish tradition. He was the last of the primitives, a master of the Northern Renaissance, a mannerist in contact with Italian art, an illustrator, a genre painter, a landscape artist, a realist, a painter who was consciously transforming reality and adapting it to his own format and beliefs.

The subject matter of his paintings covers an amazing and impressive range. He introduced landscape painting to the world. In addition, he painted conventional biblical scenes, parables of Christ, and mythological renderings and illustrations of proverbial Flemish paintings. His allegorical compositions are often of a religious nature, but they include social satire as well. Although the scenes he drew from peasant life are very well known, there often seems a deeper significance.

Beneath the superficial meaning of the work, he often makes sociological, religious or psychological statements. His paintings comment on the hypocrisy of the "pious peasants" while, at the same time, celebrate their joy of life. He speaks of the folly and destructiveness of political leaders of the time, and the follies of common and not-so-common man. In all of Bruegel's works, as in the works of many truly great artists, we see below the surface of the people and the landscapes, into their hearts and minds and understand the life issues they confronted during their times. Bruegel was a man of his times; he was limited by his times; he portrayed his times; yet his art will endure for all time.

Lawrence Warick is a Los Angeles psychoanalyst in private practice, an Assistant Clinical Professor in the Department of Psychiatry, UCLA School of Medicine, and a member of the faculty of the Southern California Psychoanalytic Institute. Dr. and Mrs. Warick are the authors of A Biographical Sketch of W. H. Auden *and* Transitional Process and Creativity in the Life and Art of Edvard Munch, *published recently in the* Journal of the American Academy of Psychoanalysis.

Elaine Warick is a medical writer who has collaborated with her husband on a number of articles and presentations related to psychoanalysis and creativity. Her experience includes art therapy with Vietnam veterans at the Sepulveda Veterans Administration Hospital and with terminally ill children at UCLA Medical Center.

My afflictions belong to me and my art—they have become one with me.
Without illness and anxiety, I would have been a rudderless ship.

—Edvard Munch

Edvard Munch
A Study of Loss, Grief and Creativity
by Lawrence Warick, M.D., Ph.D. & Elaine Warick, B.A.

Toward the end of the 19th century, at about the same time Sigmund Freud was investigating unconscious phenomena and the influence of childhood events on the causation of neurosis, a little known Norwegian artist, Edvard Munch (1863-1944), began to express his tormented inner world through his artistic creations, giving birth to an art style that would later be known as Expressionism.

Family Background

The most painful event in Edvard Munch's life was the premature death of his mother from tuberculosis when he was five years old. This tragedy was compounded when his older sister, Sophie, to whom he had become attached in her place, also died of tuberculosis when Munch was thirteen. In addition to these two major losses during Munch's critical stages of development, his father became emotionally unavailable when he suffered an agitated depression of psychotic proportions, associated with religious preoccupations, after his wife's death. All this trauma was intensified by the poverty experienced by the Munch family, despite the fact that Edvard's father was a physician.

177

Besides his older sister Sophie, Munch had three younger siblings. Peter Andreas, two years younger than Edvard, was a physician, who married, and died at age thirty of pneumonia. Edvard's sister Laura, four years his junior, developed a schizoaffective illness during her adolescence and required intermittent lifelong hospitalizations for mental illness. She died of cancer in 1926. The youngest child, Inger, remained unmarried, outlived Edvard, and compiled a book of family letters. Shortly after Edvard's mother died, her younger sister, Karen, came to the family home to care for the children, and it was she who encouraged Munch's art studies, despite Dr. Munch's disapproval.

Although Mrs. Munch described Edvard as a "healthy, rambunctious rascal" in a letter written to a friend a few months before her death, his health after her death was poor, marked by frequent respiratory illnesses which recurred throughout his life. It is not surprising that with Munch's background of multiple childhood losses, illness, and poverty that his art would later be described by many critics as "melancholy."

Themes in Art

Prior to Munch's formal art studies, he drew both himself and his family. He began producing self-portraits in his late teens and continued throughout his life until he died at age seventy two. A noticeable aspect concerning his self-portraits is that none of them show him smiling. In fact, in many, his mouth is turned downward, his shoulders sag, and in a number of paintings he produced furrows in his forehead, similar to Darwin's description of "grief muscles."

Munch's early art work (1880-85) fell into the category of Naturalism both because of its subject matter, which was often a critical commentary on society, and its realistic style. He broke from this school when he was 22 years old and produced what is considered his first major work—*The Sick Child.* The picture recalls a scene that occurred in reality when his sister Sophie was dying of tuberculosis. Munch painted this picture six times during the course of his life and wrote that he experienced grief in its fullest sense in the reworking of this memory of his dying sister.

In the period that followed (1890's), Munch developed his unique expressionistic style and produced a large group of paintings that dealt with his feelings and childhood memories. His themes were love, loss of love, grief, despair, loneliness, jealousy, anxiety, attachment, engulfment, separation and death. He later grouped these pictures together and called them *The Frieze of Life*. One of the most widely known pictures belonging to this group is entitled *The Scream,* which shows a disintegrating, fetus-like figure on a bridge, with an undulating sunset and coastline, along with two vaguely drawn human figures retreating in the background. Although many interpretations have been made about this picture, it seems to represent loss: loss of the self (dissolving figure), loss of the day (sunset) and the loss of his parents (two figures). Like so many of his works, Munch reproduced this picture many times, in a number of different media.

The Sick Child, 1885

Relationships with Women

During Munch's early art career, he lived in Norway where he was connected with a group of Oslo Bohemians who advocated free love. He then began a six year obsession with a married woman, "Mrs. Heiberg," who resembled his own mother in appearance and in the fact that she was married to a physician. In recalling the unsatisfying relationship, Munch wrote, "Is it because she took my first kiss that she took the perfume of life from me?"

179

The Scream, 1895

Munch spent most of his time in Germany during the 1890's, as a member of the Berlin Bohemians. He became infatuated with the wife of another member of the group, an exiled Norwegian named Dagne Juell, repeating his earlier frustrating and ultimately painful attachment to a married woman. This involvement resulted in a number of pictures in which he, Dagne, and a man appear.

At about this same time, Munch also became entangled with a wealthy Norwegian, Tulla Larsen, who pursued him relentlessly and tried to trick him into marriage. This relationship led to a violent quarrel and an accidental shooting, which cost him the loss of the top two joints of one of his fingers on the left hand, causing him considerable physical and emotional pain.

Munch's disappointing relationships with women resulted in a number of heavily affect-laden paintings. In 1893, he painted a picture called *Death and the Maiden* which shows a woman embracing a skeleton. In *Vampire* (1893), a woman's head is buried in a man's neck and in the picture *Harpy*, he produced a birdlike woman tearing out a man's innards. During this period, he also painted a series of pictures depicting a dying or dead mother with a child near her bedside, indicating that his most unfulfilled relationship with a woman was the interrupted attachment between him and his mother due to her premature death.

Hospitalization

While Munch's art flourished in the early 1900's, his emotional and physical health deteriorated. He had a number of hospitalizations for respiratory problems, "nerves," and alcoholism. He suffered from chronic depression and many phobias (agoraphobia, germ-phobia, etc.). He complained of insomnia and had many somatic symptoms (chest pains, gastrointestinal problems and headaches). He was suspicious of people, and when he used alcohol, his paranoia increased to the point where he got into barroom brawls. He also experienced hallucinations, usually during alcoholic bouts or febrile illness.

Harpy, 1901

After a three-day alcoholic binge in the autumn of 1908, Munch admitted himself to Dr. Daniel Jacobson's psychiatric clinic in Copenhagen for an illness characterized by depression, anxiety, phobias and paranoid ideation. For seven or eight months, Munch received a spa and massage daily, low current electricity treatments, pine needle baths, open air treatments, a healthy diet and attention from the nurses and his physician. He was encouraged to continue his artwork and during his hospital stay he painted his doctor, nurses, fellow patients and a few friends who visited him. Several months after entering the hospital he wrote to his Aunt Karen:

> There is a competent doctor here and kind people—I hope after a few
> months to be able to put behind me the old unpleasantness and become
> a new person.

Later years

Munch's hospitalization seemed to cure him of his alcoholism. He returned to Norway, at age forty-five, a changed man. Although major changes in his work had already occurred as early as 1902, after his psychiatric treatment in 1908-09, the content of his art seemed to deal more with the positive aspects of the external world and less with his troubled intrapsychic world. He continued, however, to rework his old themes, intermittently, until the end of his life.

During the last thirty-five years of his life, Munch lived in Norway, becoming a recluse, avoiding human contact and devoting himself to his work. He abstained from alcohol, cigarettes and women. He continued to experience anxiety, depression and somatic symptoms, but these did not interfere with his ability to work. Although he was encouraged by his physician, Dr. Schreiner, to seek help for his emotional problems, he said he felt his creativity might be destroyed if he were treated.

Munch maintained a correspondence with his Aunt Karen, who died in 1931, and his sister Inger throughout his life, but did not enjoy visiting them. He had housekeepers, but they usually quit working for him, complaining that Munch would never talk to them. In addition to his few physician friends, he had a relationship with a businessman/art dealer, Rolf Stenersen, who wrote his biography at Munch's request, entitled *Edvard Munch: Close-up of a Genius.*

Stenersen says later in life Munch developed a very intense relationship to his paintings and actually talked about them as if they were living people. When he was offered a large amount of money for a painting he did not want to part with, he said, "I must have some of my friends on the walls." Although Munch was always attached to his paintings, after his illness in 1908, they seemed to replace his relationships with people.

Edvard Munch died on January 23, 1944, at the age of eighty, of pneumonia, complicated by cardiovascular disease. He had spent the morning working on a portrait of his old friend from his Oslo Bohemian days, Hans Jaeger, who had died over thirty years earlier.

Discussion

Munch's contribution to the world of art was his presentation of familiar objects in a new expressive form (often distorted) that conveyed feelings. In this respect his art is a major link between representational and non-representational styles—a stepping stone on the path from Realism to Abstract Expressionism.

The sources of Munch's art can be found in his inherited natural talent, his identification with his mother, aunt and other family members who were artists, as well as his need to record his feelings and experiences in his lifelong attempt to understand himself and the meaning of his life.

Munch was greatly affected by the many losses he experienced in his life, and his grief became a major motif in his art. In attempting to work through his grief, Munch visually re-created his mother, father and sister, many times. In a normal grief process, this would allow gradual diminishing of the pain of loss. For Munch, this was not to be.

The death of Munch's mother was the major disruption of attachment in his life, and this trauma severely affected the development of his subsequent object relationships. Although some children may experience an adaptive mourning process, it appears from all evidence available (Munch's art, diaries, letters, autobiographies and the observations of those who knew him), that Munch waged a lifelong struggle to recover his lost love object, using a group of defenses often seen in pathological grief reactions, according to Bowlby.

Munch's longing for reunion with his mother and his inability to give her up is manifested in his repeated paintings of her (and symbolic representations of her) in an attempt to recreate his lost love object. This action is best described by M. Robbins: "The creative process is set in motion when painful affects related to object loss and object hunger threaten to become conscious... In this way the artist creates his own world of objects which he may then possess and maintain, thus avoiding for the time, the pain of loss."

Despite his efforts to resurrect his lost mother, both in his art and in his relationships with older, married women, Munch was

183

doomed to an unending repetition of failure and disappointment when fusion and re-union did not occur. Munch's development of life-long respiratory illness (similar to the disease that took his mother's life) may have been related to a pathologic identification with her.

Although Munch's repressed hostility toward his mother for leaving him was transferred to other women (both in reality and in his art), he was able, through the process of splitting, to preserve the good mother with whom he would be reunited in heaven (she had promised this to her children shortly before her death), while, at the same time, attacking the bad mother (including women he had encountered in his adult life) who had abandoned him. Munch saw the union between man and woman as leading to ego dissolution or death. Hence women were seen, via a projection of his own oral aggressive wishes, as sadistic vampires who sucked life's blood from men.

In spite of the fact that there appears to be a more positive change in the way Munch depicts women in his paintings after his

treatment with Dr. Jacobson, there also seems to be evidence of even further withdrawal from any real relationships. After his hospitalization, Munch removed himself to a solitary existenc where he could create a controlled environment and where he could maintain a semblance of self-autonomy without the fear of disintegration or engulfment. Munch's self-imposed exile and schizoid withdrawal helped him

The Dead Mother and the Child, 1899-1900

avoid the revival of regressive anxieties, paranoid ideation and painful feelings of jealousy, depression and anger that relationships with people engendered. While isolated, he was able to spend all of his time painting, and through his creativity he was able to gratify many of his needs.

Through his art he could visually recreate the dead members of his family, thereby denying his loss and the painful feelings associated with his tragic past. He could project emotions onto his paintings that he found unacceptable in himself—jealousy, hostility, and sexuality. He was also able to express feelings toward his paintings—to love them and scold them. The paintings allowed Munch to diminish his feelings of envy toward the reproductive and nurturing woman through his fantasies that he also could give birth and nurture. He was the mother/father unit to his "children." He could reduce his anxiety and depression so long as he was around his artwork

His paintings allowed him to deal with his dependency needs by providing him with money. Hence, he had the illusion of independence. He experienced fame (he received the Order of St. Olaf from Norway in 1909), which was narcissistically gratifying and assured him a form of immortality, thus mitigating his own fear of death. Munch's art also helped him cope with his guilt for the imagined responsibility he felt (like most children) over his losses by creating a product via the reparative process.

Harry B. Lee believes that the artist creates in order to deal with anxiety due to an intense dread of loss of love from maternal figures. The artist's hostile destructive impulses, when frustrated, lead to guilt and a need for punishment. Creativity is an attempt to undo the loss and win forgiveness and approval. The artist wants a fantasized reunion with the frustrating bad mother, symbolically, via the newly created aesthetically satisfying product, in order to recapture infantile magical omnipotence.

The infant deals with stress through the use of a transitional object, for example, a pacifier. Volkan and Josephthal report that the adult who suffers separation anxiety and pathologic grief may reactivate in his regression just such an archaic way of dealing with stress, through the use of a transitional object as a linking object to the departed person. "Put into the external world, the linking object helps the patient *externalize* the work of mourning."

There is good reason to believe that Munch's creativity saved him from psychological disintegration and eased, to some extent, his painful journey through life. At the same time, this remarkable artist left the world a wonderful legacy.

Reinhold Heller, one of Munch's many biographers, seems quite accurate when he says, "Despite a recurring schizoid near-psychosis, actualized through alcoholic over-indulgence, Munch remained in tight control of his creative powers."

Summary

Edvard Munch's life and art reveals his lifelong struggle with pathologic grief. Although Munch was not able to relinquish his lost love objects and establish new human relationships, which ideally occurs in the adaptive grief process, he was successful in obtaining a certain degree of psychic equilibrium through his art. There is little doubt that Munch's creativity saved him from complete psychological disintegration and eased, to some extent, his painful journey through life. At the same time, Munch left both aesthetically satisfying products and a graphic legacy which offers a fascinating study in the correlation between early childhood loss, pathologic grief and creativity.

Melissa Robertson is Director of Southern California Psychological Services and in private practice in Whittier and Brentwood, California. Originally from Chicago, Dr. Robertson, who specializes in the issue of women and creativity, received her Ph.D. degree from the California School of Professional Psychology in Los Angeles.

Everything great in the world is created by neurotics. They have composed our masterpieces, but we don't consider what they have cost their creators in sleepless nights and, worst of all, fear of death. —*Marcel Proust*

Sylvia Plath
A Blind Girl Playing with a Slide Rule of Values
by Melissa Robertson, Ph.D.

Throughout history, few women have been recognized as geniuses. Sylvia Plath's life and death may cast light on this issue. The difficulty for Plath was her inability to make what was for her an impossible synthesis, a synthesis that demanded that she live her life as the creative genius she was, while simultaneously maintaining the commitments of a wife and mother during the 1950's and early 1960's.

By the 1970's, the advent of a strong women's liberation movement allowed large numbers of women to see themselves as a group with common external and internal oppressive forces. This common viewpoint enabled a significant expansion to occur in women's previously circumscribed sex role, along with increases in opportunities and positions of power. However, certain opportunities still remain elusive for women, not the least of which is the achievement and acknowledgment of women as creative geniuses.

Sylvia Plath's story may shed some light on the obstacles.

Plath found herself at age twenty, in her 3rd year of full scholarship at Smith College, "upborne on a wave of creative, social, and financial success." On November 3, 1952, she wrote in her journal:

> Five years ago, if I could have seen myself now, at Smith (instead of Wellesley) with seven acceptances (publications) from Seventeen and one from Mademoiselle, with a few lovely clothes, and one intelligent, handsome boy—I would have said, 'that is all I could ever ask!'

The stage was set: outstanding success, and public recognition of her exceptional intellectual and creative ability:

> Hundreds of dreaming ambitious girls would like to be in my place. They write me letters, asking if they may correspond with me.

Yet the same day she wrote the above excerpts, she also wrote:

> God, if ever I have come close to wanting to commit suicide, it is now... I fell into bed again this morning, begging for sleep, withdrawing into the dark warm, fetid escape from action, from responsibility."

Clearly, she was describing the symptoms of a major depression: hypersomnia, loss of energy, fatigue, loss of interest in usual activities, and suicidal ideation.

The available biographical material suggests that such episodes were previously unusual and uncharacteristic of Sylvia Plath. Professor Davis, for example, recalled how refreshing it was "to have a completely wholesome, healthy, yet creative student" like Sylvia, and how he "had never had a talented writer in his creative writing class who was not a little neurotic or something, except Sylvia." What precipitated such a severe depression that fall day in November?

She continued:

> I am afraid... I want to kill myself to escape from responsibility, to crawl back abjectly into the womb. I do not know who I am, where I am going. I am the one who has to decide the answers to these hideous questions...

> Why did Virginia Woolf commit suicide? Or Sara Teasdale or other brilliant women? If only I knew. If only I knew how high I could set my goals, my requirements for my life. I am in the position of a blind girl playing with a slide rule of values. I am now at the nadir of my calculating powers.

Herein lies the heart of the matter. Contained within this quote is the essential dilemma. In a brilliant insight, Sylvia was aware of the seeds of her own downfall. In a flash of light she saw herself for who she was, what she represented: a blind girl playing with a slide rule of values. She is afraid of the unknown. She has walked straight up to a giant void, blackness, nothingness—as though she has been catapulted into space, where she is suspended, floating, and all that surrounds her is empty, black space. She is confronting her own tremendous power to create. She is facing her own genius. What she wants to know is, what danger is there in that void? What will happen if she dares to go there? How does she dare decide to go where so few women have been before?

"Let's see," she might have thought to herself, "there is Virginia Woolf, who clearly was a female genius, but look what happened to her, she killed herself... and so did Sara Teasdale, and other brilliant women. I, too, could be destroyed if I dare to enter that unknown."

The only women she knows who have dared to enter that void, the only maps she was taught, the only scenario she has heard, is that women who have realized their brilliance have ended up destroyed. And here is Sylvia, having to make the "hideous" decision of whether she wants to leap into that void. She would have to be a fool to take that chance. So what does she do? The blind girl decides to drop "the slide rule of values" altogether, and runs in terror at the notion of a woman of twenty having to calculate new female values for herself, and having only tragic role models as guides.

In the next paragraph she wrote:

> The future? God, will it get worse and worse? Will I never travel, never integrate my life, never have purpose, meaning? Never have timelong stretches, to investigate ideas, philosophy—to articulate the vague seething desires in me? Will I be a secretary—a self-rationalizing, uninspired housewife, secretly jealous of my husband's ability to grow intellectually and professionally while I am impeded?

> Will I submerge my embarrassing desires and aspirations, refuse to face myself, and go either mad or become neurotic?

Is there anyone she can talk to who might understand? Would a woman understand Sylvia's "vague seething desires," her "embarrassing desires and aspirations"? Would a man understand why she feels she has no choice but to submerge them? She writes:

> Whom can I talk to? Get advice from? No one. I'll kill myself. I am beyond help.

191

According to Howard Parad, "Suicide threats and attempts should be understood as communication to 'significant others' in the patient's life. The patient is communicating in this way something he [she] is unable to talk about. We have found that people do not commit suicide while they are in communication with other persons."

Perhaps, if Virginia Woolf were around, Sylvia could talk to her, communicate with her, she would understand.

She concluded writing in her journal on that bleak November day with a graphic description of the kind of affective state which accompanies radical emotional and social isolation:

> I go plodding on, afraid that the blank hell in back of my eyes will break through, spewing forth like a dark pestilence, afraid that the disease which eats away the pith of my body with merciless impersonality will break forth in obvious sores and warts, screaming, "traitor, sinner, imposter."

She went into the infirmary, under the auspices of having "bad sinus," and wrote *Infirmary Blues*, a poignant poem that catches the loneliness, vulnerability, self-hatred and despair she felt at that time:

> You push the button and the voice comes out of the wall
> Hygienic and efficiently impersonal
> "What can we do for you? What can we do?"
> And you
> Say to the waiting voice inside the wall:
> "I don't think I want my supper meal.
> My stomach feels queer and I don't want to eat at all."
> There is a distant click and soon the soft-soled footsteps come down
> the hall;
> And she hands you a glass of white medicine
> That tastes like peppermint, cool-flavored and milk-thin.
> She says: "There will be toast and tea for you and junket
> by and by."
> And you say all right and turn your face away because you
> are going to cry.
> Outside the picture window the rain is pouring on the ground
> And all the things you ever did or will do wrong are
> falling down without a sound
> Out of the yesterday sky
> To where all the little stillborn cretins of tomorrow lie.

Plath, men and sex roles

Over the next six months her severe depression gradually lifted. Late in November, she met a man she "could want to see again and again." Two months later she wrote:

> I am probably at the peak of my sexual desire, and I should not wonder at my smoldering passion.

She thought a great deal during these months about the kind of love and type of man she wanted to marry. What emerged is a very common coping mechanism for women. As a flight from her own deeply private, personal, existential dilemma, along with its implied social sex role conflict, she becomes absorbed in an "other." She goes on to outline in great detail what she fears in such a relationship:

> O.K., here is a certificate guaranteeing you 50 years
> during which she will
> love your faults, honor your bestialities,
> obey your whimsies, ignore your mistresses,
> nurse your progeny, paper your walls, and
> adore you as her dying mortal god,
> conceive babies and new recipes in labor and travail.

This was her fantasied world of traditional sex roles, and good old-fashioned love. However, on May 12, she learned that she had won the 1953 Mademoiselle guest editorship. There she was to spend a month in New York, among other things, interviewing famous writers. Asked to pick four writers to interview, she chose J.D. Salinger, Shirley "The Lottery" Jackson, E.B. White of New Yorker fame, and Irwin Shaw. She wrote to her mother, "I hope one of these illuminaries consents to be with me."

Immediately following the news of this great success, she plummeted again into the same depression of six months earlier. On May 14, two days later, she wrote:

> It was good to walk faceless and talk to myself again, to ask where I was going, and who I was, and realize that I had no idea... Is anyone anywhere happy? No, not unless they are living in a dream or in an artifice that someone else has made.

She was forced again to acknowledge that she cannot fit into the artifice that American society in the 1950's had made for women. She tried to fly away from her creative self, the genius within her that does not fit into society's scheme of things, but instead threatened her with temptation into the unknown. In metaphors, she wrote of the terror of her own genius and the unknown ramifications of public recognition of that genius:

> I want to love somebody because I want
> to be loved. In a rabbit fear I may
> hurl myself under the wheels of the
> car because the lights terrify me, and
> under the dark blind death of the wheels
> I will be safe. I am very tired, very
> banal, very confused. I do not know
> who I am tonight.

A suicide attempt

The following entry is the only excerpt which survived the Guest Editor experience at Mademoiselle, and the only one preceding her suicide attempt on August 24, 1953.

> Stop thinking selfishly of razors and self-wounds and going out and ending it all... Believe in some beneficent force beyond your own limited self...

Journals have disappeared if they existed for the two years after Sylvia's suicide attempt and "breakdown" that August. The attempt was, as far as suicide attempts go, a very serious one. In a letter she wrote, but never sent, she "kept a record" of how she felt at the time. One year after the attempt she gave it to her mother. She describes her suicidal intentions:

> Well, I tried drowning, but that didn't work; somehow the urge to life, mere physical life, is damn strong... The body is amazingly stubborn when it comes to sacrificing itself to annihilating directions of the mind.

Virginia Woolf committed suicide by drowning. Sylvia states directly that by trying to drown, she was trying to "duplicate" Virginia Woolf. Four years later she wrote in her journal:

> Virginia Woolf... Bless her. I feel my life linked to her somehow. I love her... But her suicide I felt I was reduplicating in that black summer of 1953. Only I couldn't drown.

194

Instead she took a bottle of 50 sleeping pills, crawled into the cellar and "blissfully succumbed to the whirling blackness that I honestly believed was eternal oblivion." However, she vomited them while unconscious and "instinctively" called for help. Her brother found her and she was brought to the hospital. Her first words were a moaned "Oh, no!" She said weakly, "It was my last act of love...'" She wrote in a private letter that she felt

> ... hatred toward the people who would not let me die, but insisted on dragging me back into the hell of sordid and meaningless existence.

Her attempt at suicide was intended to be a final one.

Sylvia's suicide attempt can be seen as a communication to a "significant other," Virginia Woolf. She was trying to reveal a sense of communion with her, a sense of sharing in common, of being connected, of being "linked" with her, "somehow." Somehow! Even after reenacting Woolf's suicide, Sylvia did not consciously know, herself, why she felt this common bond.

What message was she communicating through this act of identification with Woolf, of which she herself was only vaguely aware? The underlying message can be described as follows: Women who assert their brilliance are violating an ancient taboo; the violation of an ancient taboo demands punishment; therefore, women who assert their brilliance demand to be punished. Woolf, a genius, committed suicide for violating an ancient taboo. Like Woolf, Sylvia Plath is a woman who asserted her genius and thereby violated an ancient taboo. Sylvia Plath must therefore be punished. Suicide is a form of punishment. Therefore, Sylvia Plath must commit suicide.

She was still playing with the terms of the contract, even though the contract itself was already set. Questions such as "How high is too high?" and "How far can she reach, and still be safe?" arose. But she quickly realized she was playing a game of Russian Roulette, where there were no safe answers. No one could tell her where to stop safely before brilliance and genius. And so she stopped playing this dangerous game of achieving. It was safe enough for a while, getting published here, getting published there, but of late she had been getting too many publications and other significant professional recognition of her work. The game became more dangerous; she felt herself in the dark. Approaching the ominous and lonely frontier of female genius, she came face to face with a prohibition as primitive and ancient and as firmly embedded in the female psyche as the incest taboo.

The only solution: to end her life, do the inevitable, hasten her fate, enact the punishment which, if not now, will be her inevitable due. Still, she believed, hoped, someone somewhere would understand, with a bird's-eye-perspective, her blind struggle. To whom could she turn for advice? What woman had been there and lived to tell the tale?

She made a last desperate appeal, before walking to what she believed was her inevitable doom:

> God, god, god: Where are you? I want you, need you, the belief in you and your love and mankind.

But no god answered.

Following her suicide attempt, she was hospitalized, and underwent shock therapy, with some lifting of her depression. Most of her struggle was blind; it was not on much of a conscious level (except, perhaps, in the beginning). After her recovery, she still did not know why she had tried to commit suicide. She wrote in her journal:

> Why, after the 'amazingly short' three or so shock treatments [following the suicide attempt] did I rocket uphill? Why did I feel I needed to be punished, to punish myself...

Marrying and merging

Sylvia now wanted to marry and merge herself with another human being:

> I deserve that, don't I, some sort of blazing love that I can live with. My God, I'd love to cook and make house, and surge force into a man's dreams... I can't bear to think of this potential for loving and giving going brown and sere in me.

She wanted love, even if it meant conforming to the then traditional role of self-sacrificing wife. The day after she wrote this, she met the poet, Ted Hughes, at a party:

[He] came over and was looking hard in my
eyes and it was Ted Hughes... and bang
the door was shut and he was sloshing
brandy into a glass and I was sloshing
it at the place my mouth was when I last
knew about it... and then he kissed
me bang smash on the mouth [omission]...
And when he kissed my neck I bit him long
and hard on the cheek, and when we came
out of the room blood was running down
his face. [Omission.] And I screamed in
myself, thinking: oh, to give myself
crashing, fighting, to you.

Four months later, while she was in England on a Fulbright,
they married. She was now able to merge herself, passionately, but
found her impulse to create quite gone, and her self-development at
a standstill:

I am stymied, stuck, at a stasis...
I feel really uncreative... my whole
being has grown and interwound so completely
with Ted's that if anything were
to happen to him, I do not see how I
could live. I would go either mad, or
kill myself... But I must get back
into the world of my creative mind:
otherwise in the world of pies and
shin beef, I die.

She confronted her dilemma here. If she merged herself with
another as a female and traditional wife, her creativity would cease,
her self-actualization would came to a standstill. But if she lived in
the world of the creative mind, she risked isolation, punishment, and
possible ramifications, now, of outshining her husband. She wrote:

I am so glad Ted is first... his rejections more than double my sorrow and
his acceptances rejoice me more than mine... That's why I could marry
him, knowing he was a better poet than I and that I would never have to
restrain my little gift, but could push it and work it to the utmost and still
feel him ahead.

"Daddy"

As stated earlier, suicide attempts are often very desperate efforts at communication. With whom else may Plath have been attempting to communicate through her attempts to kill herself? An answer is furnished by her poem, *Daddy.*

> You stand at the blackboard, daddy.
> In the picture I have of you,
> A cleft in your chin instead of your foot
> But no less a devil for that, no not
> Any less the black man who
> Bit my pretty red heart in two
> I was ten when they buried you
> At twenty I tried to die
> And get back, back, back to you
> I thought even the bones would do.

John Bowlby has observed that it is quite common for children who experience the death of a parent to yearn for reunion. The child wishes either that the parent will return to this world, or else the child may hope to die and thereby be reunited with the deceased parent in the beyond.

Sylvia's mother, Aurelia

Based on the writings of Sylvia Plath, it is evident that the process of mourning and bereavement was not fully experienced either by Sylvia or her mother, Aurelia. Aurelia Plath's method of coping became compulsive care-giving, described by Sylvia as "abnormally altruistic" behavior, which appears at bottom to have been a thinly disguised plea to be taken care of by her daughter. It is clear that Sylvia felt responsible for her mother's happiness. Bowlby found that it is not uncommon that the child, after the loss of a parent, comes to feel responsible for the happiness of the other parent.

While in psychotherapy at age 26, she wrote in her journal of her mother:

> What do I expect by "love" from her? What is it I don't get that makes me cry? I think that I have always felt that she uses me as an extension of herself, that when I commit suicide or try to, it is a shame to her, an accusation.

Aurelia Plath was herself exceptionally intelligent and a talented writer. She had helped her husband in his writing. After he died, she taught shorthand and typing (which, according to Sylvia, she hated and resented) to support her children. It is evident that Aurelia Plath's own creativity had been thwarted, and that she lived vicariously through Sylvia's professional recognition, publication, and awards "as if it had been [her] own." Her mother thus passed on to Sylvia the complicated legacy of thwarted female creativity and genius, expecting Sylvia to live out her dreams without warning her of the obstacles.

Therefore, it is quite understandable that Sylvia would feel rage both at her father for deserting her and at her mother for expecting Sylvia to live the life that her mother wanted but could not have for herself. To a great extent Sylvia fulfilled her mother's dreams—the daughter of the teacher of the rudiments of writing, shorthand and typing, became one of the most recognized and celebrated writers of her generation.

From December, 1958 to 1959, Sylvia returned to psychotherapy with Dr. Ruth Beuscher, the therapist she had worked with following her first suicide attempt. Psychotherapy had a profoundly therapeutic effect upon her, and helped give rise to her first major work: *Poem for a Birthday*. She wrote in her journal,

> Have been happier this week than for six months. It is as if R.B. (therapist), saying, 'I give you permission to hate your mother,' also said, 'I give you permission to be happy...'

Unfortunately, Sylvia terminated therapy when she and her husband left the country to live in England.

Sylvia gave birth to her first child, a daughter, Frieda Rebecca, in 1960 after four years of marriage. She gave birth to a son, Nicholas Farrer, in 1962. From 1962 to 1963, Sylvia experienced a period of immense creativity. A. Alvarez, who was one of Sylvia's closest confidantes in the last years of her life, wrote of her during this period, "No longer quiet and withheld, a house-wifely appendage to a powerful husband, she seemed made solid and complete, her own woman again... There was a sharpness and clarity about her. I understood why as I was leaving. 'I'm writing again,' she said. 'Really writing.'"

The Bell Jar

Sylvia Plath wrote her novel, *The Bell Jar*, in six weeks. *The Bell Jar* was Sylvia's novel, an autobiographical account of her mental breakdown and suicide attempt.

During this period of extraordinary creativity, her husband began an affair with a woman. It was rather obvious for some time, but when it became quite blatant, she asked him to move out. The betrayal and abandonment by her husband reawakened with even greater intensity her feelings of betrayal and abandonment by her father. During the period following her separation from her husband, her creativity continued to flourish as she gave poetic expression to her anger at her father, her husband, and the patriarchal nature of society in general. More from the poem, *Daddy*:

> Daddy, I have had to kill you.
> You died before I had time.
> Marble—heavy, a bag full of God
> Ghastly statue with one gray toe
> Big as a frisco seal
>
> Every woman adores a Fascist
> The boot in the face, the brute
> Brute heart of a brute like you.

Living alone, solely responsible for the care of her two young children, she continued a prolific period of creative output. She wrote thirty poems in thirty days, by estimates her greatest work, the poems of *Ariel*. She wrote to her mother at this time,

> Living apart from Ted is wonderful—I am no longer in his shadow.

During this extraordinary period, she was able to say to herself and to the world:

> I am a genius of a writer; I have it in me. I am writing the best poems of my life; they will make my name.

In another letter she wrote:

> For a genius there are no bonds and bounds.

Two months after her "realization," *The Bell Jar* came out under the pseudonym Victoria Lucas, with excellent reviews. A month later she wrote the poem, *Edge*.

> The woman is perfected
> Her dead
> Body wears the smile of accomplishment,
> The illusion of a Greek necessity
> Flows in the scrolls of her toga
> Her bare
> Feet seem to be saying:
> We have to come so far, it is over.

"Perfected," "dead body," "accomplishment," "necessity," "Greek necessity," all terms of which the stuff of ancient tragedy is made. Her struggle is now over, she has seen the brilliant light of day, she has entered the land with no bonds and no bounds, freely, she has crossed the prohibited threshold of creative genius and it no longer terrifies her. She can go in peace to meet her "Greek necessity" for she is perfected now, and wears "the smile of accomplishment." She said of the moon, which she called her muse:

> The moon has nothing to be sad about,
> Staring from her hood of bone.
> She is used to this sort of thing.
> Her blacks crackle and drag.

Six days later, Sylvia went up to the children's room and left a plate of bread and butter and two mugs of milk. She went into the kitchen and sealed the doors and windows with towels and laid her head in the oven. This time, there were no mistakes. Nevertheless, she had sent a letter to a psychotherapist requesting an appointment. The therapist's reply arrived a day or two after she died.

Summary

If Sylvia's life is ever to be given its rightful value, it will be as a tragedy, born out of ancient female oppression. At nineteen years of age, she wrote a most fitting epitaph:

> Being born a woman is my awful tragedy.
> From the moment I was conceived I was
> doomed to sprout breasts and ovaries

rather than penis and scrotum; to have
my whole circle of action, thought and
feeling rigidly circumscribed by my inescapable femininity.

Sylvia Plath lived and died before the advent of the women's liberation movement. This "blind girl playing with a slide rule of values" was alone in her life-and-death struggle with her genius as a writer, and her conflicting roles as wife, mother, and finally, single parent. She perceived no female genius role models to guide her, other than the tragic and self-destructive Virginia Woolf.

Plath was terrified of the unknown social and psychological consequences of becoming a female genius. As long as she had Ted, her genius husband, ever with and before her, she was safe. She could push and work her "little gift... to the utmost and still feel him ahead." However, it was not until they separated and she was no longer "under his shadow" that she could actualize her genius to its fullest. But for her, life as a female genius was profoundly lonely, devoid of love, and ultimately, demanded to be punished.

Comment by invited discussant Benjamin Garber, M.D.:

Dr. Garber is the Director of the Barr-Harris Center for the Study of Separation and Loss in Childhood. He is a training and supervising analyst for the Chicago Institute for Psychoanalysis, and a member of the attending staff at Michael Reese Hospital.

Sylvia Plath, one of the most gifted poets of our time, died in 1963 at the age of 31. She committed suicide after an abbreviated lifetime of prodigious creativity in poetry and in her novel, *The Bell Jar.* Due to her creative genius and self-revelatory writings she has become a frequent subject of psychologically oriented researchers.

Mental health professionals and psychoanalysts in particular have always been fascinated by the twin mysteries of creativity and genius, and their relationship to psychopathology. Starting with Freud's *Jensen's Gradiva* and the use of applied psychoanalysis, psychoanalysts have pursued the understanding of the creative genius with fervor.

Dr. Robertson, with her interesting study of Sylvia Plath, tries to fathom the reason for her suicide at such an early age, when she was at the height of her creative powers. Dr. Robertson's thesis is that Sylvia, having recognized the extent of her genius, was unable to integrate her creativity with her role as a wife and a mother. The culture of the 1950's and 60's did not support the synthesis of these roles. Other women geniuses, Virginia Woolf and Sara Teasdale, committed suicide for similar reasons. With limited role models to emulate, Sylvia felt impelled to follow in their footsteps.

I would like to address some additional issues of Sylvia's life and how they also contributed to the final outcome.

The psychoanalytic examination of an author's life or work involving the thorny methodological problems of "analysis in absentia" is sometimes facilitated by picking a subject with a relatively simple lifeline, whose psychological preoccupations occur with regularity in a thinly disguised form. A justification for using Plath's works to understand her psychologically is the almost perfect agreement between statements about herself, the description of events and feelings of her fictional heroine, Esther Greenwood in *The Bell Jar*, and the personae in her poems. Although I do not believe we can analyze someone from their literary works alone, much can be learned about the creator.

The experience of loss in the lives of many writers is a recurrent finding. The break-up of Sylvia's marriage to Ted Hughes echoed the earlier loss of her father at age eight, and contributed to a hostile-dependent relationship with a depressed and unempathic mother, factors that lent linearity to the events that ultimately culminated in suicide. In her poems and in her novel, Plath demonstrates a daughter's rage toward the mother as she talks about pounding against an empty unresisting and unresponsive space.

While Sylvia's father died when she was eight, he was sick from the time she was four. During this time and after his death, Sylvia's mother had to work and support herself and her two children. There is evidence that she was a chronically bitter, depressed, and angry woman, incapable of supporting and mirroring her daughter's bril-

203

liance and creative talents. At times she was competitive with Sylvia and depreciated her lack of practicality.

Dr. Robertson begins the events of Sylvia Plath's creative life, and in a parallel sense her psychopathology, in the third year of college. At this time Sylvia began to realize her genius, its possibilities, as well as the inherent dangers in such a discovery. However, I believe that her depression may have had much deeper roots than the realization of her genius.

Sylvia's preoccupation with death and the fact that she wrote and spoke of dying at a young age point to a life-long depression. There is evidence that Sylvia made a suicide attempt at age ten, although it was never documented. The suicide also may have been an attempt to merge with her dead father whom she longed for, indicating that she never resolved her feelings about the loss. How much was unresolved grief and how much was an identification with a depressed mother will never be known.

Kligerman makes a reference to the specific meaning of creativity in which the created work serves to replace a part of the self. Many creative persons suffer a structural defect, often related to early object loss, which may be temporarily healed by the artistic productions. Kligerman implies that the part of the self the created work stands for in fantasy is the lost, narcissistically experienced person who provided mirroring or affirmation or emotional nurturance of the artist at an early age.

For Plath the creative urge and the need for literary success were intertwined with her need to overcome her depression and her narcissistic withdrawal from the people around her. Her poetry gave her a chance to check and ameliorate her strong aggressive and destructive urges by constructive activity. Her poetry afforded her the opportunity to establish order and control over her desires and the emotional storms that tore her apart. Why there came a point in her life when these adaptations did not work any more is something that awaits an answer.

I agree with Dr. Robertson that Sylvia needed a female role model to help her come to terms with her overwhelming conflicts about her genius and creativity, one better than Virginia Woolf or Sara Teasdale. If she had had the support, the responsiveness, and the validation of her ambitions by an empathic, non-competitive mother, then perhaps she would have had a better chance to resolve her conflicts. The only female to respond to her needs was her therapist, Dr. Beuscher, and that relationship was abbreviated when Sylvia left for England with her husband.

Sylvia Plath made a valiant but unsuccessful attempt to make use of her literary gifts to resolve the powerful, unconscious emotional conflicts of a severe depressive and narcissistic disturbance. We still do not possess a complete understanding of why, at the height of her creative powers, recognized and appreciated on both sides of the Atlantic, and the mother of two children who needed her, she chose to end her life.

Warren L. Jones, M.D., was born in Portland, Oregon and graduated from the University of Oregon Medical School. Internship and residencies included service in Navy hospitals during the Korean War. Dr. Jones was instrumental in the development of the Pasadena Mental Health Center, a pioneer program in paraprofessional counseling services. He has numerous faculty appointments, including the Southern California Psychoanalytic Institute. Regarding creativity, Dr. Jones' personal view is that madness or mental illness is an impediment, rather than an impulse to creativity; and holds the controversial opinion that Leonardo was one of the world's greatest underachievers.

Why is it that all men who are outstanding, in philosophy, poetry or the
arts, are melancholic?   *—Aristotle*

The Missing Mothers of Leonardo and Magritte
by Warren L. Jones, M.D., Ph.D.

It seems that I was always destined to be deeply concerned with vul-
tures; for I recall as one of my earliest memories that while I was in my
cradle a vulture came down to me, and opened my mouth with its tail,
and struck me many times with its tail against my lips.

Leonardo da Vinci

My recollections of early childhood are few, and all bizarre. What I
remember especially, in a kind of vision, is a large wooded chest standing enigmatically near my cradle. I also remember when I was a year old,
two balloonists arrived suddenly one day, dressed in leather and wearing helmets, and dragging down the stairs the deflated envelope of their
balloon, which had become entangled on the roof of our house.

René Magritte

The earliest memories: bird and balloon

These are the earliest memories recorded by two incredible
artists, Leonardo da Vinci and René Magritte. Separated in time by
about 450 years and a Zeitgeist of even more disparity, each illumi-
nated the spirit of his age with brilliance, while cloaking himself in
tantalizing enigma and obsessive privacy. Even the cradle memory of
each is striking, with one believing a vulture (or kite, another type of
bird, in a better translation) landed on his lips, and the other certain
that a hot air balloon landed on his roof. The bird's tail entered

Leonardo's mouth in his remembrance; the balloon and the men in it entered Magritte's home through the roof, and left down the stairs. Neither has revealed much more, at least in writing that has survived, about his early life, and other sources must be searched for information.

Leonardo: background of a bastard

In 1452, Leonardo was born to a peasant woman, Caterina, and Ser (the title of a notary) Piero in Vinci, Italy. Leonardo's parents were not married, and he has been described by Stendhal as "the natural child of Ser Piero, notary of the Republic, and as lovable as a love child." The name of Leonardo's mother was not recorded in his birth entry, a usual omission in cases of illegitimate birth, although the baptismal priest and the ten witnesses to the baptism were named. Caterina is thought to be about age 22 at the time, and the daughter of peasants. She may have been employed as a servant at an inn, or on a farm. Leonardo's later observation, "Have you not seen peasant girls in the mountains, clad in their poor rags, bereft of all ornament, yet surpassing in beauty women covered with adornments?" lends itself easily to speculation that his mother may have been the object of that admiration.

Soon after Leonardo's birth, his mother married a man nicknamed The Quarreler, a farmer, and they soon had four daughters and a son. Many biographies speculate that, in keeping with the custom of the time, Leonardo's father probably arranged for Caterina to keep the infant until he was weaned. In the same year of Leonardo's birth, his father married the 16-year old Albiera Amadora, who remained childless and died twelve years later. Leonardo's father and his young wife lived most of the time in Florence, at least a day's journey from Vinci, where documents suggest that Leonardo remained in the care of his aging paternal grandparents. It is not unlikely that he continued to see his mother who lived about a half-hour's walk from the town, particularly on festive occasions such as fairs and feast days. Thus, the contact he had with his parents was one of constant reminder of his separation from them. He probably saw his mother increasingly surrounded by other children who returned home with her, and his stepmother as progressively fragile until her early death at age 28.

Leonardo's thoughts regarding these missing mothers are not directly available, but certain riddles he recorded suggest he had strong feelings regarding the situation. Examples of riddles written in one of his notebooks take the form of a prophecy for which the answer is the riddle-definition. These include:

> The time of Herod will return, for innocent children will be snatched from nursing mothers and will die of great wounds inflicted by cruel men. (The answer, or to what this riddle is referring, is "Baby goats.")

> Many children will be torn from the arms of their mother, with pitiless blows, and thrown to the ground to be mutilated. (Answer—"Walnuts, acorns, and olives.")

> A tender and kind mother to some of your children, you are a cruel and implacable stepmother to others. I see your sons sold into slavery and their lives serving the oppressor. (Answer—"Donkeys.")

> We will see fathers and mothers take more care of their stepchildren than of their own son. (Answer—"Trees, which allow their sap to nourish grafts.")

Although such examples may have lost something over time and in translation, the common theme seems to be the separation of children from their parents.

Magritte: background of a bourgeoisie

Magritte came from a far different background, one of surface calm and ordinariness. His father was a "small-time" businessman who sold foodstuffs. As a youngster, his favorite game was dressing up as a priest, and conducting mock masses with great seriousness before an altar he had constructed. Summers and holidays for him and his two younger brothers were spent with his grandmother and aunt in Soignies, Belgium, where he particularly enjoyed playing with a little girl in an old abandoned cemetery. "That little girl in the cemetery returns to haunt my daydreams," he wrote many years later. One of their favorite pastimes was to lift up the iron trap-doors and descend into the underground vaults. Magritte's fascination with the vaults and graves seems a symbolic continuation of the "large wood-

209

ed chest standing enigmatically near my cradle" from the early child-hood memory. One day, when coming up out of a vault, Magritte saw an artist who had set up his easel among the tombstones and was painting. It was his first view of an artist, who seemed to be perform-ing some sort of magical activity as he transcribed the scene and objects before him onto a canvas. The artist-magician, the cemetery, and the little girl became fused in his mind together with an intense feeling he could not yet identify, but which he knew would drive him toward some goal.

The death of Magritte's mother

Just as Leonardo's stepmother died as he was entering puberty between age 12 and 13, at the same age Magritte lost his mother. Of this critical event, only the most terse of details is recorded:

> She shared the room of her youngest son (Paul) who, waking to find him-self alone in the middle of the night, roused the rest of the family. They searched the house in vain; then noticing footprints outside the front door and on the sidewalk, they followed them as far as the bridge over the Sambre, the river which ran through the town. She had thrown her-self into the water and, when they recovered the body, they found her nightgown wrapped around her face. It was never known whether she had covered her eyes with it so as not to see the death she had chosen, or whether she had been veiled in that way by the swirling currents.

To his later intimates, Magritte may have provided more infor-mation, but none for public consumption. There is no elaboration of why his mother, Regina, had been sharing the room of his youngest brother, or of any family discussion or exploration of the tragedy. Even the image of following footprints out the door and onto a bridge seems odd and unlikely in reality. A woman so depressed as to take her own life in such a way must have become increasingly inaccessi-ble to her family for some time prior, but Magritte has claimed to remember little more than "a certain pride at being the center of attention in a drama in which I was identified as the son of the dead woman."

Sexuality and privacy

After the death of his mother, Magritte turned his attention increasingly toward painting when he was not attending films about phantom murderers and reading Edgar Allen Poe. As he became older, he was able to identify the feeling behind his fusion of painter-magician, little girl companion, and cemetery:

> It was a pure and powerful feeling: eroticism. The little girl I had known in the old cemetery was the object of my reveries, and she became involved in the animated ambiences of stations, fairs, or towns that I created for her. Thanks to this magical painting, I recaptured the same sensations I had in my childhood.

When he was age 15, two years after the death of his mother, Magritte met a young girl, Georgette, on a merry-go-round at a fair, a setting much like that he imagined or animated for the little girl of the cemetery. A few years later, while studying painting, Magritte married Georgette. From then until his death, she would be his constant companion and primary model. Privacy and insulation became the rule. Magritte hated to travel, and became increasingly housebound. Painting was done primarily in the dining room, between meals. Five clocks, set in synchronicity, rang out each quarter hour as he painted.

Sexuality and secrecy

Leonardo had also begun to study painting in his teenage years. It was most fortunate for him to have such talent because, as an illegitimate son, he would not have been able to enter into the guild of magistrates and notaries, the professions of his paternal family, nor would he have been able to enter a university to become a doctor, apothecary, or nearly any other bourgeois career.

Shortly after the death of his first wife, Leonardo's father married the second of what would eventually be four wives, marriage and childbirth being often more fatal than fulfilling for women of the time. Up until his early 20's, however, Leonardo remained the only child of his father. He had, therefore, remained singular and unique, even if denied that position in his mother's life, as well as excluded from all careers to which any legitimate son could aspire.

But at that point in Leonardo's life, one of his father's succession of wives gave birth to the first child of what would eventually become a legitimate family of nine sons and two daughters. One month later, Leonardo (along with a goldsmith, tailor, and doublet maker) was accused of sodomizing a 17-year old apprentice goldsmith. Although the Florentines had a tolerant view toward homosexuality at times, at other times, the penalty could be death at the stake.

During the months between the accusation and the dismissal of charges, Leonardo may have returned to the home of his mother. This speculation by some biographers is based partly on the assumption that Ser Piero could not have been too pleased by the scandal just as he was again becoming a father, but primarily on notes written by Leonardo during this period on the subject of animal characteristics. Writing of the lion and the lioness, Leonardo may have been referring to his father and mother. The lion, he writes,

> fears nothing so much as the sound of empty wagons and the crowing of cocks (symbols of gossip in that day). The sight of them troubles him greatly, he looks at their crests with terror, falling prey to strange distress, even if his face is covered, whereas the female is ready for any sacrifice to defend her cubs and prevent their being captured.

In the same vein, speaking of the partridge, Leonardo writes:

> It is transformed from a female into a male and forgets its first sex. Being envious, it steals the eggs of other birds and sits on them, but the young always return to their true mother.

He may have been referring to his own sense of having been emasculated by the scandal, when he writes of the beaver:

> When it is pursued, knowing that it is being hunted for the medicinal properties of its testicles, if it cannot escape, it stops and in order to be left in peace by its assailants, bites off its testicles with its sharp teeth and abandons them to the enemy.

From that period, Leonardo apparently decided to live less openly, writing that he would henceforth conduct his life "secretly, with only the darkness of the night for witness." He also wrote, "Many men hate their fathers and lose their friends when upbraided for their faults," and apparently as a warning to himself, "If freedom is dear to you, do not reveal that my face is the prison house of love."

212

Freud studies artists

No less an art critic than Kenneth Clark has referred to Leonardo as "the Hamlet of art history," in reference to the enigma of his life and work onto which so many projections have been offered. And no less an analyst than Freud has attempted to explain this enigma through his own projections. In an October, 1909 letter to Jung, Freud writes:

> The riddle of Leonardo da Vinci's character has suddenly become transparent to me.

Despite the amount of criticism that was heaped on this illumination (including the mistranslation of kite into vulture), a decade later Freud still wrote to Lou Andreas-Salome that his study on Leonardo, centering around his cradle memory of the bird tail parting his lips, was "the only beautiful thing I have ever written." Jung, in friendlier days, responded, " 'Leonardo' is wonderful."

In his study of Leonardo, Freud relates the supposed infant's imagery both to a reminiscence of being suckled at the mother's breast, as well as an unconscious concern with "the idea of an act of fellatio," or desire for a passive homosexual experience. Freud, concerned with the familial contributions to the development of homosexuality, postulated that Leonardo's early family constellation, in which his mother, Caterina, had been over-affectionate to him at the same time that his father was playing a very small role in his life, was the classic situation which would tend to produce homosexuality, i.e., the over-indulgent or smothering mother and the absent father. When Leonardo was returned to his father's household to the care of a young and childless wife, or to his aging grandparents, the severe repression of his close erotic attachment to Caterina would have resulted in an identification with the mother, a consequent homosexual orientation, and the eventual sublimation of much of his sexual energy into curiosity and a craving for knowledge.

Artists study Freud

If artists were a subject of study for Freud, particularly the Renaissance giants Leonardo and Michelangelo, Freud in turn became a subject of study for the Surrealists, the group of painters whose popularity climaxed between the world wars. The work that especially inspired most of this group was Freud's *The Interpretation of Dreams*, with its identification of the four principal means utilized by the dream to disguise its fulfillment of a repressed infantile wish, fulfillment which, if recognized, would cause such disturbance that the dreamer would awake. Modern revisionists believe that Freud had it backwards when he theorized that dreams occur in order to protect sleep, rather than sleep occurring in order to produce dreams. Nevertheless, Freud's formulation of the dream as servant to sleep remains profound.

In any case, the Surrealists enthusiastically began to incorporate condensation, displacement, symbolization, and secondary revision onto their canvases, which, like the dream, simultaneously revealed as it concealed. Because Freud also defined the dream as a primary process involving images more than words, the Surrealists felt a particular affinity existed between dreaming and painting. Amid the general enthusiasm of Surrealists for the findings of Freud, Magritte stood out as the most overtly hostile to psychoanalysis, which he often criticized. Nor did he find "dream-like" to be the compliment to his art which other Surrealists appreciated and for which they strove. Magritte argued:

> My paintings are not like sleeping. Dreams are involuntary and imprecise, qualities that do not apply to my paintings.

In a paradox that matches the imagery of his painting, Magritte was both the exemplar and the exception to the Surrealist ideals. As Salvador Dali's popularity has faded, Magritte's has only increased. But whereas the creed of most Surrealists was the expression of primary process, the power of the unconscious, in life as well as in art, Magritte's life was a study in control. Referring to his life as well as his paintings, Magritte's favorite descriptive adjectives were "neat, precise, orderly, formal, private, and controlled." If one part of his mind roamed in cemeteries and with phantom murderers, propelled by eroticism, the other part required the sanctuary of the safe bourgeois life that had existed before his identification as "the son of the dead woman." He made "a calculated choice to live without history,

214

including my own, and without style," a denial of his identity as the dead woman's son that could only have grown painful after the first forbidden, narcissistic thrill.

The art of dialectics and dreams

Magritte refused to use the Freudian concepts employed by the other Surrealists in describing their artistic process. Rather, he resorted to the Hegelian dialectic of contradictions, in which a union of opposites operated as a fundamental dynamic. A painting, according to Magritte, was "a problem that must be solved." The problem was how to create a paradoxical dialectic, so that "the synthesis through paradox which brings conflicting possibilities into a unified focus suggests the ambivalent nature of reality itself." The right paradoxical juxtaposition of "thesis" and "antithesis" would produce a meaningful "synthesis."

Thus, the "problem of rain" was resolved for Magritte in *The Song of the Storm* with a synthesis of rainy landscape and an enormous storm cloud on the ground. The "problem of woman" was resolved in *The Rape*, in which female sexual parts are juxtaposed onto a woman's face. In *The Human Condition*, a painting placed in front of a window reveals exactly the scene outside that is covered by the painting. The "problem of shoes" resolves in *The Red Model* in which "the union of a human foot and a shoe is actually a monstrous custom."

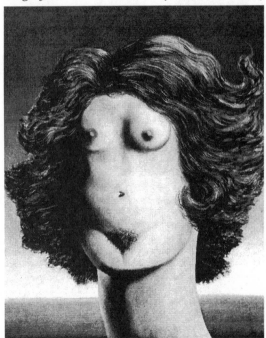

The Rape

215

The Red Model

As Magritte came to "the problem of the sea," he did acknowledge that, "The special problems the painter must resolve are psychological in nature." For the resolution of the problem of the sea, Magritte created *The Collective Invention*. Of this painting, he writes :

> *The Collective Invention* was the answer to the problem of the sea. On the beach I laid a new species of siren, whose head and upper body were those of a fish and whose lower parts, from stomach to legs, were those of a woman.

Hegelian dialectics aside, a psychoanalytic observer might speculate that the problem of the sea was that it had killed Magritte's mother, throwing her dead body back up with revealed sexuality and concealed humanity.

In Magritte's later description of that event, it is notable that he wondered not why his mother acted so drastically, but whether she had intended that the nightgown be wrapped around her face. What dialectic problems Magritte has solved in his paintings of *The Lovers, The Heart of the Matter,* and *The Invention of Life* with the repetitive image of every head completely wrapped in a cloth, seem better explained by the language of condensation, displacement, symbolization, and secondary revision of his mother's inability to mirror her abandoned son.

The Collective Invention

The last years of Leonardo's mother?

From a journal entry in one of Leonardo's notebooks which reads, "16 July/Caterina came, 16 July 1493," some biographers have concluded that the housekeeper named Caterina who came to live with Leonardo in Milan on that date was his mother, Caterina. Only a very few of Leonardo's many thousands of journal entries have a date doubly recorded in the above manner, such as the notable entry of his father's death. By 1493, Caterina would have been 66, her son 43. Two of her daughters had died by that time, as well as her other son. A tax register tracks her until about that time, living in humble circumstances in Vinci. An earlier note by Leonardo states, "What la Caterina

The Lovers

wishes to do," possibly interpreted as an invitation to her to come. Lending more credence that these notations do refer to his mother, on the other side of the page that notes the date of Caterina's arrival, Leonardo also lists names from his childhood: "Antonio (his grandfather), Lucia (his grandmother), Piero (his father), Leonardo (himself)."

There is scarcely any other mention of this Caterina until a year or two later when a list, entitled *Expenses of Caterina's Burial*, including wax, the bier, the cross, priests, clerks, gravediggers, bell, book, and sponge appears, along with a short list of *Earlier Expenses* for a doctor, sugar, and candles. The expense, although not great, is larger than would be expected for a servant who had only been in the home two or three years.

Freud interprets the Mona Lisa

If *The Collective Invention* solved a problem regarding what was probably both an earlier and final loss of his mother in terms of primary process imagery, did the *Mona Lisa* serve a similar function for Leonardo? Regarding this painting, Freud addressed two primary issues: the subject's enigmatic smile, and the artist's characteristic inability to finish the painting.

Freud believed the enigmatic smile of the *Mona Lisa* was a smile that reminded Leonardo of his mother, as well as the qualities and virtues he looked for in a woman: gentleness, understanding, indulgence, patience, constancy. Several observers have speculated that the face so resembles Leonardo's at a certain period that he may have been painting himself. Or again, he may have been painting his mother's face which could well have resembled his. The painting was commissioned by a rich man who wished a painting of his third wife, Lisa di Gherardini, who would have been in her mid 20's when Leonardo began the sketching.

Some biographers report that the subject in the painting had lost a child not long before the project began, and that Leonardo had to coax smiles out of her by surrounding her with musicians, singers, and clowns. Most observers agree it is a fleeting smile, with nothing of seduction in it, and little of happiness, although Freud saw the smile quite differently, believing that it:

> awakened in Leonardo, as a grown man, the memory of the mother of his early childhood, and in her smile he saw his mother's happy smile of sensual rapture. The face was the perfect representation of the contrasts which dominate the erotic life of women; the contrast between reserve and seduction, and between the most devoted tenderness and a sensuality that is ruthlessly demanding—consuming men as if they were alien beings.

It may be that the smile, faint or sensual, that the subject bestowed on Leonardo was so beautiful to him because it reflected the love of a mother seeing her lost child as she gazed at Leonardo. The mirror he thus looked into would be his idealization of the look he most wished to see bestowed on himself: his mother mourning his loss, rather than simply rapidly replacing him with other legitimate children. (It had, at least, taken his father more than 20 years and four wives to do the same.)

Freud notes that Leonardo's next painting of the sacred trio of child, mother, and grandmother, *The Virgin, Saint Anne, and the Christ Child*, places the same *Mona Lisa* smile on both women who appear to be about the same age as his own mother and first step-mother would have been, thereby depicting idealizing mirrors of those two formative figures beaming at a somewhat naughty little Jesus with a lamb. (In pressing a mistaken image even further, Freud is able to discern the outline of a vulture in the skirt of one of the women.)

After four years of effort, everyone gave up hope that the painting would ever be finished. Indeed, one of the characteristics of Leonardo was his striking inability to finish most of the few paintings he ever attempted. Some biographers believe that Leonardo could not give up the image of his dream woman, placed in front of a phantasmagorical landscape, and painted entirely without collaborators

The Virgin, St. Anne, and the Christ Child

(a rare style in those times). By procrastinating on the *Mona Lisa* until the commissioner no longer wished it, Leonardo would have been able to keep it in his own possession.

An additional unconscious motivation, according to Freud, was Leonardo's identification with his father who had begotten and then abandoned him, reflected in Leonardo's passionate beginning of his paintings, followed by his inability to carry through the tedious detail of bringing them to completion. In Freud's analysis, then, Leonardo's identification with his mother had caused his passive homosexuality, and his identification with his father, his procrastination. Further, by rebelling against his father, Leonardo rejected authority for science, into which pursuits he was able to sublimate his sexuality.

In short, there was something for everyone to either love or hate in Freud's analysis of Leonardo or, as he said, "will please all friends and will, I hope, arouse the abhorrence of all strangers."

Dualism, dialectics, and dreams

The Renaissance, of which Leonardo was a primary exemplar, focused on beauty and spirituality, and the artistic achievements were grand and titanic. Good is depicted as triumphant, and evil as tormented. The Surrealists, of whom Magritte was arguably the most skilled, were unalterably opposed to the Western dualistic view of good and evil, a duality espoused in the Renaissance without doubt or irony. Strongly influenced by Freud, as well as by the political currents of the time, Surrealists brought about a synthesis of paradox in their work, just as the unconscious does through its dream work. If the Renaissance celebrated the Superego and the Enlightenment the Ego, the Surrealists recognized the intense power of the Id as a source not only of creative activity, but also the repository of dangerous tendencies.

Conclusion

Artistic, cultural, and political fashions come and go, even though they appear sweeping and universal at the time. What remains when all the tumult and the shouting die, according to Freud, is an individual's primal relationship to the parents. And whether the heated visions of the Renaissance or the cool dreams of the Surrealists are the mode of imagery, the great works of art express repressed primal wishes and fears. The *Mona Lisa* and *The Collective Invention*, for all their superficial differences, may on one level simply reflect the wish of two individuals to see themselves mirrored in the eyes of their mothers as irreplaceable and beloved. In that sense, these paintings have found the missing mothers.

Alma Bond is a diplomate in Psychoanalysis, American Board of Psychotherapy, and a fellow and training analyst at the Institute for Psychoanalytic Training and Research. She was among the first U.S. nonmedical analysts admitted to membership in the International Psychoanalytic Association. in 1989. Dr. Bond now devotes full time to writing. She is the author or co-author of Is There Life After Analysis *(Baker Book House, 1993),* Dream Portrait *(International Universities Press, 1992),* America's First Feminist: The Courage of Deborah Sampson *(Paragon House, 1992),* Who Killed Virginia Woolf, A Psychobiography *(Human Sciences Press, 1989), and* Diary of a Grandmother: A Psychoanalyst's Personal Odyssey *(Bridge Works, in publication). She has written many articles for psychoanalytic journals, and is the winner of the* American Literary Press *short story contest; her winning story,* The Latch That Wouldn't Lock, *was published in* Top Ten Stories of 1993. *She is a member of the American Society of Journalists and the Florida Freelance Writers Association.*

Seeing the truth of people and events and things needs imagination.

—Joanna Field

Virginia Woolf
Manic-Depressive Psychosis and Genius
by Alma H. Bond, Ph.D.

Virginia Woolf, one of the greatest women writers who ever lived, was diagnosed as a manic depressive by physicians and family alike. She suffered at least four major psychotic breakdowns in her lifetime, and took her own life by drowning at the age of 59. This paper is an attempt to understand some of the sources both of her genius and of her pathology, to understand them in the light of Margaret Mahler's theory of separation-individuation, and to reopen that dark and insufficiently explored territory, the disease of manic depression.

The manic polarity of the disease of manic depression has been relatively neglected in the annals of psychiatric literature, as compared with the volumes published on depression. This phenomenon may well be due to the realities of treating manic patients. They are often quite demanding and perhaps more difficult for the therapist to treat than any other diagnostic category. Research in this area in recent years has been largely biochemical and genetic. Psychoanalytically, work seems to have stopped in the '50's, and the little that has been done, with a few exceptions, deals mainly with fixations of psychosexual development. Freud himself, unbelievably, deals significantly with mania only in two short references, and mania is not even listed in the Abstracts of the Standard Edition of the Complete Psychological Works of Sigmund Freud. His statement about mania, "Here are happenings rich in unresolved riddles," is almost as true today as it was then.

In her landmark discussion of genius, Phyllis Greenacre remarks, "I am myself largely convinced that genius is a 'gift of the gods,' and is already laid down at birth, probably as a sport development which finds especially favorable soil for its evolution in families where there is also a good inheritance of intellect and a favorable background for identification."

Virginia's Illustrious Family

If ever an artist met Greenacre's criteria for genius, that artist was Virginia Woolf. She was born on January 25, 1882, as a result of what her biographer, Quentin Bell, called "the imperfect art of contraception in the nineteenth century." There is no doubt that she, like many artists, began life as a sensitive, sensuous, superbly endowed individual. She belonged to one of England's great literary families. Her father was Sir Leslie Stephen, critic and editor of the renowned Dictionary of National Biography. His first wife was the daughter of Thackeray. Generations of his ancestors had been involved in literature. Virginia's great-grandfather, grandfather, uncle, and cousin were all prominent authors. Her mother was Julia Jackson, herself a published writer and the granddaughter of a French nobleman who was page to Marie Antoinette. Virginia's sister, Vanessa, became a celebrated painter who married the critic, Clive Bell, while her brother, Adrian, was a distinguished psychoanalyst, writer and editor.

Virginia married Leonard Woolf, author and publisher. Her closest friend and homosexual lover was Lady Vita Sackville-West, descendant of an ancient house of nobility, and an illustrious poet and novelist of the time. Virginia's godfather was the great American poet, James Russell Lowell, one of a coterie of famous men and women who frequented the Stephen household and to whom Virginia addressed her first recorded letter at the age of six.

If Virginia Stephen received the "gift of the gods" at birth, the devil apparently gave her a gift as well. For it is widely accepted today in the psychiatric world that the disease of manic depression has an inherited, probably metabolic, substructure, and indeed Virginia's biographer reveals that many of her close relatives were known to be psychotic. Virginia's half-sister, Laura, a schizophrenic, was institutionalized most of her life. Sir Leslie Stephen, Virginia's father, underwent a series of "nervous collapses" in his fifties. Her cousin, the poet James Stephen, was a floridly psychotic manic depressive, who took his own life at the age of 33. Virginia's uncle, the eminent James Fitzjames, deteriorated rapidly after the death of his own son and became unable to function, dying two years later. Virginia Stephen, then, born to a family of geniuses and madmen, was at birth already a candidate for both of these human conditions.

Her mother, Julia Stephen, was a gifted woman who had a talent for symbiosis. She and Virginia were wondrously matched the first four or five months of Virginia's life. Virginia's writing makes clear that Mrs. Stephen was able to provide a luxuriously sensual atmosphere for her which could lift the exquisitely endowed child to heights of ecstasy. Virginia later called the idyllic experience of this early period "the base upon which life stands." Out of this base, the uniqueness of Virginia Woolf would emerge. Woolf describes one of her first memories, her early intoxication with her mother:

Virginia Woolf

> My mother would come out onto her balcony in a white dressing gown. There were passion flowers growing on the wall; they were great starry blossoms, with purple streaks, and large green buds. If I were a painter I should paint these first impressions in pale yellow, and silver, and green. Everything would be large and dim; and what was seen would be at the same time heard.

Mahler's Phases of Development

Margaret Mahler and her co-workers, in their book, *The Psychological Birth of the Human Infant*, describe the phases of normal development of the infant:

1. The *autistic* phase. For a few weeks the infant functions almost entirely on a biological and instinctual level.

2. The *symbiotic* phase. A time, from one to five months, of social and biological interdependence, in which the infant functions as though she and her mother were a single omnipotent unity.

3. The *separation-individuation* phase. From around five months to two and a half years, it consists of four sub-phases:

> a. *Individuation:* As the infant learns to crawl, her total dependence on her mother decreases.
>
> b. *Practicing:* The infant moves further away from her mother, and enjoys her developing skills.
>
> c. *Rapprochement:* The infant needs to return to mother for refueling and reassurance.
>
> d. *Consolidation:* The infant begins to consolidate her individuality as a separate entity.

When the symbiotic period of complete interdependence is a joyful one (as seems certain in the Mrs. Stephen-Virginia couple), the infant is free to follow normal developmental processes that eventually lead away from mother.

The separation-individuation phases, however, requires different psychological skills of the mother. Now the mother must enjoy and be in tune with her baby's excitement in exploring, touching, and reaching out to the world.

Mrs. Stephen almost certainly was not as good a "mother of separation" as she was of symbiosis. In *To the Lighthouse,* the character of Mrs. Ramsey who, Virginia states, was modeled almost entirely on her mother, seeks continuous involvement with others to ward off a sense of inner emptiness and loneliness. Woolf writes,

226

If one is a Mrs. Ramsey, one can never let go of relationships because they all are needed to sustain life.

Such a mother could hardly allow Virginia to remain at her own play when the mother needed all attention directed to herself. Mrs. Ramsey muses on just such feelings:

Oh, but she never wanted James to grow a day older! or Cam either. These two she would have liked to keep forever just as they were... nothing made up for the loss...Why should they grow up so fast? Why should they go to school? She would have liked always to have had a baby. She was happiest carrying one in her arms.

Such demands on the infant Virginia must have exerted a tremendous force to keep her from growing up. But the strength gained in the richness of the symbiosis, coupled with the mighty push of developing ego faculties, temporarily stimulated the child to fight off the encompassing needs of her mother. Greenacre, in her discussion of future genius, says,

Rapid unfolding of the inner...pressure for unusual growth in some way [is] inherent in the child himself.

In my opinion, these inner demanding pressures are especially strong in the incipient manic, as they are in the genius-to-be.

In *A Sketch of the Past*, Woolf describes this phenomenon:

One must get the feeling that made her press on, the little creature driven on as she was by growth of her legs and arms, driven without her being able to stop it or to change it, driven as a plant is driven up out of the earth, up until the stalk grows, the leaf grows, buds swell.

Virginia Woolf's pathology may have begun at this early phase of develpment, out of the conflict between yielding to the magnetic pull of her mother, and the strident organismic thrust to individuation.

The tragic life and early death of her older half-sister, Stella Stephen, must have served as a warning to Virginia. Stella, described by Virginia as being "without any ambition or character of her own," yielded up her own identity, to be the handmaiden of her mother. According to Kaplan,

Were the toddler to succumb to the absolute bliss of oneness before carving out his own space in the world, the child would be reabsorbed into the being of his mother. His surrender would be tantamount to ceasing to exist.

Virginia, unlike Stella, escaped, for a time, through her momentous push to action. Virginia Stephen chose to live in her own ego instead of her mother's. Virginia clearly was able to "carve out her own space in the world."

However, like Stella, Virginia never completely outgrew her symbiotic attachment, but, in a psychological sense, remained part of her mother forever.

Standing by a flower bed at St. Ives, Virginia muses:

I was looking at a plant with a spread of leaves, and it seemed suddenly plain that the flower itself was part of the earth; that a ring enclosed what was the flower, and that was the real flower; part earth, part flower.

Here she expresses that, on the deepest level, mother and child, earth and plant remained symbolically intertwined. This theme, that each individual is but a part of a larger unit, appears and reappears throughout her works, and climaxes in *The Waves*, that unsurpassed study of the establishment and dissolution of identity throughout the life cycle.

According to Freud, the factor that brings about psychosis is a conflict between the ego and a reality that has become intolerable. All her life, Virginia Woolf was caught in the conflict between yielding to the pull of regressive inner forces and the clamorous organismic thrust of development. The terrible reality she had to bear was the loss of her mother forever. For Virginia, there was no "going home."

The practicing period

According to Mahler, the phase of differentiation blends imperceptibly into the practicing period. So excited is the child by the process of exploring the new-found world that her mother fades into the background for long periods of time. The infant becomes more interested in exploring the world and feeling the exhilaration of his growth. Greenacre calls this period the "love affair with the world."

While the practicing period is exhilarating for most toddlers, it must have been magnificent for Virginia, the artist. Imagine, for example, the exaltation experienced by Virginia first toddling down the hills of St. Ives to the "thick escallonia bushes whose leaves one picked and pressed and smelt," or see her energetically carrying oak apples and acorns back and forth among the great ferns of the Stephen children's "fairyland" playground, or following with widening eyes the wonderful, wandering butterflies soaring over the gardens.

Her third memory, which took place during her second summer at St. Ives, hints of the love for her mother that became transformed into her "love affair with the world":

> All these colours and sound memories hang together at St. Ives... It still makes me feel warm; as if everything were ripe; humming; sunny; smelling so many smells at once...The gardens gave off a murmur of bees; the apples were red and gold; there were also pink flowers; and grey and silver leaves. The buzz, the croon, the smell, all seemed to press voluptuously against some membrane...It was rapture rather than ecstasy.

According to Freud, there is always an "economic condition" to be fulfilled before the individual can experience exuberance. In all states such as joy and triumph, a volume of energy, previously inhibited, suddenly becomes available. The larger the volume of energy inhibited and suddenly released, the greater the degree of exaltation. Restrained during the period of differentiation by a needy mother, the sheer amount of power suddenly released must have led to an ecstatic practicing period indeed. It is this great biological surplus of energy, originally held back, that fuels the great organic force of energy released in the manic state.

The surge to action remained characteristic of Virginia all her life, even during her well periods. For example, her niece, Angelica, informs us,

> Virginia danced around her [Vanessa] like the dragonfly round the water-lily, darting in to attack and soaring away before Vanessa could take action... Virginia's attitude was far from sitting, it was striding; long narrow thighs and shins in long tweed skirts, loping over the downs,

across the water-meadows, beside the river, or through the traffic in London, under the trees in the park and round the square. She was never placed, never quite at rest.

Rapprochement

About the middle of the second year, the toddler, who could conquer the world, suddenly finds his omnipotence punctured. Bewildered by his inability to make it alone, dim memories of bliss and ease lure him back to mother. So the recalcitrant toddler decides to try mother again. What a shock to discover there is "nobody home." Mother has invested her energy elsewhere. There is no place for baby to return. Mahler terms this fateful crossroad the *rapprochement crisis*. Each child seals his future fate by the way he deals with this crisis. For Virginia, the rapprochement crisis was never resolved, but was acted out all her life in alternating states of mania and depression.

She writes of her mother,

> I can see now that she was living on such an extended surface that she had not time, nor strength, to concentrate... upon me... Can l ever remember being alone with her for more than a few minutes?

Her sister, Vanessa, and her brother, Thoby, had "some technique for making the toddler, Virginia, look purple with rage," and turn "the most lovely flaming red." Such experiences, in all likelihood led to Virginia's feeling that she was "quite unable to deal with the pain of discovering that people hurt each other." Surely Virginia at that time felt as Rhoda did in *The Waves* when she said,

> I shall fall alone thru this thin sheet into a gulf of fire. And thou will not help me. More cruel than the old torturers, you will let me fall, and will tear me to pieces when I am fallen.

Flooded with rage and feelings of helplessness, Virginia, like many of us, must have wondered why her mother was not available to help protect her. As an older girl, in what is possibly a screen memory, Virginia remembered the incredible agonies she suffered while waiting for her mother to come home from one of her innumerable charity ventures. Louis, in *The Waves*, says,

> I am always the youngest, the most innocent, the most trustful! You are all protected. I am naked.

Thus must Virginia have felt at the hands of her sadistic siblings, which left her little alternative but to chance the terrors of re-engulfment and return to her mother's lap.

Through the character of Rhoda in *The Waves*, Woolf says,

> I am afraid of the shock of sensation that leaps upon me, because I cannot deal with it as you do—I cannot make one moment merge into the next. To me they are all violent, all separate; and if I fall under the shock of the leap of the moment, you will be on me tearing me to pieces.

In a later work, she says,

> For the reason that it destroys the fullness of life, any break—like that of house-moving—causes me extreme distress; it breaks, it shallows; it turns the depth into hard thin splinters.

It seems likely that the "first break that destroyed the fullness of life," occurred when she tried to re-enter the symbiotic state with her mother and found the place already filled by her new brother. Woolf's feelings on the death of her mother can serve equally well to illustrate the effect on the 22-month-old child of being dethroned by her brother:

> It was the greatest disaster that could happen; it was as though on some brilliant day of spring the racing clouds of a sudden stood still, grew dark, and massed themselves; the wind flagged, and all creatures on earth moaned or wandered seeking aimlessly...

Flush, that whimsical dog created by Virginia, reigned at the feet of his famous mistress, Elizabeth Barrett Browning, until he was dethroned by his successor, Robert Browning. The painful rupture of his paradise, and the resulting agonies of jealousy he suffered sound autobiographical, and in all likelihood were inspired—originally, at any rate—by Virginia's own fall from grace.

An earlier reflection of her jealousy and vengefulness (as reproduced by Henig) can be seen in the *Experiences of a Paterfamilias*, Virginia's first recorded story, written at the age of ten. It concerns the domestic foibles of a man and his wife, and centers on the husband's jealousy of the new baby. It begins:

> My wife a month ago got a child and I regret to say that I wish he had never been born, for I am made to give in to him on everything.

A letter concerning her sister Vanessa's new baby, when Virginia was 30 years old, confirms that her feelings about infants had not changed very much. She writes:

> I doubt that I shall ever have a baby. Its voice is too terrible, a senseless scream, like an ill-omened cat.

Superego development

In the formation of her superego, it seems that there were at least two great areas in which Virginia's psychological development was immature: in the establishment of the superego as a control system, and in its ability to serve as a regulator of self-esteem.

According to Meissner, when parental images have not been internalized, the superego cannot assume the functions of parental control. The superego of the manic depressive fails to modulate mood. Hence the individual remains dependent for this on the outside world.

Virginia's "purple rages" inform us that her superego was not functioning well as a control system. While still in the nursery, Virginia,

> ...knew how to create an atmosphere of thunderous and oppressive gloom, a winter of discontent. It was done without words, somehow her brothers and sisters were made to feel that she had raised a cloud above their heads from which, at any moment, the fires of heaven might burst.

The following story, charming as it is, also predicts difficulties in the internalization of parental demands. The two and a half-year-old Virginia had scratched her four year-old brother and was told by their father to apologize. Virginia responded with "Why have we got nails, Papa?"

The need for approval and affirmation

The second great area, the conflictual need for mother's approval and affirmation, also presented Virginia with difficulties. Her sister Vanessa relates an incident that illustrates the manner in which Mrs. Stephen received Virginia's "gifts." Virginia, age ten, was the chief writer of a little newspaper, published by the Stephen children, called "The Hyde Park Gate News." Virginia and Vanessa surreptitiously laid a new copy of the paper on the table next to Mrs. Stephen. They then crept into the next room to watch their mother's reaction. As they looked, Vanessa reported, Virginia "trembled with excitement." They saw their mother's figure outlined in the lamplight, sitting by the fire. For a long time, Mrs. Stephen ignored the paper. Then she picked it up and began to read. The girls held their breath as they watched.

"Rather clever, I think," said Mrs. Stephen, and laid the paper down. This minimal response, according to Vanessa, "was enough to thrill Virginia." If Virginia could be "thrilled" by such an unenthusiastic reaction, it would seem that praise from her mother must have been rare indeed. The incident speaks of deep feelings of unworthiness in Virginia, which made her yearn for her mother's approval. When the infant's first offerings are devalued by the mother, self-esteem may be undermined for life. And there is no reason to assume that Virginia's first "gifts" were met with any greater enthusiasm than the "gift" of the ten-year old child.

Here, in capsule form, is concealed Virginia's latent psychosis. Intimidated by a sense of worthlessness about the value of her production, Virginia pressed to win her mother's approval. Hoping for a positive response from Mrs. Stephen, Virginia, with great excitement, threw off the deprecation of her own superego, only to have it return and crush her.

In an important passage from *Between the Acts*, Miss LaTrobe, a playwright who has just witnessed a successful production of her play, says,

> The bells had stopped; the audience; also the actors. She could straighten her back. She could open her arms. She could say to the world, you have taken my gift! Glory possessed her—for one moment! But what had she given? A cloud that melted the other clouds on the horizon. It was in the giving that the triumph failed. Her gift meant nothing.

In adulthood, Virginia's triumph, like that of Miss LaTrobe's, was in the writing. At the conclusion of each of her major works, she experienced a terrifying depression. Many of her major novels ended with Woolf entering a psychosis.

If each work represented an early gift to the mother, with all of the expectations of glory, each ended with crushing disappointment. Virginia Woolf could not bear to reread anything she had written, and any copy of a journal in which she was published was completely ruined for her. "Is the time coming," she wailed, "when I can endure to read my own writing in print without blushing-shivering, and wishing to take cover?" Mrs. Stephen's rejection of Virginia's gifts during infancy and latency was a paradigm, when introjected by Virginia, of her later failure to meet her own standards.

Virginia Woolf was a feminist

Virginia Woolf was a feminist 50 years before feminism became popular. Pippett suggests that "as a little girl, Virginia would like to have been the one thing she could not be, a tom-boy." In the cultural and social climate of the times, in which men were the grossly favored sex, various passages in Woolf's work suggest that envy of the positions and trappings of power men enjoyed played a central role in her pathology. Virginia's overwhelming feelings of jealousy and envy may well have found their impetus at the birth of Adrian, his mother's favorite. For Bell states that "in the nursery it was believed that all Stephens were born with tails seven inches long."

In her famous treatise on feminism, *A Room of One's Own*, Woolf writes a hilarious comparison of food served to men and women scholars at the fictitious University of Oxbridge. In it, she shows how the dinners symbolically illustrated the status of the sexes at the time. The men were served the "whitest of sauces, partridges many and varied, with all their retinue of sauces and salads—the sharp and the sweet; their sprouts foliated as rosebuds." The women were fed gravy soup, and plain beef with attendant greens and potatoes, "a homely trinity" suggesting to Woolf "the rumps of cattle in a muddy market." Associating this outrageous discrimination to the plight of the Manx cat, that "tailless creature from the Isle of Man," Woolf asks,

> Was he really born so, or had he lost his tail in an accident? The tailless
> cat...is rarer than one thinks....What a difference a tail makes.

If the Oxbridge meals refer to the food of love served to Virginia and her brother Adrian in the nursery, and if the "cat without a tail" gets to eat only "the rumps of cattle in a muddy market," no wonder Virginia refused to eat during her psychotic periods. And if only a boy with a penis can "think well, love well, sleep well," no wonder Virginia Woolf left behind her a history of homosexuality, her continuing attempt to reunite with the early mother.

Virginia's progress in separation-individuation can be measured by indicators such as the quality and measure of her wooing behavior as a toddler, the intensity of her anger, and a readily discernible ambivalence conflict—a tendency to alternately cling to and try to excape from the other person.

Virginia's wooing behavior

Virginia was known to family and friends alike for her persistent wooing behavior, and it remained characteristic of her to woo the important women in her life with a vengeance. Bell states,

> As a child she would ask her sister 'Do you like me better than - - - -?' naming a list of friends and relatives. As a woman in her fifties she played the same game with Vanessa, who could never adequately respond to her sister's declarations of love... To satisfy that need, as imperative in its way as a junkie's, Virginia turned to women of a different sort, to women who had retained the knack of expressing simple affection. But even when she obtained the enormous infusions of affection and esteem that she required, the effects soon wore off, for she did not have that irrational, unshakable sense of her own worth which...is found in people who have been extravagantly wanted and loved as children.

"Purple rages"

Children who have experienced difficulties in earlier subphases get angrier than other children, what Bowlby called their "continued protest." The "purple rages of a lovely flaming red" and the "atmosphere of thunderous and oppressive gloom" she was able to generate in the nursery speak of a "continued protest" of the highest order.

235

"Drawing near and receding"

Another diagnostic indicator is pointed out by Mahler, Pine and Bergman, who have observed that, in troubled children, "the ambivalence conflict is discernible during the rapprochement subphase in rapidly alternating clinging and negativistic behavior." Woolf beautifully describes this conflict in her second novel, *Night and Day*:

> It seemed to...[Mary] that Katherine possessed a curious power of drawing near and receding, which sent alternate currents thru...[Mary] far more quickly than usual, and kept her in a condition of curious alertness.

This "curious power" apparently invaded all of Virginia's relationships, for Bell states,

> There was no one whose stock did not rise and fall in the uncertain market of her [Virginia's] regard.

A photograph of Virginia in her third year graphically demonstrates that the conflict was present at the rapprochement period. In the portrait, Mrs. Stephen is lovingly looking down at her small daughter, who is sitting on her lap. But Virginia, perhaps startled by the flash of the camera, is dramatically demarcated from and turned away from her mother. In an adequately developing toddler in the rapprochement phase, one would like to see greater mastery of aggression, and the ability to contain her anger, which would have enabled her to turn to her mother for comfort.

She had only two basic moods: elation and despair. Each subphase of separation individuation has a basic mood most characteristic of it, which "leaves its mark upon the individual throughout the life span." As a manic depressive, Virginia Woolf alternated between two basic moods all her life. The depressive mood, in all likelihood, crystallized during the rapprochement period when Virginia first became aware that she and her mother were two separate people. At this time, quite probably, she felt as Bernard did in *The Waves*, when he said,

> I do not believe in separation. We are not single...

And she learned that, with all her talents and appeal, she was unable to coerce her mother to return to their former state of bliss.

This "dark part of the human condition" is superbly described by Rhoda in *The Waves*:

> Lord, how unutterably disgusting life is! Here we are among the bread crumbs, and the stained napkins again. That knife is already congealing with grease... Always it begins again; always there is the enemy... Call the waiter. Pay the bill... We must pull ourselves up out of our chairs. We must find our coats. We must go... Must, must, must—detestable word. Once more, I, who had thought myself immune, who had said "Now I am rid of all that," find that the wave had tumbled me over, head over heels, scattering my possessions, leaving me to collect, to assemble, to heap together, summon my forces, rise and confront the enemy.

But Virginia Woolf's most characteristic mood was elation. In her well periods, she was filled with the delight of discovery experienced by the practicing infant. Bell expertly captures this quality:

> It was in movement that she was most truly herself. Then she reminded one of some fantastic bird, abruptly throwing up her head and crowing with delighted amusement at some idea, word, some paradox, that took her fancy. Her conversation was full of surprises, of unpredictable questions, of fantasy and of laughter—the happy laughter of a child who finds the world more strange, more absurd and more beautiful than anyone could have imagined.

Beck paints a picture of the manic patient which in many ways makes a brilliant portrait of Virginia Woolf:

> [The manic] conveys a picture of complete lightness of heart... such as, 'I am bursting with joy.' Capable of getting gratification from a wide variety of experiences, the intensity of his gratification far exceeds that of his normal phase—a leaf falling from a tree may cause feelings of ecstasy. He experiences a thrill when he thinks about all his attributes... (and) plunges into his various interests with abundant zest. He experiences a broadening as well as an intensification of interests, full of fun, optimistic about anything he undertakes and tends to deny the possibility of any personal weakness, deficiencies, or problems. In his expansive way, he wishes to take in everything life has to offer and at the same time, demonstrate to an ever increasingly greater extent his superior attributes. In summary, he tends to be energetic, aggressive, animated, and overactive; and he presents a demeanor of impulsivity, boldness, and lack of inhibition. He is generally sociable, genial, and exhibitionistic.

The manic condition—regression to the practicing subphase

The similarity between the manic patient and that of the infant of the practicing subphase of separation individuation cannot be a coincidence. Many manics, as was Virginia Woolf, are well-endowed individuals who frequently were considered, before their illness, as the most promising members of the family. As such, they were able to experience particularly rich and exciting practicing subphases. The fright of the regressive pull to engulfment experienced in the pre-manic state leads to a return to a caricature of the practicing sub-phase of development. The manic condition, then, is a desperate compromise between the attempt to avoid further regression to the symbiotic state of dissolution of self, and the frantic urge to ward off a painful reality.

Virginia Woolf, at terrible crises of her life, such as the death of her mother, in order to ward off unspeakable pain and depression, conceivably experienced a tremendous regressive pull back to the stage of symbiosis. To avoid this double jeopardy of deep depression and/or loss of self, Virginia "chose" a middle path, a travesty of the one so beautifully carved out by the normal infant, who evades the depression caused by loss of symbiotic bliss as well as the engulfing arms of her mother by running to the welcoming arms of the world.

The actual death of her mother, which took place when Virginia was 13, on the eve of adolescence, that second biological upsurge toward individuation, was a repetition of the great loss of her mother during the period of differentiation, a reality too terrible to bear; for shortly after her mother died, Virginia experienced her first psychotic breakdown. Frances Baudry, in a paper presented to the National Psychological Association for Psychoanalysis, stated that Virginia Woolf used sensation to replace emotion. It would be more complete to say that Woolf regressed during the period of rapprochement from the painful emotions of loss and despair to the sensate world of the practicing period of separation-individuation.

For at least four periods of her adult life, Virginia avoided the pain of loss and depression and the dissolution of a deeper regression by turning to the ecstatic, lively, manic state. Her use of this affect as

238

a defense is illustrated in the section previously referred to from *A Room of One's Own* on the "tailless Manx cat," when she "burst out laughing" at the sight of the "abrupt and truncated animal."

Virginia Woolf's regression to the *practicing subphase*, ordinarily one of nature's most beautiful and creative growth periods, helped both to exalt her art to its loftiest peak and to steer her descent into madness and the depths of human despair.

Summary

Virginia Stephen was a member of one of England's great literary families, many of whom were also mentally ill. An exquisitely endowed infant, she was beautifully matched with her mother during the symbiotic state of development, and later called this period "the base upon which life stands."

Difficulties began as early as the differentiation subphase of separation. Mrs. Stephen appeared to be a narcissistic woman, who required constant affirmation, and thus was unable to respond to the needs of a developing child.

Virginia probably was rescued from engulfment by a powerful biologically determined practicing period of separation-individuation, a great organismic surge as characteristic of toddlers who are incipient manics as of future genius. Because of the strong regressive pull, Virginia experienced a particularly high-powered glee in evading the field of her mother.

Deflated by events such as the sadism of her siblings, Virginia attempted to return to her mother. But Mrs. Stephen was not available. As a result she was unable to proceed to an age-adequate level of development. The raw rage lay smoldering within until many years later, when it burst forth to power her manic attacks. This failure of rapprochement presumably deflated Virginia, and resulted in a basic mood of depression, already apparent in the nursery, and of manic elation, characteristic of her even in her well periods.

Sara Epstein is an Assistant Clinical Professor at Los Angeles County-University of Southern California School of Medicine. She did her undergraduate work at Smith College, her medical training at the Medical College of Pennsylvania, and her psychiatry residency at LAC-USC Psychiatric Hospital in Los Angeles. She then took psychoanalytic training at the Psychoanalytic Center of California, with special interest in creativity, depression, and public sector psychiatry. She is also a gifted writer and musician.

"Early in 1986, my mother gave me an article about Elizabeth Layton which proved so interesting that by that October, I traveled to Kansas to have the privilege of meeting her. I was able to speak with her several times, as well as with Don Lambert and Robert Ault, who had played critical roles in making her known to the world.

I not only gained additional respect for Layton's achievements in artistic expression and outstanding sublimation, but also for her as a person—generous, whimsical and plucky. I present the following in appreciation and admiration of Layton and my mother, who "discovered" the artist for me. The contributions of both of these women in their later years have been of great and enduring value." *Sara Epstein*

In the next two chapters, two authors talk about Elizabeth Layton from different perspectives. Psychiatrist and musician Sara Epstein describes Layton's early life, her personal experience of depression and shock therapy, and her recovery after taking up contour drawing. Then gerontologist Vivian Rogers discusses the significance that Layton's remarkable development and achievement in old age has for all of us.

Elizabeth Layton
Life-Long Depression, with Healing Through Creativity in Later Life
Sara Epstein, M.D.

Elizabeth Converse Layton was born in Wellsville, Kansas, population 550, in 1909. Father Asa owned the local newspaper. He was a favorite of the press, a dapper dresser and a critic of proposals for art in Topeka (ironic in view of our subject's later career). Mother May was Kansas poet laureate in the 1920's, and a featured columnist on the paper. Her column often dealt with private events in the Converse family. Mother's twin sister Maude, a pioneering female photographer, took myriad pictures of the young Elizabeth in fanciful poses and costumes. Layton described growing up feeling lonely and yet, between mother's newspaper column and aunt's photographic studies, exposed.

Layton finished high school in 1926. She had two years of college at Ottowa University in Kansas, and then married Clyde Nichols, a milkman with whom she had attended high school. They moved to Colorado and proceeded to have five children in a ten year period. She experienced her first mood swing in the form of depression after the birth of her first child. The marriage was stormy with multiple separations during which Elizabeth would return to Wellsville to work on the family paper.

After her father's death in 1942, Layton became managing editor of the paper, initiating a 15-year marital separation. She had many feelings about what she saw as the shame of divorce; after all, she said, at that time, divorced peoples' books were even banned in public libraries. The divorce was finalized in 1957. That same year, Layton was hospitalized for depression in Robinson Neuropsychiatric Clinic in Kansas City, where she underwent a series of 13 electroshock treatments. She recalled this experience in a piece called *Transverse Shadows*:

> Nameless terror lurked in the stifling air above... choking me with its intensity... absolute acquiescence was my only protection against the threatening horror... if I lay immobile long enough, the ghastly thing, whatever it was, would go away... screams kept splitting the darkness... through this upheaval words came to me, "Please stop crying. The nurse will take you away again tonight."... I wondered vaguely to whom my roommate was talking... when my eyes adjusted to the brightness of the flashlight I could not only feel but see this danger, so I was not afraid of it. "Shut up," it said, "Do you want to wake up all the patients?"
>
> I put my head against the muscular forearm, pushed until I worked my face with all my might against it. Instantly I gave a jerk with wide open mouth and clamped my teeth with all my might into the hard flesh. Blood gushed into my mouth. It sickened me, and I could not hold back the vomit. With my arms pinned behind my back the night nurse marched me through our room, down the chasm to the elevator... we made our way through a maze of wriggling white cots. I felt myself forced onto a cot that was not squirming. I knew the comfort of wide straps... "Don't get excited. We're just going to give you another electroshock treatment. This is your 13th..."
>
> Even before I opened my eyes, I could feel it—a familiar sensation harking back to childhood days... while it is not a painful sensation, neither is it pleasurable. It is a little like coming out of the foyer of a strange movie theatre, and not knowing which way was home. Part of it is fighting cobwebs with no way out. "Disjointed!" That is the reason there is no pain, the head is completely severed from the body.
>
> The body lies here on this cot and the walls push in on it... the head floats airily just above the corner of the ceilingless room. It is detached and lazy, calmly interested yet not affected by what it sees..."
>
> At last I was dismissed to go home, "cured." To all outward appearances I was well, and definitely would have been the first to say so. I gave all

the expected answers glibly. These easy responses were unrelated to my inner feelings... I laughed and laughed because I knew all the time that black is not black. Black is white. Sometimes it is a beautiful royal purple or a soft mauve tint. I knew the answers by rote but not by faith. I was a disbeliever...

Today, much is being done for the emotionally and mentally disturbed and for their families. Many vital needs remain, and one of the greatest of these is for understanding... I have simply tried to set down for you some of my feelings as a disoriented person, so you may understand these things with me; help may be needed even after the cure is pronounced. The strict discipline drives away the terror by night. Confining straps are security, not cruelty. Nameless, I would break faith with all who feel pointed at. Signing my real name is the very beginning necessity of our new relationship. Now we are no longer strangers..."

Bag Lady

"There is a potential bag lady in her which the wind can blow in, unexpectedly, at any time, alone, sad, and homeless."

Layton was particularly interested that this image be shown to mental health professionals to enhance their understanding of the personal experience of illness.

Layton married her second husband, Glenn Layton, in March, 1957. He had lived in town since the mid-1940's, having switched from oil to real estate. Layton had helped him nurse his first wife during the latter's terminal illness, and Elizabeth's daughter had married Glenn's son. After the remarriage, she stopped newspaper work and remained home, baby-sitting and sewing, and experiencing mood swings. As described to Robert Ault, Menninger art therapist:

> Sometimes it was a tremendous homesickness (for what?)... sometimes it was a great tiredness, when I'd sleep 20 hours out of the day. I couldn't move. Sometimes I'd scream, the top of my head hurt so bad. Years ago, I'd try one way or another to die. Never felt the same way all the time... I never got happy or excited. Shall we say agitated. My brain spun round and round. I used to beat my head and yell "You're stupid, you're stupid," to myself. Sometimes I'd get panicky and hide in the closet. When I felt this way, I often hated the town and everybody in it. Frustration, I expect. No sleep, then I used to throw away all but one or two of my clothes because I didn't deserve them, anything good or bad... I lived quite a few years on amphetamines... then I got to taking downers too and for some years before and after Glenn and I were married, I must have been a mess. I don't know how he stuck it out. I feel that I inherited a lot of this depression and that I have passed it on to my kids.

She was seen at the Ottawa Guidance Center around 1971-3, receiving a diagnosis of *adjustment reaction of later life*, and prescriptions for Elavil and Tofranil, which she stopped taking because they made her feel "unnatural."

In 1976, Layton lost a son to liver disease. Her grief was all-consuming and prolonged. Her sister, Carolyn, suggested that Layton take some drawing classes to keep her mind off the loss. Layton at age 68 in 1977 enrolled in Pal Wright's contour drawing class at Ottowa University.

Contour drawing is a technique introduced in 1941 by Constantin Nicolaides, in which the artist looks at the subject, not the paper, while drawing, so as to bypass self-censure and to draw what is felt. This technique seemed to provide Layton an explosive catharsis and possible exorcism. In the fall of 1977, she worked feverishly, obsessively, as long as 10 hours a day, drawing and writing powerful commentaries about her views. Over a period of nine months, her crativity and search for inner peace resulted in a lifting of her depression. Within a year, complete healing of her depression occurred and never returned. Through her art, she found a creative purpose for her life which blessedly continued until its end.

Intensive Care Room.

Layton said she could not work on this steadily, so it took over a month to finish: "This is the room where my son died. They had all these tubes... there was always blood coming down... I couldn't draw the face so I put the pillow there. They gave him 4 gallons of blood... I couldn't wait till I could go again and give blood to somebody else. They wouldn't take me because I was taking a medicine... think of the people I've killed. Well it isn't that... the Red Cross just has certain rules."

The Wink

In this picture, we see a love-chase between Layton in her size 40 see-through nightie with her teeth out, and her husband. Art therapist Ault of Menninger's wrote that, stripped of all pretense and in a state of complete honesty, Layton still found herself attractive to another person.

245

Indian Pipes

In commenting on this picture, Layton spoke of elder Indians being put out to die, and society ignoring the potential productivity of its elder citizens. Here an old chief makes arrowheads, and an old squaw, booties. The title derives from Indian pipes, saprophytic herbs which help by cleaning up dead or decayed matter.

Acknowledgements:

Thanks to the Mid-America Arts Alliance for their permission to quote and paraphrase from *Through the Looking Glass; Drawings by Elizabeth Layton.* Thanks to Robert Ault, ATR, MFA for his permission to quote from *"The Foxy Squaw from Gettysburg."* Thanks to Ann Stephenson of the Arizona Republic for a quotation from her article, *"Lines on Life,"* and much appreciation to Don Lambert for permission to reprint four of Layton's drawings here. Finally this rendering is lovingly dedicated to the memory of Elizabeth Layton, a spirited and inspirational artist.

Vivian Rogers, Ph.D., a gerontology counselor, is presently visiting scholar and guest lecturer at the University of North Carolina, Wilmington. Before moving to Wilmington in 1988, she was founder and director of the Adult Life Resource Center at the University of Kansas and directed the Center for Education for Women at the University of Michigan.

For the most part, what I draw is for other people like me who may be troubled by their feelings...It's not whether this is art or not. I don't care.
—Elizabeth Layton

Elizabeth Layton
Maverick Model of Personality Growth in Late Life
by Vivian Rogers, Ph.D.

The artist, Elizabeth Layton, defied traditional rites of passage to old age. Her point of departure was a 30-year crisis of manic depression and the cruelest blow of all—the death of a child. Yet ahead was an astonishing 16-year journey of creativity and personality growth.

A period often characterized as one of overwhelming physical decline and psychological pathology, Elizabeth Layton made into a time of extraordinary productivity, healing, and hope, despite physical problems that might have deterred a less hardy spirit.

Was hers an uncommon experience of old age? Researchers who have studied how old people function in everyday life conclude it is more common than many may think. Uncannily, as a maverick challenging the stereotype, Layton "did" old age developmentally right.

The death of a son precipitated a psychological crisis when she was 67 and was the turning point in Layton's late life development. A class in blind contour drawing prodded her to turn inward to confront her new terror head-on, tracing the details mercilessly until it became something she could live with. Self-acceptance, new directions and an intractable optimism were to be her rewards.

Layton was doing what developmentalist Erik Erikson said was the major task of *later adulthood.* She was examining the whole bolt of her life, the successes and the setbacks and, in the process, finding, at long last, purpose in her life and reason to accept herself. It had been a rocky road, with a lingering sadness that began in childhood, a failed first marriage, the need to support five young children, and life in a small midwestern town where, as county newspaper editor, her liberated views often put her at odds with her readers. Thirteen electroshock treatments, lithium and psychotherapy failed to bring any lasting relief. A successful second marriage and the support of loving friends and family also proved inadequate to buffer the pain.

In her grief, Layton took her sister's advice to enroll in an art class at Ottawa University, not far from her home town, Wellsville, Kansas. The class available was in contour drawing. The instructions were to look at the subject when drawing, and to look at the paper only to get one's bearings. The theory behind the technique is that the brain has two sides, the creative right side, and the more logical left side that governs functions like writing, doing math and keeping things in proper order. The idea is to use the right side of the brain, the more visual side, so the artist can *experience* what she draws, rather than just drawing what she sees.

"Draw yourself"

"If you have nothing to draw, then draw yourself," the instructor advised. Layton drew herself with every wrinkle, every blemish, every extra pound in her body showing. But other things also came out: her indignation at society's treatment of the old; her sense of having no control over a deteriorating body; the heartbreak of seeing life ebb in a son still in his prime.

About one early drawing, *On the Death of a Child,* a self-portrait of herself as an old woman nursing the child she lost, she said:

> If we have an emotion, if we can just face it head on, look right at it and do something and talk about it, our problems seem to get better. I was feeling grief. So I decided to draw a picture of this grief. I picked out what to me was the hardest subject I could find. And I drew that. And as I drew it, I got a little used to the idea, and by the time I did some more I got more used to the

idea, and the first thing I knew, it was something I could live with. It never goes clear away but then it isn't something you sit around and mourn, because you're used to it.

From that inward search, carried on through drawings so stark she could hardly look at them, Layton's depression lifted, and healing came within the year, and her bi-polar symptoms never returned.

At first convinced that it was the contour drawing technique alone that cured her, Layton was later to conclude that it was both the act of blind contour drawing and the finding of meaning in her drawings that made her well. She thought that those who do contour drawing experience some sort of catharsis, some relief from the pain of their emotions as, after the images mysteriously take shape on the page, the artists reflect on the meanings of what they have drawn.

On the Death of a Child, 1977

Layton is "recognized"

Lambert, a young reporter, discovered Layton's work in a University of Ottawa student art show, and thereafter promoted her work with unflagging enthusiasm. In 1978, by now director of the Topeka Arts Council, he showed her work to Robert Ault, one of the founders of the American Art Therapy Association and resident art therapist at the Menninger Foundation.

Seeing Layton's work, Ault recognized it was more than just "patient art." It had imagination, an intuitive sense for composition, wit, intelligence and tremendous power. He immediately agreed to

251

show her art at the Menninger Foundation and asked Lambert to introduce him to the artist.

In that meeting in Layton's bedroom studio that lasted several hours, biographer Lynn Bretz wrote: "Layton poured forth tales from her life, thoughts and worries she had harbored for years until drawing about them." She later wrote to students in Ault's class who were studying the influence of contour drawing on the artist:

> Bob Ault said: "Tell me about these." What a welcome release to talk about them.

Ten years later, Ault and six of his graduate students in an art therapy class at Emporia State University set about trying to identify what it was about Layton's technique that could affect psychological change. Both teacher and students experimented with doing self-portrait contour drawings and discussing the meanings each attributed to his or her drawings. Ault reported that within a year he and all six students had experienced positive, significant life changes traceable to insights gained in the experiment. For him, Ault said, it was the richest kind of psychological growth he had ever experienced.

Layton first drew, then wrote

Layton's written commentary, which often accompanied her drawings, was another way she explored and shared meaning. She confided that as a journalist, she had often been frustrated in trying to communicate through her writing. Drawing and writing about what she drew were apparently a more compatible combination. Layton said the commentary also provided closure.

From Layton's inner search, a profound new interest in the world around her also emerged. It was an outer world she could never have understood so fully nor drawn with such compassion had she not first turned the mirror on herself.

This became clear in a self-portrait, entitled *All Were Myself,* which she drew as the artist-in-residence for a national conference on adult development held in 1982 at the University of Kansas.

In the drawing, Layton, smiling, with a spray of flowers in her outstretched hand, approaches the viewer. Smaller self-images crowd the background. Pinned on her housedress is the inevitable rainbow. The artist explained:

> My feeling is that if I can't understand myself, how can I ever understand others? Some coming toward me are friendly, one is Numero One, one is begging, one is angry, another is holding me off. Skins are all colors. All are female, so in one pocket there is a Hershey bar with just He showing to include males—along with a computer print-out of Sakei-an:
>
> "I saw people coming towards me. But all were the same man. All were myself."

When Layton turned her attention to the world, she drew its problems and joys with characteristic honesty. By turns tender and satirical, lyrical and shocking, she empathized with those hurting in that world—the crack babies, the victims of discrimination, the AIDS patients, the Jonestown suicides. She celebrated the dovetailed relationship she enjoyed with her husband, Glenn, her favorite model, and delighted in the independence of the grandmother serving Kentucky Fried Chicken for Thanksgiving dinner.

Creativity and intelligence

Much has been written regarding Layton's ability to deal honestly with her emotions. That she did so powerfully through her art is undisputed. But there is also in her art undisputable evidence of a keen intellect at work that enabled her to cope successfully with the many complicated aspects of her inner and outer worlds. Layton's skillful coupling of creativity and

All Were Myself

253

intelligence would not have confounded researchers Patricia Haensley and Cecil Reynolds. Their studies of creativity led them to believe that creativity and intelligence are interrelated and to propose that "creativity is not just another 'breed' of mental processing, but is the ultimate expression of that finely honed system of thinking we know as intelligence."

While Layton subscribed to the theory that contour drawing could enable the artist to access a more creative side of the brain, she also valued the influence of the logical left side of the brain. As she told Dwain Workman, a Kansas sculptor who interviewed her in 1982:

> When you live with or are involved with something in your right brain, paradoxically, it helps you to think logically. If I'm doing something with my drawings, I think through this problem without a bit of trouble. It becomes very clear. But you just can't live completely on your right side. If you did, you'd be a guru sitting cross-legged on the mountain side for 50 years. Is it helping you? Is it helping anybody? The issue is balance.

The issues to which Layton drew attention through her art were complex personal and social dilemmas before which she neither flinched nor despaired of remedy. On display in her art is a rare intelligence, rich in understanding and bright in hope.

Recently, developmental psychologist Paul Baltes reported research which sought to understand what is possible in intellectual functioning as persons grow older and what is not. He did what is rarely done in such testing, he tested people at the limits of their capacity.

What he found was that the functioning of the mind is multifaceted and that intelligence is not a single category. He identified two kinds of intelligence and allowed that there might be more. One kind he identified as the neurophysiologic make-up of the brain, based in genetics and biology. To use a computer analogy, the neurophysiologic make-up of the brain would be the hardware of the mind and involve such matters as speed, accuracy of information, and visual and motor memory.

The other kind of intelligence could be understood as the culture-based software or content of the mind, reflecting the knowledge about the world and human affairs that people acquire in the course of living. Examples would be reading and writing, language comprehension, knowledge about self, and mastery of life-coping skills.

Baltes found that as older adults approached their limits of functioning (often through debilitating illness or advanced old age), their age had a pronounced effect on speed and accuracy of memory. This seems reasonable in light of the genetic and biological base of the neurophysiologic make-up of the brain influencing these functions.

But, in presenting people with real life dilemmas, the researchers found the 70-year-olds did just as well as the 30-year-olds and the 60 to 70-year-olds produced as many of the top 20% performers as younger adults.

The issue around which Baltes did his testing was, of course, wisdom.

From any study of her life and work, it cannot be denied that Layton, in late life, faced and dealt well with such daunting dilemmas as fear and depression, homelessness, the arms race, inequity, discrimination, poverty and genocide.

Layton's faith

When Layton's children were of Sunday school-age, she met with her minister to explore questions about the religion in which she was raised. When his answers failed to satisfy her, she terminated her church membership. She later told an interviewer:

> I spent 15 years trying to figure out religion and I keep struggling with it. I would hope that I always keep on struggling with it. I think if you get any pat answers, they're not the right answers because we can't know. I don't know what I am going to believe tomorrow. But at this point, I believe this life and the human mind are the most wonderful things in the world. I just try to accept that they are wonderful, and try to keep myself open. Breaking down the barriers and feeling myself at one with you is important to me. Then we don't try to belittle each other. We don't try to blame each other. We accept each other.

From what we know of Layton's life, the search for answers to questions of personal and public morality was one that deeply concerned her all her adult life. When she was a young adult, her position against capital punishment led to a year-long stand-off with her father, a state legislator, who had voted in favor of the death penalty. Her powerful drawing, *Capital Punishment*, evidenced that the issue continued to engage her passionately in old age.

Theologians Paul Tillich, H. Richard Niebuhr, and James Fowler believe that faith is a universal human concern, not always religious in its content.

Tillich asked the hard questions: What ultimate concerns have centering power in our lives? Is the ultimate concern centered in our own ego or its extensions—work, prestige, power and wealth? Or is it centered in a power sufficiently worthy to give our lives unity and purpose? Faith so understood, Fowler concluded, governs how we put our lives together to make our lives seem worthwhile.

Niebuhr saw faith taking form in infancy and developing over the lifespan as we experience trust and fidelity, or mistrust and betrayal, in relationships.

Fowler studied the stages of faith development from earliest years to old age. He asked: What makes you get up in the morning? On what or whom do you set your heart? To what vision of right-mindedness between humans, nature and the transcendent are you loyal? What grounds of hope animate you and give shape to your life?

From the answers, Fowler mapped a faith journey from the basic trust of the infant in the caretaker to the "universalizing faith" of the person for whom:

- the community is universal;
- life is both loved and held to loosely;
- a readiness for fellowship with all exists;
- a radical commitment to justice is present;
- and there is a selfless passion for a transformed world.

Among his age 61 and older subjects, (there were 62 people in this group), Fowler found only one "universalizing faith stage" respondent. Had Fowler interviewed Layton, perhaps that number would have doubled.

Very old age development

In concluding, I'd like to return to the Erikson model to the stage he called *very old age,* (75 to death). The major tasks of this stage, he said, are coming to grips with one's declining physical powers and coming to terms with one's own mortality, both tasks presuming the ability to adapt to change.

In old age, Layton came to accept that development implies change and the need to deal with change. It was a lesson her mother tried to teach her earlier when Layton expressed sadness that a childhood friend was moving away. "Well, everything changes," her mother had said. Years later, in talking about this incident, Layton confessed that she had only come late to the conclusion that it does, and to the view that adaptability to change was highly important.

Over the last 16 years of Layton's creative life, the artist faced many changes as she came to grips with her own declining physical powers. High blood pressure, osteoporosis, and osteo and rheumatoid arthritis assailed her. A surgery in the mid-80's for a detached retina left her with severely diminished sight in one eye and she suffered a minor stroke in the late 80's. But, as Rollo May once observed, limitations can also frame the picture. Layton continued to draw right up to the final stroke which precipitated her death in 1993.

During her career as an artist, Layton often used death as the subject of her drawings. In her late 80's, one drawing, a statement on the right to die, depicted a dying woman attached to all the life-support devices known to medicine.

Not long afterward, Layton drew the *Magic Gate,* a drawing eight years in the making. The Magic Gate, she explained, is death. With a radiant smile, the woman in the drawing stands partly through the gate. The woman was happy, Layton explained, about where she was going and about leaving the world behind. Everything behind her is in the world, the happy and the sad—a flower here and a rainbow there, Glenn and her children, the cross, dropping bombs, a Nazi concentration camp, a merry-go-round, a dove nesting on this side and on the other side, a dove flying.

Would there be another drawing after the woman goes through

the gate? Layton replied:

> "No I don't think so. How could I draw it when I don't know what it will be? But I feel whatever it is, it's going to be a good place. I feel so strongly that there is one life and we are all a part of that life and it will go on forever."

Layton was coming to terms with her own mortality.

According to psychiatrist Robert Lifton, we achieve some form of immortality through our biological and adopted children, students and "mentees." We can also achieve and express a sense of immortality through a variety of other means. We can do this through: our belief in an afterlife; our creative achievements and impact on others; our ideas of participation in the chain of nature; and a feeling of a continuous present that can be equated with eternity.

The Magic Gate

Confronting this last developmental task, Layton expressed conviction that her work had many purposes (the most important being that others, through art, might also be healed), that the "one life that is in all living creations" would continue, and that hope was a human requirement.

Her wish that others would see her work and be encouraged by her example was a purpose Layton lived to see fulfilled on a scale far beyond her imagination. She never sold a drawing for fear the magic would go away. She gave close to 1100 of her 1200 drawings to friends, family members, and charity. Yet she managed somehow to keep together enough major works for two major exhibitions which have crisscrossed this country and Canada many times and have been seen in over 200 communities.

Artistic acceptance

Artistic acceptance came early. In 1980, she won first prize in the Mid-Four annual juried art exhibition held at the Nelson Atkins Art Museum in Kansas City. In 1982, she was one of five older artists invited to exhibit at the *White House Conference on Aging*. SoHo 20, a women's cooperative gallery, was the first gallery to show Layton's work in New York City. The Museum of Modern Art acquisitioned a drawing. The first major exhibition of the National Museum of Women in Art in Washington, D.C. was a one-woman show of Layton's work. In 1992, the Smithsonian Institution scheduled a one-artist showing of Layton's drawings at the National Museum of American Art. The exhibition, *Elizabeth Layton: Drawing a Life*, lasted for three months and brought together 60 of Layton's drawings from two separately touring exhibitions.

Two years earlier, when the word was out that the Smithsonian would exhibit Layton's work, AP reporter Michael Bates went to Wellsville to ask Layton if she was impressed by the Smithsonian recognition. Layton said she had received letters from people who had seen the new exhibition when it was first shown at Stephens College. "You can't say they liked it when it's that horrible looking. But they did seem to relate to it."

Bates concluded: "She considers little about whether her work is considered art. If she draws something representing a private feeling, and if it makes an emotional connection with someone who sees it, then the drawing is successful."

What was clearly important to Layton about the exhibitions was the chance to inspire others to understand that through the creative process, life can be renewed at any age.

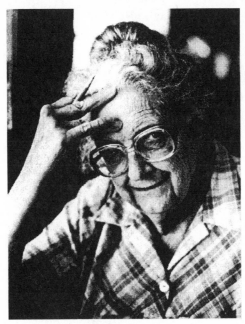

Elizabeth Layton

Comment by Evelyn Virshup, Ph.D., A.T.R. As an art therapist, I am most impressed by Elizabeth Layton's experience. She discovered what is known to art therapists—that the expression of one's inner experience graphically allows the artist, who is willing, the opportunity to examine, understand, and accept that experience. Not all artists are willing to do this. Some, like Pollock, deliberately avoid confronting their inner life, and lose this opportunity for emotional growth. Whether or not others "like" our art is, then, not very important, although it is gratifying when others can relate, through our art, to our own essential, inner being and find their own through the same process.

In my experience working with drug abusers, documented in *Right Brain People in a Left Brain World*, I saw, time and time again, that when my clients had found their images through projective techniques and then wrote or talked about the significance of the image, they reached powerful truths about themselves, long denied, or forgotten. In addition, they found self esteem when they discovered their "latent" creativity and received praise from their peers.

The process of drawing first, then writing or talking about the image, has no peer in bringing suppressed experiences and emotions to consciousness, and resolving paralyzing and debilitating conflicts.

In regard to Paul Baltes' comment that intelligence is multifaceted, Roger Sperry's Nobel Prize-winning work on hemisphericity and Howard Gardner's treatise on *Multiple Intelligences* demonstrate clearly that we have many different styles in how we learn. Right brain dominant people lose a lifetime of self-expression when they are not exposed to and trained at an early age in the "language" in which they excel—i.e. music, drama, dance and art. Imagine what Elizabeth Layton's art might have been if she had had a lifetime in which to draw! Imagine how different her life could have been!

C. Kate Kavanagh is Clinical Assistant/Associate Professor at the University of Wisconsin Departments of Psychiatry, Pediatrics, Surgery, and School of Nursing. She is the author of 11 published articles on psychology and nursing, and an editor and co-author of the book, Psychiatric and Mental Health Nursing. *She has delivered 78 professional presentations, including four for the Creativity and Madness conferences. The proprietor of Shorewood Psychiatric Associates, she is on the medical staff of Parkway and University Hospital/Madison and an active member of Greenpeace, the Center for Environmental Education, the Union of Concerned Scientists, The Costeau Society, and People for Ethical Treatment of Animals.*

Creative art and actual experience are one and the same. A bit of mystery remains for the creator as well.

Gustav Mahler

Picasso
The Man and His Women
by C. Kate Kavanagh, R.N., Ph.D.

Picasso created over 40,000 works of art. His masterpiece, *Guernica*, was created to denounce the destruction of the city of Guernica during the Spanish civil war. This painting, however, was not the only metaphor he used to portray destruction. More than two thirds of his paintings from 1930–40 consisted of deformed women, their faces and bodies flayed. Behind captivating female beauty, he saw disintegration, decomposition, and death.

In his art, Picasso mercilessly lays bare what he believes to be the illusions of synthetic beauty. In his life, beautiful women under his influence also became similarly transformed, through physical and emotional abuse. Picasso destroyed both the women in his life and his children. For them, Picasso became an addiction that cost some of them their sanity and their lives.

Early History

Picasso's early life, from his birth, October 25, 1881, to age three was apparently unremarkable, except that the five women in the household, his mother, grandmother, two maids, and a nurse, adored him, to the point of being smothering and intrusive. Dona Maria, his mother, ruled over her introverted, depressed husband and household while believing in Picasso unconditionally. Totally absorbed in her son, she described him as "an angel and a devil." According to her, Picasso could draw before he could speak, and drew incessantly, with his father, also an artist, as his first teacher.

When Picasso was three, the Malaga earthquake occurred. It was a catastrophic earthquake, with 60 major shocks in three days, during which 600 people died. During the earthquake, his mother gave birth to his sister, Lola. Immediately, all the attention he had been receiving stopped, his narcissistic glory ended, and his care was transferred to his depressed father. What could he have thought? We know that as an adult, when his women were pregnant, he experienced severe anxiety and stress.

When he was six, his sister Conchita was born, and died two years later. Picasso had very tender feelings for her: "so blonde, so tender, so vulnerable." It has been said that he loved her so much, he made a pact with God that if Conchita lived, Picasso would give up his art. When Conchita died, Picasso decided that God was evil. At the same time, knowing he could never have kept his end of the bargain, he was haunted his entire life with a feeling of responsibility for the death of his sister.

He developed separation-anxiety that affected his relationships for the rest of his life. To avoid Picasso's hysterics at being left at school, his father would leave his walking stick with him. "If he left the stick with me," said Picasso, "I was sure he would return."

At the age of 10, his family moved to Coruna on the northern coast of Spain, and then, when he was 16, to Barcelona.

At school, his inability to read or learn, or to deal with rules, curriculum, or any type of structure, is consistent with what we know today as dyslexia and, perhaps, attention deficit disorder. "The bad student," "running wild," he was often removed from class and banished to a bare cell. However, he liked it there because he took along a sketch pad and pencil and drew. As a child of 12 he boasted: "I draw like Raphael." Unable to learn, he was passed, year by year, until finally, at age 16, he left school.

It has been said that his mother had said to him as a teenager: "If you become a soldier, you will be a general; if you become a monk, the Pope." At this point, neither seemed likely.

When his family moved to Barcelona, he became the leader of a group of young men who spent their time drinking in night clubs, and visiting brothels. Briefly, his family sent him to an art school in another city, but he returned to Barcelona, probably because of homesickness. Finally, at 20, supported by his father, he went to live in Paris to become an artist. With him went his best friend, Casegemus. Tragically, Casegemus became enamored of a prostitute, and, because of her infidelities, he first shot her (without, however, killing her), and then shot and killed himself.

Women in his life

1. Ferdinand

Picasso's first great love, Ferdinand, had a mass of reddish hair, green almond-shaped eyes and long prehensile fingers. She was indolent, self-indulgent, and promiscuous; also beguiling, easy going and affectionate. She left her husband who beat her after a miscarriage left her unable to bear children, and she was "picked up" the same day by Picasso, who entreated her to be his model. This fateful meeting occurred in Paris in 1904. It was a thundery evening and Ferdinand was on her way home. Picasso was chatting with a friend on the street. Laughing and blocking her path, he held out a tiny kitten to her as she passed. She accepted his invitation to see his studio.

When their affair began, both Ferdinand and Picasso were involved with other people. Picasso pressured Ferdinand to come live with him. Though she would spend days, weeks with him, a year passed before she moved in.

Opium played a significant role in their relationship. Picasso started smoking the drug regularly in 1904. It has been suggested that the languid magic and beauty of Picasso's work between 1904-1906 can be attributed in part to the "black blood of the poppy." It would be a mistake, however, to minimize the effect of Ferdinand, once referred to as "Picasso's door to Manhood." She was the other half of his first real relationship. For the first time, Picasso committed himself to a woman.

Ferdinand was attracted to Picasso's "inner fire." She was magnetized by him, and offered him passionate and abandoned sex at any time he wanted her. Yet, Ferdinand observed, "There always seemed to be a great grief within him."

However, even during that first very passionate year of his relationship with Ferdinand, Picasso continued to see another woman, Madeline. And when World War I broke out, Picasso stopped being the gay, wild, brilliant, lively, but tender and kind man she knew in Paris, and became jealous and violent.

By 1912, Picasso supposedly said that "To live on one woman was not to be thought of." But to leave a woman was for him emotionally no less difficult. So he waited for Ferdinand to take the first step, which she did with a young Italian painter in 1912.

2. Eva

The second significant woman in Picasso's life (and supposedly his "first love") was Marcelle, whom he renamed Eva. Eva filled the void left by Ferdinand. In 1915, when she was hospitalized, Picasso who had to live alone for the first time in years, visited daily. At the same time he began an affair with a beautiful 27 year old, Gaby Lespinasse. "My life is hell," Picasso said of this period, apparently because he had less and less time for work. Eva's illness, probably tuberculosis, ended in her death. Eva's death made matters worse for Picasso as feelings resurfaced about the death of his sister and his sense that "death was always winning."

3. Olga

The void was filled by Olga. In 1917 at age 36, while doing sets for the ballet in Paris, Picasso met and married Olga Koklova, a Russian ballerina. Picasso's paintings of Olga, which she insisted be naturalistic, reveal a toughness, possessiveness, and obstinacy in her nature. Weary, disappointed, tired of daring, burnt by the fire within him, he hoped to find with Olga a haven of dignified tranquillity. He was said to have "sleep-walked" to his wedding with Olga, and into her world of boundaries, limitations, and artificial conventions. When he "awoke," however, he realized that he wanted something else.

Shortly after their marriage, Picasso's friend, Apollinaire, an art critic and poet, died.

"Woman with a Fan" (Olga), 1920

Picasso now had experienced several deaths: his sister Conchita, Eva, Casegemus, and now, Apollinaire. With each death, something withered in him and the chain of mortality around his heart became heavier.

In 1931, when Picasso was 40, Olga became pregnant, and bore him a son, Paulo. He was not happy about the news. Pregnancy, possibly related to his sister's birth when he was three, caused Picasso severe anxiety. Olga's growing self-absorption, irrationality and demands for attention, exasperated him and confirmed his fears of the "devouring woman." Olga's considerable desire for power had now changed focus from a drive for social recognition to a no less obsessive drive to possess her husband. He withdrew from her in response. He would frequently suddenly leave her to go off to another house to work and retreat. She, feeling angry and betrayed, lashed

Les Demoiselles d'Avignon, 1907

out at him. Anger begot rage and rage violence. Picasso began to obsess about the women who had possessed him in the past and who might possess him in the future. Picasso's paintings at this time began to reflect savage decomposition of the human body. All the while, Olga's presence in Picasso's life grew even more oppressive. As a result, there was an explosion of violence, mostly against women, in his work, not unlike an earlier period when he tried to put all of life on one canvas, *Les Demoiselles d'Avignon.* He sought, at the same time, freedom and control.

4. Marie-Therese

Picasso found both in the fourth woman in his life, Marie-Therese Walter, whom he "picked up" on the streets of Paris. "I'm Picasso. You and I are going to do great things together," he said. Only 17, she was impressed.

On the day of her 18th birthday, he took Marie-Therese to bed. Picasso experienced this as his own rebirth. Picasso found that he could explore the limits of sexuality with Marie-Therese, the "greatest sexual passion of his life." She was an endlessly submissive and willing pupil, accepting all sexual experience, including sadism. She was a willing object he alone possessed. Picasso, of course, was not about to "sneak around." So, he had his affair with Marie-Therese right under Olga's nose. Ultimately, he installed her in an apartment across the street from his and Olga's home!

For Picasso, women were either goddesses or doormats. Those who knew him well observed that nothing gave him greater pleasure than transforming his women into doormats, making him a "perverse kind of Henry Higgins." Women then, as many do now, allowed this, in fact, became addicted to the trampling. One of the addicts, Marie-Therese, when asked what happiness was for Picasso, said, "First he raped his woman, and then he worked."

Picasso's "War Against Women" was declared on his canvases in his bullfight pictures. One, done in July, 1934, depicts Marie-Therese as a wounded matador, carried off on the back of her horse, mortally wounded, while the bull (Picasso) observes with sadistic satisfaction. He painted the Minotaur (mythical beast: half man, half horse) carrying off a woman victim frequently during this period, many of the paintings untitled, but clearly representations of Picasso's (the Minotaur) relationships with the women in his life.

Picasso collected women. Unlike most men, he did not move from one to another. Despite the fury, conflict, and self-hatred that relationships with women engendered, he couldn't bear the thought of parting from any of them. Apparently, the separation-anxiety of his childhood persisted throughout adulthood.

5. Dora

The fifth woman in Picasso's life, Dora Maar, first appeared at the time of his and Marie-Therese's daughter Maya's birth. Picasso was struck by Dora's powerful profile and her career woman status. Picasso admired Dora as an artist in her own right. He also admired her courage in entering into a man's world, her independence, and her spirit. But she was not to be an exception to the goddess-doormat transformation her lover had perfected. From the very beginning of their relationship, Picasso began her ruination, although this time combat was waged on a lioness rather than wasted on a mouse (Marie-Therese).

Initially, Dora unknowingly met Picasso's insatiable narcissistic needs. A painter and photographer, she had the advantage of being in the world of art herself and so could more easily relate to it and to him. In the process, however, she became less and less the independent woman and more and more Picasso's increasingly dependent "official" mistress.

At the same time, Picasso was still married to and "living with" Olga; Marie-Therese continued to hold the title of "secret lover;" and Ferdinand remained an important figure in Picasso's life. Only Eva was lost, through death.

Marie-Therese's reaction to Picasso's emotional abandonment of her for Dora included constructing a fantasy (actually a delusion) that she lived in a world that contained only her and Picasso. There was no room even for their daughter, Maya. When Picasso was not crushing Marie-Therese with transparent deception, he bound her with flowery declarations of love and the insistence that she write to him daily. Again and again he told her: "I love only you."

Weeping Woman (Dora), 1940

Of Dora Maar, Picasso said: "I wasn't in love with Dora Maar—I liked her as though she were a man. I told her, 'You don't attract me; I don't love you.'" It is said that often Picasso beat Dora into unconsciousness.

The death of his mother in 1939 was a major trauma for Picasso. She had been a haven of unconditional love and acceptance, even if years passed by without his seeing her. While she existed, the possibility of that kind of loving acceptance existed for him; when she died, it died with her. He wrote a poem after her death about the center of an infinite void that was dragging him down to its dark and destructive limits. He described himself as oscillating between self-adulation and self-disgust without a resting point.

When his mother died, Picasso stayed in Paris and never spoke of her again. His paintings, however, began even more to reflect deformed women, thought by many to represent his universal hatred for all women.

His behavior did not always reflect his dynamics or his art, however, since at this time he would frequently take evening walks on the beach with Dora; and continued to write passionate letters to Marie-Therese. He also still visited Olga regularly. Picasso turned what for many would have been a nightmare— to collect and continue intimate relatinships with so many women—into a "sport."

Picasso constantly sought ways to make things "more interesting" and began to create tension among the women in his life by setting up confrontations between them. He introduced Dora to Marie-Therese, telling her Marie-Therese was the only woman he ever loved. The enraged Marie-Therese threw Dora out, but Picasso brought Dora back "to console her." The incident was one of Picasso's "choicest memories."

6. Francoise

The next important woman in Picasso's life was Francoise Gilot, a woman with an intensely rational mind and androgynous beauty. When he began to pursue her, she didn't resist, which he told her was "disgusting." But she said she wasn't interested in playing games or in being a victim or turning others into victims.

Woman Flower (Francoise), 1946

271

Picasso once told Francoise:

> Happiness, like everything, exists in limited quantity. So we mustn't see each other too often. Everything in my life weighs me down and shuts out the light. This thing with you seems like a window opening up. I want it to remain open.

Picasso was seeking to protect what had begun to blossom with Francoise from the monster within him that experience had taught him he could not control. Francoise eventually became psychologically merged with Picasso, and she too denied his rejections and betrayals. Specifically, Picasso continued his relationships with Dora, Marie-Therese, Olga, and began a new one with a friend of Dora's, Genevieve. Picasso arranged for Dora and Francoise to meet at a social event, insuring that Dora would be publicly humiliated. Francoise was extremely upset by Dora's ultimate "breakdown" after this event.

Eventually, Francoise refused to help Picasso annoy Dora any more and left him to spend the summer in Brittany. The first woman in his life to see that Picasso's urge to seduce was not love, but possession and destruction, Francoise managed to escape for a while. However, Picasso's claim that he didn't have long to live, as well as Francoise's grandiose belief that she could succeed at anything she tried, including overcoming the destroyer in Picasso, resulted in her return to him.

Now 65, Picasso's need to demonstrate total control through cruelty and manipulation became an addiction. He told Dora how marvelous Francoise was in front of Marie-Therese, taking special care to point out her athletic prowess, a knife in the heart of the formerly very athletic Marie-Therese. Then he dragged Francoise to Dora's apartment for the purpose of telling Dora directly that there was nothing between them. Shortly afterwards Picasso began taking Francoise to Dora's country house (a gift from Picasso) on holiday, making sure Dora knew about it. Once he went so far as to make sure Dora would find them there.

He now transferred his outrageous, infuriating and self-centered behavior, not to mention sadistic abuse, to Francoise. Once he held a burning cigarette to her cheek. She said to Picasso at the time,

> You can destroy my beauty…but you are not going to destroy me… Look
> at it, it's ugly and you did it, and you'll have to look at it now.

Another time, while Picasso and Francoise were vacationing in Dora's country house, Francoise awoke to find three scorpions crawling by her head. Picasso, laughing at her terror, said,

> That's the kind of crown I like to see on you. They're my sign of the zodiac.

And Picasso never resisted a chance to remind Francoise of the other women in his life. During their "honeymoon," he read Francoise passages from Marie-Therese's continuing daily letters, commenting that she really loved him.

When Francoise became pregnant, Picasso refused to allow her to see a physician. Phobic of doctors and hospitals, he was certain they would bring bad luck. Not totally under her lover's thumb, however, Francoise went anyway.

Picasso's reaction to the birth of Claude was far from paternal. In his words: "Getting a woman with child is for me taking possession and helps to kill whatever feelings existed. I constantly feel the need to free myself."

Olga, to whom he was still married, was berserk with jealousy and anger. She began coming uninvited to their home, physically assaulting Francoise, especially if she was holding Claude in her arms, and telling visitors that she, Olga, had been rightfully reinstated as the woman of the house.

When Francoise became pregnant with their second child, Picasso left for Paris. He didn't write, or return when she expected him. When he did return, she welcomed him home with a slap and locked herself in Claude's room for the night. Yet again they found a new intimacy, and for a time, Francoise and Picasso were together constantly. By 1949, however, Picasso, unable to tolerate the new-found closeness, again began to flee.

Paloma was born. Francoise didn't fully recover immediately from Paloma's birth; she became ill, and their sex life decreased. Nevertheless, Picasso expected more from her than ever. He slept till noon while she ran the household. When her health steadily declined, Picasso complained that he didn't like sick women, and blamed her for everything.

Picasso's loving feelings for his children were non-existent. Descriptive of his attitude toward them is his now famous remark,

They are elephants—they take up so much room.

He described his son, Paulo, as "the most disgusting son in the world." To a friend, Picasso said:

My works are much more my children than the human beings that claim to be my children.

Commenting on an apocryphal story of a celebrated ceramist who had burned all his furniture so his kiln would not go cold, Picasso said,

I would gladly have thrown my wife and children in, if that was necessary to keep the fire going.

Surely, no one felt this more than his children. He is said to have told his son Claude,

I am old and you are young—I wish you were dead.

When, later, his father disowned him, not out of malice, more out of lack of interest, Claude attempted suicide.

By 1953 Francoise finally concluded that life with Picasso was a sickness. Having met a man in Paris, Francoise left with the children.

Picasso, suffering from separation anxiety and fear of abandonment, had repeated again and again, "Nobody leaves a man like me."

Francoise proved him wrong. This was defeat, old age, death for him. He grieved her loss through working maniacally, producing 180 drawings in two months, at age 72.

He tried to get Francoise to return by entreating,

There is no one I can talk to the way I can with you; it was hard living together, but it is worse living apart.

7. Jacqueline

In 1954, he met Jacqueline Roque. Picasso treated Jacqueline as abusively as her predecessors. Indifferent towards her at best, he told her to do what she wanted (stay or leave). She begged him to let her stay and take care of him.

In 1954, Olga died of cancer. Their son, Paulo, was with her. Picasso stayed in Paris, and, in Jacqueline's presence, phoned Marie-Therese and told her "Olga is dead," then asked her to marry him. For 30 years she had lived only for him, but she refused.

So Picasso and Jacqueline settled into a life of being devoured and devouring each other. Picasso had never been lonelier and less able to drown the loneliness in frenzied activity. He was happy only when working, but he seemed to have nothing of his own to work on. He took up themes of other painter's pictures. He played like a child, decorating pottery others had made for him.

By 1958 all the women in his life, with the exception of Jacqueline, were gone. He told a friend:

> You live in Paris; you have a house and know where you are. I'm not anywhere, don't know where I live—you can't imagine how awful that is.

Still carrying Picasso in her heart, Francoise decided to return to him. Divorced and on her way to her former lover, Francoise found out

Picasso had married Jacqueline 12 days earlier. Francoise went on to fight for and ultimately prove Picasso's paternity of her children so they wouldn't be left out of his estate.

Picasso now painted mostly pictures of Jacqueline, more than 70 in one year. His separation-anxiety in full-bloom, he couldn't tolerate even an hour's absence from her.

Portrait of Jacqueline, 1954

275

After marrying Jacqueline, Picasso stopped sending the monthly checks to Marie-Therese, her only means of support. In his growing paranoia, she had become a monster from whom he had to protect himself. In addition, he refused to sign the unsigned works he had given her, rendering them worthless.

In Picasso's last years, he wanted only to be left alone. He refused to see any of his children. He wrote Marie-Therese that she was the only woman that he ever loved. In 1973, as he lay gasping for breath, in Nice, he said his last words to his physician: "You are wrong not to be married. It's useful." He was 91 at the time of his death.

After Picasso died, Jacqueline continued to live as if he were alive. She even set a place for him at table at mealtime. She refused to acknowledge his death as she (and he) refused to acknowledge his children, the "elephants."

Picasso left behind 1885 paintings, 1228 sculptures, 2880 ceramics, 18,095 engravings, 6112 lithographs, 3181 linocuts, 7089 drawings, 149 notebooks, 11 tapestries, and 8 rugs.

Jacqueline inherited the largest portion of his estate, valued at 260 million. But wealth and great art were not Picasso's only legacy. On the day of his funeral, his grandson by Paulo, Pablito, Picasso's namesake, after begging to attend his grandfather's funeral and being refused by Jacqueline, committed suicide. Three years after Picasso's death, his son Paulo died of alcoholism. Five years after his death, Marie Therese hanged herself. And Jacqueline, after arranging for a showing of Picasso's works in Madrid, killed herself. Of all the women in Picasso's life, only Francoise survived. She married Jonas Salk, of Salk vaccine and Salk Institute fame, and today is a successful artist herself.

What was Picasso's power? Narcissistic men are often attractive, even charismatic. They seem to draw women like flies to honey—only to leave them caught in what often turns out to be a web of rejection, projective identification (of the man's self-hatred), and the elusive promise of the perfect love that she inspired.

One biographer, Richardson, has said of Picasso:

More than any other great artist, Picasso harnessed his sexuality to his work. Ultimately he equated the creative with the procreative act. As long as he could create, he lived. For Picasso, work and sex were the only weapons he could pit against death, his great adversary. So he was driven to work late into the night, often all night— not alone, but with a woman constantly at his side.

Last Self Portrait, 1972

C.G. Jung did not see Picasso as the narcissistic victim of his own rage. Though he felt his art reflected his psychic fragmentation, he saw him less as mad than as evil. I agree. He described him during his lifetime as

a man... who (did) not turn toward the day-world, but (was) fatefully drawn into the dark; who (followed) not the accepted ideals of goodness and beauty, but the demoniacal attraction of ugliness and evil.

277

References

I Vincent Van Gogh

Arenberg, I. K., 1990. Van Gogh had Meniere's Disease, not epilepsy. *Journal of American Medical Association*, 264:491-493.

Heiman, M., 1976. Psychoanalytic observations on the last painting and suicide of Vincent van Gogh. *International Journal of Psychoanalysis*, Vol. 57: 71-79.

Lee, T. C., 1981. Van Gogh's vision: digitalis intoxication. *Journal of American Medical Association*, 245:727-729.

Nagera, H. 1967. *Vincent van Gogh, a psychological study*. NY: International Universities Press.

Stone, I., 1937. *Dear Theo: the autobiography of Vincent van Gogh*. NY: Doubleday.

II Jackson Pollock

Cardinal, R., 1972. *Outsider art*. NY: Praeger.

Ernst, J., 1984. *A not-so-still life*. NY: St. Martin's/Marek.

Feldman, T., 1989. Creativity and narcissism: a self-psychology examination of the life and work of Jackson Pollock. *The Arts in Psychotherapy*. NY: Pergamon Press, Vol. 16: 201-209.

Friedman, B., 1974. *Jackson Pollock: energy made visible*. NY: McGraw-Hill.

Guggenheim, P., 1979. *Out of this century: confessions of an art addict*. NY: Universe Books.

Henderson, J., 1985. Personal interview.

Kligman, R., 1974. *Love affair: a memoir of Jackson Pollock*. NY: Murrow.

MacGregor, J., 1989. *The discovery of the art of the insane*. NJ: Princeton U. Press.

McKinzie, R., 1973. *The New Deal for Artists*. NJ: Princeton U. Press.

Naifeh, S. and Smith, G., 1989. *Jackson Pollock, an American saga*. NY: Clarkson Potter.

Naumberg, M., 1966. *Dynamically oriented art therapy: its principles and practice*. NY: Grune & Stratton.

—1950. *An introduction to art therapy: studies of the "free" art expression of behavior problem children and adolescents as a means of diagnosis and therapy*. NY: Teachers' College Press, Columbia.

O'Connor, F., 1967. *Jackson Pollock*. NY: The Museum of Modern Art.

—(Ed.), 1975. *Art for the millions, essays from the 1930s by artists and administrators of the WPA Federal Art Project*. Boston: New York Graphic Society.

—and Thaw, E., (Eds.), 1978. *Jackson Pollock: A Catalogue Raisonné of Paintings, Drawings and Other Works*. New Haven: Yale University Press.

Potter, J., 1985. *To a violent grave: an oral biography of Jackson Pollock*. NY: Putnam.

Prinzhorn, H., 1972. *Artistry of the mentally ill*. NY: Spring-Verlag.

Rose, B., 1983. *Lee Krasner: a retrospective*. NY: Museum of Modern Art.

—1981. *Krasner/Pollock, a working relationship*. NY: New York University.

Solomon, D., 1987. *Jackson Pollock, a biography*. NY: Simon and Schuster.

Virshup, E., 1979. *Right brain people in a left brain world*. Los Angeles: Guild of Tutors Press.

ing behavioral, narcissistic, and laterality theory. In E. Klinger, (Ed.). *Imagery: concepts, results and applications, Vol. 2.* NY: Plenum Press.
—and Riley, S., 1993. The Art of Healing Trauma. *California art therapy trends.* E. Virshup, (Ed.). Chicago: Magnolia Street Publishers.
Wysuph, C., 1970. *Jackson Pollock/psychoanalytic drawings.* NY: Horizon.

III Richard Wagner

Berkowitz, D., 1977. The vulnerability of the grandiose self and psychotherapy of acting-out patients. *International Review of Psychoanalysis.*
Cook, D., 1979. *I saw the world end.* London: Oxford University Press.
Gay, P., 1983. Blame Wagner? *NY: Vogue Magazine.*
Gutman, R., 1968. Richard Wagner—the man, his mind, and his music. NY: *Time.*
Hall, C., 1983. Wagnerian dreams. *Psychology Today.*
Henderson, W., 1923. *Richard Wagner: his life and his dramas.* NY: Knickerbocker.
Kernberg, O., 1975. *Borderline conditions and pathological narcissism.* NY: Aronson.
Kohut, H., 1977. *The restoration of the self.* NY: International University Press.
Krammer, F., 1985. Audiotape of lecture at the Seattle production of *The Ring Cycle.*
Shirer, W., 1960. *The rise and fall of the Third Reich.* NY: Simon and Shuster.
Wagner, R.,1853. *Letter to Franz Liszt,* Feb. 11.
—1854 *Letter to Rockel.*
—1954 *Siegfried, Der Ring des Nibelung,* Libretto.

IV An Artist Destroys His Work

Andreasen, N., 1988. Bipolar affective disorder and creativity: implications and clinical management. *Comprehensive Psychiatry,* 29(3):207-217.
Berman, L., 1987. Role of the primal scene in the artistic works of Max Ernst. In *Psychoanalytic Perspectives on Art,* Vol 3. Hillsdale, NJ: Analytic Press.
Eissler, K., 1967. Psychopathology and creativity. *Imago,* 24:35-79.
Greenacre, P., 1957. The childhood of the artist: libidinal phase development and giftedness. *Psychoanalytic Study of theChild,* 12:47-72.
—1958. The family romance of the artist. *Psychoanalytic Study of the Child,* 13:9-36.
Jamison, K., 1989. Mood disorders and patterns of creativity in British writers and artists. *Psychiatry,* 52(2):125-34.
Kris, E., 1952. *Psychoanalytic Explorations in Art.* NY: International University
Lowenfeld, H., 1941. Psychic trauma and productive experience in the artist. *Psychoanalytic Quarterly,* 10:116-130.
Niederland, W., 1976. Psychoanalytic approaches to artistic creativity. *Psychoanalytic Quarterly,* 45:185-212.
Pollock, G., 1975. On mourning, immortality, and utopia. *Journal of the American Psychiatric Association.,* 23:334-362.
Richards, R., 1989. Compelling evidence for increased rates of affective disorder among eminent creative persons. *Comprehensive Psychiatry,* 30, 3:272-3.
Trilling, L., 1949. Art and neurosis. In *The Liberal Imagination.* NY: Harcourt Brace.

V Frida Kahlo

Arnborg, H., Barnkob, L. & Venge, A., 1984. Feminine aesthetics: utopia through fragments. *Bidrag: Bevidsthedssociologis Tidisskrift*, 18:22-68.

Bergman-Caron, J., 1993. Like an artist. *Art in America*, 81:35-39.

Bierhurst, J., 1990. *The mythology of Mexico and Central America.* NY: Morrow.

Brett, G., 1987. Diego Rivera and Frida Kahlo. *Art Monthly*, 109:7-9.

Butterfield, J., 1977. Replacing women artists in history. *Artnews*, 76:40-4.

Chadwick, W., 1985. *Women artists and the surrealist movement.* London: Thames and Hudson.

—1985. The muse as artist: women in the Surrealist movement. *Art in America*, 73:120-129.

Chessick, R., 1977. *Intensive psychotherapy with the borderline patient.* NY: Aronson.

de La Fuente, J. & Alarcon-Segovia, D, 1980. Depression as expressed in pre-Columbian Mexican art. *American Journal of Psychiatry*, 137:1095-1098.

Dominguez, L., 1993. Mystery and history: sexuality and the Hispanic woman. *Health and Sexuality*, 3:9-11.

Drucker, M., 1991. *Frida Kahlo.* New York: Bantam.

Franco, J., 1989. *Plotting women: gender and representation in Mexico.* NY: Columbia University Press.

Gadon, E., 1989. *The once and future goddess.* San Francisco: Harper and Row.

Grimberg, S., 1990/1991. Frida Kahlo's memory: the piercing of the heart by the arrow of divine love. *Woman's Art Journal*, 11:3-7.

Helland, J., 1990/1991. Aztec imaging in Frida Kahlo's paintings: indigenousness and political commitment. *Woman's Art Journal*, 11:8-13.

Herrera, H., 1983. *Frida: a biography of Frida Kahlo.* NY: Harper & Row.

Herrera, H., 1983. Frida Kahlo: the pallette, the pain, and the painter. *Artforum.* 21:60-67.

Herrera, H., 1993. Beauty to his beast: Frida Kahlo and Diego Rivera. In *Significant others, creativity and intimate partnership.* Chadwick, W. & Courtivron, I. de, (Eds.). NY: Thames and Hudson, 119-135.

Jenkins, N., 1991. Callalilies and Kahlos. *Artnews*, 90:104-105.

Kohut, H., 1984. *How does analysis cure?* Chicago: University of Chicago Press.

Kozlof, J., 1978. Frida Kahlo. *Women's Studies*, 6:43-59.

Lee, R. & Martin, J., 1991. *Psychotherapy after Kohut: a textbook in self psychology.* Hillsdale, NJ: The Analytic Press.

Lee, R., (in press). *Cohesive functions of the self and creativity.*

Lowe, S., 1991. *Frida Kahlo.* NY: Universe.

Morrison, C., 1978. Shadow heroines; a post-Freudian look. *Format*, 1:1-14.

Orenstein, G., 1973. Frida Kahlo: painting for miracles. *Feminist Art Journal.*

—, 1990. *The reflowering of the Goddess.* NY: Pergamon Press.

Poniatowska, E., 1992. Diego, I am alone: Frida Kahlo. In *Frida Kahlo, the camera seduced.* San Francisco: Chronicle Books, p. 124.

Sander, H., 1980. *Women in art*, Vol. 1. Frankfurt Am Main, G.F.R.: Suhrkamp.

Stern, D., 1985. *The interpersonal world of the infant.* NY: Basic Books.

Zamora, M., 1990. *Frida Kahlo, the brush of anguish.* San Francisco: Chronicle.

VI Rossini

Burrows, B., (Ed.), 1993. *The opera quarterly*, Vol.9, No.4. North Carolina: Duke University Press.

Gossett, P., 1980. *New Grove dictionary of music and musicians*, Vol. 16: 226-229. London: Macmillan.

Jaques, E., 1965. Death and the mid-life crisis. *International Journal of Psychiatry*. 46: 502-514.

Osborne, R., 1986. *Rossini*. London: J.M. Dent.

Schwartz, D., 1965. Rossini: A psychoanalytic approach to the great renunciation. *Journal of the American Psychoanalytic Association*, 133: 551-569.

Till, N., 1983. *Rossini, his life and times*. NY: Midas Books.

Toye, F., 1954. *Rossini: a study in tragi-comedy*. London: Baker.

VII Edgar Allan Poe

Bloom, H., 1985. *Edgar Allan Poe: modern critical views*. NY: Chelsea House.

Brooks, C, Lewis, R. W. B., and Penn, R., (Eds.), 1973. *American literature: the makers and the making*. Vol. 1. NY: St. Martin's.

Foucault, M., 1965. *Madness and civilization: a history of insanity in the age of reason*. NY: Random House

Hoffman, D., 1972. *Poe, Poe, Poe, Poe, Poe, Poe, Poe*. NY: Doubleday.

Levin, H., 1985. *The power of blackness: Hawthorne, Poe, Melville*. Chicago: Ohio University Press.

Meyers, J., 1992. *Edgar Allan Poe: his life and legacy*. NY: Scribner.

Regan, R, (Ed.), 1967. *Poe: a collection of critical essays*. NJ: Prentice Hall.

Silverman, K., 1991. *Edgar Allan Poe: mournful and neverending remembrance*. NY: Harper Collins.

Szasz, T. S., 1961. *The myth of mental illness*. NY: Harper and Row.

VIII Michelangelo

Anthony, E., & Koupernik, C., (Eds.), 1974. *The child in his family: children at psychiatric risk*. NY: John Wiley and Sons.

Anthony, M.D., James E., and Cohler, J., 1987. *The invulnerable child*. NY: Guilford Press.

Coughlan, R., 1978. *The world of Michelangelo*. NY: Time-Life Books.

Goldscheider, L., 1953. *Michelangelo: painting, sculptures and architecture*. NY: Phardon Publisher.

Lamarche-Vadel, B., 1986. *Michelangelo*. London: Chartwell

Liebert, R., 1983 *Michelangelo, a psychoanalytic study of his life and images*. New Haven: Yale University Press.

Leites, N., 1986. *Art and life: aspects of Michelangelo*. NY: New York University Press.

Sterba, R. & Sterba, E., 1978. The personality of Michelangelo Buonarroti: stone reflections. *American Imago: a Psychoanalytic Journal for Culture, Science and the Arts*.

Wolin, S. J. & Wolin, S., 1992. *The resilient self: how survivors of troubled families rise above adversity*. NY: Villard.

IX Pieter Bruegel the Elder

Martin, G., 1978. *Bruegel.* NY: St. Martin's Press
Marijnissen, R. H. and Seidel, M., 1984. *Bruegel.* NY: Harrison House.
Martin, G., 1986. *The complete paintings of Bosch.* NY: Harry N. Abrams.
Campbell, J., 1968. *The hero with a thousand faces.* 2nd ed. NJ: Princeton University Press
DeTolnay, 1952. *The drawings of Pieter Bruegel the Elder.* NY: The Twin Editions.
Stetchow, W., 1990. *Pieter Bruegel the Elder.* NY: Harry N. Abrams

X Edvard Munch

Heller, R., 1973. *Edvard Munch: the scream.* NY: Viking Press.
Lee, H. A., 1940. A theory concerning free creation in the inventive arts. *Psychiatry, 3:*229-293.
Munch, I., 1949. *Edvard Munch's family letters* (In Norwegian). Oslo: Johan Grundt Tanum Forlag.
Robbins, M., 1969. On the psychology of artistic creations. *Psychoanalytic Study of the Child.* NY: Int. Univ. Press.
Stenersen, R., 1944. *Edvard Munch: close-up of a genius.* Oslo: Gyldendal Norsk Forlag.
Stang, N., 1972. *Edvard Munch.* Oslo: Johan Grundt Tanum Forlag, 1972.
Volkan, V. & Josephthal, D., 1980. The treatment of established pathological mourners. In: *Specialized techniques in individual psychotherapy.* NY: Brunner/Mazel.

XI Sylvia Plath

Alvarez, A., 1968. *The savage God.* NY: Random House.
Bowlby, J., 1980. *Loss: sadness and depression.* NY: Basic Books.
—1979. *The making and breaking of affectional bonds.* London: Tavistock.
Butscher, E., 1976. *Sylvia Plath: method and madness.* NY: Pocket Books.
Parad, H. J. (Ed.), 1965. *Crisis intervention: selected readings.* NY: Family Service Association of America.
Plath, S., 1971. *The bell jar.* NY: Harper and Row.
—1960. *The colossus and other poems.* NY: Random House.
—Hughes, T., (Ed.), 1981. *The collected poems.* NY: Harper & Row.
—McCullough, F., Hughes, T. (Eds.), 1982. *The journals of Sylvia Plath.* NY: Dial Press.
—Plath, A., (Ed.), 1981. *Letters home.* NY: Harper & Row.
Garber, B., 1981. Mourning in children: towards a theoretical synthesis. *The Annual of Psychoanalysis,* 9:9-21.
Kligerman, C., 1970. The dream of Charles Dickens. *Journal of the American Psychoanalytic Association,* 18:783-799.
Kohut, H., 1974. Thoughts on narcissism and narcissistic rage. *The Journal of the Psychoanalytic Association,* 18:783-799.
Orgel, S., 1974. Sylvia Plath: fusion with the victim and suicide. *Psychoanalytic Quarterly,* 43:262-287.
Panel, 1972. Creativity. C. Kligerman, reporter. *International Journal of Psychoanalysis,* 53:21-30.
Pollock, G., 1975. On mourning, immortality, and utopia. *Journal of the American*

Psychoanalytic Association. 23:334-362.

Silverman, M. and Will, N., 1968. Sylvia Plath and the failure of emotional self-repair through poetry. *Psychoanalytic Quarterly.* 55:99-129.

Weisblatt, S., 1977. The creativity of Sylvia Plath's Ariel period: toward origins and meanings. *The Annual of Psychoanalysis.* 5:379-404

XII Leonardo and Magritte

Bramley, S., 1991. *Discovering the life of Leonardo da Vinci.* NY: Harper Collins.

Freud, S., 1957. Leonardo da Vinci and a memory of his childhood. *Standard Edition of Collected Works of Sigmund Freud.* London: Hogarth Press.

Gablik, S., 1972. *Magritte.* Greenwich, CT: New York Graphics Society.

Gay, P., 1988. *Freud: a life for our time.* NY: Doubleday.

Philipson, M., 1966. *Leonardo da Vinci: aspects of the Renaissance genius.* NY: George Braziller.

Torczyner, H., 1977. *Magritte: ideas and images.* NY: Harry N. Abrams.

XIII Virginia Woolf

Beck, A. T., 1967. The manic depression reaction. In *Depression.* NY: Hoeber Medical Division, Harper and Row

Bell, Q. 1972. *Virginia Woolf, a biography, Vols. 1 and 2.* NY: Harcourt Brace.

Bond, A., 1985. Virginia Woolf: manic depressive psychosis and genius. *Journal of The American Academy of Psychoanalysis,* 13 (2), 191-210.

Edwards, S., I 977. *Vivien Leigh.* NY: Simon and Schuster.

Freud, S., 1957. Mourning and melancholia. *Standard Edition of Collected Works of Sigmund Freud,* Vol. 14, London: Hogarth Press.

Gibson, R. W., Cohen, M. B., and Cohen, M. A., 1959. On the dynamics of the manic depressive personality. *American Journal of Psychiatry,* 11, 1101-1107.

Greenacre, P., 1957. The childhood of the artist: libidinal phase development and giftedness. *Psychoanalytic Study of the Child,* 12:27-72.

Kaplan, L., 1978. *Oneness and separateness: from infant to individual.* NY: Simon and Schuster.

Kris, E., 1952. *Psychoanalytic explorations in art.* NY: International Universities.

Mahler, M., Pine, F. and Bergman, A., 1975. *The psychological birth of the human infant.* NY: Basic Books.

Noble, J. R., (Ed.), 1972. *Recollections of Virginia Woolf.* NY: William Morrow.

Pippett, A., 1953. *The moth and the star, a biography of Virginia Woolf.* Boston: Little, Brown.

Rose, P., 1978. *Woman of letters, a life of Virginia Woolf.* London: Oxford University Press.

Woolf, L., 1963. *Beginning again, an autobiography of the years 1911 to 1918.* NY: Harcourt Brace.

Woolf, V., 1920. *The voyage out.* NY: Harcourt Brace.

—1925. *Mrs. Dalloway.* NY: Harcourt Brace.

—1927. *To the lighthouse.* NY: Harcourt Brace.

—1929. *A room of one's own.* NY: Harcourt Brace.

—1931. *The waves.* NY: Harcourt Brace.

—1933. *Flush.* NY: Harcourt Brace.

—1937. *The years.* NY: Harcourt Brace.

—1940. *Roger Fry: A biography*. NY: Harcourt Brace.
—1941. *Between the acts*. NY: Harcourt Brace.
—1975. *The letters of Virginia Woolf*, Vol. 1, 1888-1912. NY: Harcourt Brace.

XIV Elizabeth Layton

Baltes, P., 1993. The aging mind: potential and limits. *The Gerontologist*, 33:580-594.

Bates, M., November 26, 1990. Area artist isn't impressed. Lawrence, Kansas: *Lawrence Journal World*.

Bretz, L., 1984. *Through the looking glass: drawings by Elizabeth Layton*. Kansas City: Lowell Press.

Erikson, E., Erikson, J., and Kivnick, H., 1986. *Vital involvement in old age*. NY: W.W. Norton.

Fowler, J., 1981. *Stages of faith*. San Francisco: Harper & Row.

Haensley, P. and Reynolds, C., 1989. Creativity and intelligence. In Glover, J. A., Ronning, R. R. and Reynolds, C. R. (Eds.), *Handbook of creativity*. NY: Plenum Press.

Lifton, R. J., 1973. The sense of immortality: On death and the continuity of life. *American Journal of Psychoanalysis*, 33: 3-15.

May, R., 1975. *The courage to create*. NY: Bantam Books.

Niebuhr, H. R., 1960. *Radical monotheism and western culture*. NY: Harper & Row.

Tillich, P., 1952. *Dynamics of faith*. NY: Harper & Row.

Workman, D., 1982. Selfish art: an interview with Elizabeth Layton. In V. Rogers et al (Eds.). *Developing through relationships: a reader*. Lawrence: University of Kansas.

XV Picasso

Bernier, R., 1988. *The Picasso I knew*. Rosa Mundi (Producer): NJ: Hall.
—1966. *The Picasso nobody knew*. Rosa Mundi (Producer): NJ: Hall.

Huffington, A.S., 1988. *Picasso, creator and destroyer*. NY: Avon Books.

Jung, C. G., 1934. Picasso. In: *The spirit in man, art, and literature*. Translated by Hull, R. F. C., 1966. Princeton: Princeton University Press.

Kohut, H., 1977. *The restoration of the self*. NY: International Universities Press.

Richardson, J., 1991. *A life of Picasso*. NY: Random House.

Quinn, E., 1986. *Picasso: the man and his work*. E. Quinn (Prod.), NY: Video View.

Absinthe An alcoholic drink made from wormwood, a European bitter herb. Absinthe has been banned in most countries because it can produce irreversible brain damage.

Abstract Expressionism An art movement that developed in New York in the 1940's. Initial members of the movement, Gorky, Pollock, DeKooning, Rothko, and Kline sought spontaneous, unedited freedom of expression, not limited to painting conventional forms.

Action Painting A technique made famous by Jackson Pollock in which paint was dripped, smeared, dropped, or poured onto canvas, and the act of painting was as important as the product.

Ambivalence The condition of holding two seemingly incompatible feelings, ideas, or attitudes toward a person or thing at the same time, e.g. loving and hating.

Antabuse Drug used in the treatment of alcoholism to deter drinking. A person taking Antabuse who imbibes alcohol will become nauseated, sweaty, and shocky.

Art therapy The use of art as a projective technique for bringing unconscious conflicts, unformulated ideas, and unexpressed feelings into consciousness.

Attention deficit disorder A condition, usually in childhood, in which the individual has difficulty focusing on a task, is hyperactive, impulsive and sometimes irritable.

Autistic phase In Margaret Mahler's separation-individuation theory of development, autistic phase refers to the first stage of infantile psychological development, in which the infant has no awareness of anyone or anything outside of the self. He or she is totally dominated and reactive to inner feelings and states, such as hunger, thirst, fullness, etc. Lasts from birth to 1 month.

Capriccios Italian term for caprice. In art, applied to any fantasized or imagined type of paintings. The most famous use of the term is for a series of works done by Goya, which mock society of his time.

Castration anxiety A fear of having the penis cut off. In more recent psychiatric and psychoanalytic usage, the term refers to the fear of offending and therefore experiencing some kind of retaliation from an authority figure. More generally, a loss of power.

Cohesive functions Activities or mental mechanisms that an individual employs in an attempt to maintain feelings of positive self esteem, intactness of body, awareness of self.

Consolidation phase In Mahler's separation-individuation theory, this refers to a subphase of psychological development, in which the individual becomes aware that he or she is separate from the other person, but can still keep the other person in mind when away from that person, and at the same time, can experience the self as intact and not threatened by being alone.

Cubism A movement in painting started by Picasso and Braque in 1907-1908. They sought to portray an object or person from many angles at the same time, rather than from a single perspective. Later Cubists include Juan Gris and in sculpture the work of Henry Moore is sometimes considered to have cubist elements.

Dependency State in which the individual cannot function independently. He or she needs and seeks advice, guidance, support, etc. and cannot make decisions. The presence of the other provides comforting and soothing. If this is not provided, the dependent person may turn to drugs and/or alcohol or other destructive behavior to calm the unpleasant unfulfilled feelings of neediness.

Depression Clinically, a state of sadness and lethargy, accompanied by feelings of helplessness, hopelessness and worthlessness, often one pole of a manic depressive state.

Desynthesizing The act of taking apart into component pieces. Can refer to a physical act, or to the psychological phenomenon of a coming-apart of the various functioning parts of the mind.

Differentiation phase The first subphase of the separation-individuation process, usually from 5-9 months, when total bodily dependence on the mother begins to decrease and the infant makes his or her first tentative movements away from the mother.

Digitalis A drug initially prepared from the flower, foxglove, used in the late 1800's as a treatment for epilepsy. It is used today for the treatment of heart failure

Displacement of sexual energy According to the classical theory of psychoanalysis, the individual is motivated by one of two drives—sexuality or aggression. The sexual energy or drive can be displaced from one person or object and directed toward another person or object. The energy can also be converted to another activity other than sexuality, e.g. intellectual pursuit, painting, etc.

Disintegration, psychic The disorganization of normal psychological functions, e.g. awareness of self, ability to experience and contain emotions, the ability to think and act appropriately.

Dissociation The separation of any group of mental processes from the rest of the mind. In its most severe form, it is thought to be a factor in multiple personality disorders.

Drives Biological motivations for behavior: e.g., hunger, thirst. In classical psychoanalytic theory, the basic motivating forces that determine all behavior are sex and aggression, sometimes modified to be Eros and Thanatos, life and death, or love and hate.

Dyslexia Impaired ability to read or understand what is read. Usually associated or attributed to minimal brain damage or dysfunction.

Electroshock A form of therapy, usually for severe depression, in which a small electric current is passed through the brain.

Engulfment The act, or psychologically the fear, of losing one's identity, one's sense of being a separate intact person, due to being overwhelmed by and taken in by another person. Usually accompanied by panic or terror.

Expressionism A term in art to denote the use of distortion and exaggeration for emotional effect. The paintings of El Greco, Munch, and Kandinsky are examples of expressionism.

Fragmentation Disturbance in thinking, feeling, or psychological functioning in which normal functions become vague and confused, resulting in decompensation of judgment, behavior, and the mind, generally.

Grandiose self In self psychology, this refers to a theoretical agency of the mind in which reside feelings and beliefs of omnipotence and omniscience.

Hemisphericity The theory that the right hemisphere of the brain is the seat of imagery, creativity, and spontaneity; while the left side is the seat of logic, language, and reason.

Individuation The emotional development of the individual or infant, from perceiving the self as enmeshed in and a dependent part of another, to perceiving the self as separate and able to survive and achieve alone.

Internalization of conflict The ability to take areas of conflict from the external world and to struggle with them intrapsychically, e.g. the conflict between father and son, or the conflict with an authority figure, need not be acted out between the two people, but can become an intrapsychic phenomenon or tension within the individual.

Kohut, Heinz Austrian-born psychoanalyst who lived and worked most of his life in Chicago, whose theories of the functioning of the mind and the interpersonal needs and wishes of the individual are referred to as *Self Psychology*.

Laudanum A preparation containing opium and/or morphine.

Mahler, Margaret American psychoanalyst who lived and worked in Philadelphia. Her theory, known as the separation-individuation theory, of the psychological birth and development of the human infant was set forth in her book, *The Psychological Birth of the Human Infant,* 1975.

Manic condition A state characterized by an elated or euphoric, although unstable, mood, increased physical activity, restlessness, agitation, and increased number of ideas racing through the head, and often by bizarre and inappropriate behavior.

Manic depression An emotional illness in which the subjective states of euphoria or mania, and depression alternate. Cycles may occur as rapidly as every few weeks or over periods of years.

Mannerism Term in art used initially to describe the style that developed after the High Renaissance had reached its peak. The term initially was derogatory. Later usage referred to the elements used by the Mannerists, e.g. elongation of form, as by El Greco. Thus the term has lost some of its negative connotation.

Mènière's Disease Disease of the inner ear that causes loss of balance, ringing in the ears, fainting, sweating, and, occasionally, unconsciousness and total incapacity.

Narcissism Self love or positive self regard. The term was originally used in a pejorative sense in psychoanalysis. More recent theories appreciate that it is necessary for healthy functioning in individuals, and need not be at the expense of other people.

Naturalism A term in art that refers to the artist's attempt to render subjects as they really are rather than in any stylized or emotional manner.

Neoplatonic philosophy A philosophical school originating in Alexandria about 200 AD, which modified the teachings of Plato. According to Neo-Platonism there is one ideal form, which is God. The closer any object, art, or person comes to this form, the closer it is to perfection.

Object hunger The psychological need for another person to provide or fulfill a function for the personality, e.g. a feeling of positive self-regard, or a feeling of emotional comfort.

Object loss The loss of a person who has great emotional significance for the individual.

Oedipal complex An organized set of feelings in the individual in which the parent of the same sex is seen as a hated rival to be destroyed, in order to obtain the parent of the opposite sex who is desired sexually. This all occurs unconsciously and is at its peak at age 4-5. According to Freud, this is the bedrock of all neuroses.

Organic brain syndrome A group of symptoms consisting of disorientation, loss of memory, impaired intellectual functioning, defective judgment and emotional lability, caused by a physical illness of the brain, such as syphilis, intoxication, hemorrhage.

Organismic thrust to individuation The inborn biological drive to develop one's abilities and skills—just as a flower has an innate program and need to bloom.

Parturition Childbirth.

Pathologic grief A morbid reaction to a loss, where feelings of sadness, lack of interest, loss of appetite, insomnia, etc, last well beyond the normal period of time required to mourn a significant loss.

Pathologic identification Psychological process in which an individual assimilates an undesirable aspect, property, or attribute of another person and models himself or herself after that person.

Practicing phase In Mahler's theory, the second subphase of separation and individuation lasting from 9-14 months, when the infant is aware of his or her developing motor skills and is able to actively move away and return to the mother.

Primary process A type of thinking characteristic of the unconscious that includes no awareness of time, the absence of any negatives or limitations, the wish and need for immediate gratification—in essence, thinking that is dominated by the wish for pleasure.

Psychoanalysis A method developed by Freud of investigating mental processes and of treating neuroses. It is based on the assumption that such disorders are the result of the rejection by the conscious mind of factors that then persist in the unconscious as repressed wishes, needs and fantasies. These then cause conflicts which may be resolved or diminished by discovering and analyzing the repressions, bringing them into consciousness through the use of such techniques as free association and dream analysis.

Rapprochement In Mahler's theory, the third subphase of separation and individuation lasting from 15-24 months, when the infant, now experiencing himself or herself as a separate individual, can leave and then return to the mother, without anxiety.

Regression Psychologically returning to an earlier level of development or functioning.

Repression A mental mechanism, in which the individual unconsciously repels from awareness, unacceptable thoughts, feelings, images, or memories. For example, repressed hostility is the rejection from conscious awareness of feelings of hatred toward a person or thing.

Right brain dominant people Loosely applied as a term for people who, demonstrating 'right brain functions' of imagery, fantasy, rhythmicity, and manipulo-spatial skills, are likely to be creative.

Right-left brain See Hemisphericity.

Rorschach Projective test devised by Hermann Rorschach, popularly known as "the ink blot test," in which the individual's underlying emotional issues and concerns are seen by the individual in the ink blots.

Self psychology A theory about how the mind works, and how people relate to each other, originated by Heinz Kohut and his followers in Chicago in the 1960's to 80's. The theory emphasizes empathy as a means of understanding, self-esteem regulation as a motive for and factor in relationships, and a degree of narcissism as necessary for emotional health and well-being.

Separation anxiety A feeling of dread that accompanies the awareness that one is alone, and has the perception that he or she cannot function adequately, possibly cannot survive, alone.

Separation-individuation phase According to Mahler, the phase of normal development from 4-5 months to $2^{1}/2$ years that leads from a self that is intertwined with the mother, to the emergence of a separate independent person. There are four subphases: see differentiation, practicing, rapprochement, and consolidation.

Shock treatment See electroshock.

Social realism A movement in art in the United States in the 1930's and 40's that sought to portray the hard working, often dreary lives, of the underprivileged members of society, as accurately as possible.

Splitting A mechanism of the mind, in which the individual, unable to tolerate conflicting emotions toward one person, e,g. love and hate, directs all the love toward one person and all the hatred toward another.

Superego as control system In classical psychoanalytic theory, the superego is an agency of the mind that fulfills certain functions for the individual. It is the repository of the goals, ideals, and rules that govern the individual's actions, feelings, and relationships.

Superego as regulator of self esteem According to the above, the individual's self esteem is governed to a large extent by how well he or she is meeting the goals, rules, and ideals of the superego.

Surrealism Movement in art and literature originating in France in the 1920's and 30's. Andre Breton, principal spokesman, said its purpose "is to resolve the previously contradictory conditions of dream and reality into an absolute reality—a super reality." Other surrealists include de Chirico, Dali, Magritte, and Ernst.

Symbiosis Condition or state in which the individual experiences the self only as a part of another, i.e. the mother-infant symbiosis.

Symbiotic phase Second phase of Mahler's separation-individuation process, lasting from 1-5 months, in which the individual experiences the self, not as separate and unique, but only as a part of the mother.

Transference The phenomenon of experiencing and directing feelings and attitudes toward people who are currently important in one's life, which were initially experienced in infancy and childhood, usually toward the parents.

Transitional object Something used as a substitute for an unavailable person, e.g. a teddy bear or a blanket, which the child holds fast when the mother is not able to hold him or her.

292

294

ORDER FORM

AIMED Press
American Institute of Medical Education
2625 West Alameda Avenue Suite 504
Burbank, CA 91505

Please ship____hardcover copies of
Creativity *& Madness* at $24.95 per copy.
ISBN 0-9641185-1-3

Number of Books	_ _ _ _ _
Cost per book	$24.95
Subtotal (number of books x cost per book)	_ _ _ _ _
Shipping (Add $2.00 to ship one book, and $1.00 for each additional book)	_ _ _ _ _
Tax (California residents - add $2.05 tax per book.)	_ _ _ _ _
Total	_ _ _ _ _

My check for $_____is enclosed.

Name ···

Address ··

City, State, Zip ··

To order by phone, please call **(800) 348-8441** and
have your credit card handy

❏ Please put me on your mailing list for brochures on
other books and **Creativity *& Madness*** Conferences.